A Place To Exist

The True And Untold Story of
Camp Hope
And Homelessness In Spokane

Maurice Smith

RISING
RIVER
MEDIA

Publisher
Rising River Media
P.O. Box 1395
Veradale, WA 99037
Website: www.risingrivermedia.org

Cover Art
Drone Footage by Jay Paulson
Cover design by Gale A. Smith
Composition & Layout by Lawton Printing, Spokane

ISBN 13
979-8-218-27471-9

The thought of my suffering and homelessness is bitter beyond words.
I will never forget this awful time, as I grieve over my loss.
Yet I still dare to hope when I remember this:
The faithful love of the Lord never ends!
His mercies never cease.
Great is His faithfulness;
His mercies begin afresh each morning.
- Lamentations 3:19-23 -
The New Living Translation

Speak up for those who cannot speak for themselves;
ensure justice for those being crushed.
Yes, speak up for the poor and helpless,
and see that they get justice.
- Proverbs 31:8-9 -
New Living Translation

Table of Contents

Introduction

"We can't change what we don't love;
We can't love what we don't know;
And we can't know what we're unwilling to invest
with our time, our efforts, and our resources."
~ The Author ~

Most of us have never had our existence - our right to exist - questioned. Even in our most difficult times, we always had a place to exist - a place to call "home." But this begs a question: Do you and I have a fundamental right to exist without fear of governmental harassment or prosecution simply for existing? If so, do those experiencing homelessness also have that right to exist without fear? And to what extent can the government regulate, abridge, or violate that right if or when our circumstances force us outside the confines of a house or apartment or homeless shelter. Is the simple act of existing a human right?

"Our question became, 'Where do they exist?' They can't go downtown. They can't go to a park. They can't go to public land. Where? Where's that space? We asked the city, 'Where would you like these folks to exist?' with no acknowledgment that there needed to be space."
~ Julie Garcia

In recent years, this question regarding the right to exist has caught the attention of Courts that have found it necessary to answer it with decisions involving those experiencing homelessness. Do the homeless have a right to exist outside the confines of a homeless shelter if there are not enough shelter beds to accommodate them, or if the available bed is in a shelter that is not appropriate to their needs? This is the question that became pivotal in the creation of Camp Hope.

What follows in this book is the story of how a peaceful protest over insufficient shelter beds and the human right to exist became the largest homeless camp in the State of Washington. It is the story of opposing and competing philosophies regarding homelessness: how we see and treat those experiencing it, and whether or not they have a fundamental right to exist.[1] It is the story of 2,390 people experiencing homelessness in greater Spokane with only 1,015 shelter beds to accommodate them and of 955 homeless individuals living unsheltered and wondering if another Camp Hope might be created to provide them with a safe place to exist. It is the story of an historic housing shortage of 25,000 housing units, a local rental vacancy rate of less than 2%, of not enough mental health or substance abuse treatment beds, or insufficient medical respite beds, and more. It is the story of the "perfect storm" that became Camp Hope in the Summer of 2022 - the story of a safe place to exist.

A Place to Exist

A Personal Journey

I've been working among the homeless and marginalized of Spokane for more than 18 years, following our family's own journey through homelessness and losing everything some 22 years ago. Working in the West Central neighborhood of Spokane with families struggling with poverty, drugs, and more, co-founding Feed Spokane after trying to feed the 150 people who showed up every Monday night for a weekly neighborhood outreach, and to help put more food into ministries feeding and serving those in need, serving on the board of Truth Ministries Men's Shelter for many years, serving on the leadership team for the Spokane Homeless Coalition and on the planning committee for the Spokane Homeless Connect. All of these led up to what came next: documentary filmmaking on homelessness in Spokane, in an attempt to show a better optic of homelessness, to tell a better narrative about those experiencing homelessness, and to set a better tone - a tone of building Shalom - in our community discussions about homelessness. Little did I know that it would eventually lead me into helping manage the largest homeless camp in the State of Washington (perhaps in the Pacific Northwest). There's a reason why God in His wisdom seldom reveals more of His will for our lives than one day, one step, or one project at a time. The word *overwhelmed* comes to mind.

On Any Given Night

I was producing my first documentary, *The Spokane Homeless Connect*[2], when it happened. My film crew and I were at the original Cannon Warming Shelter filming the annual Point-In-Time Count in January of 2019 for what would become Segment 2 - "On Any Given Night" - in the documentary.[3] My crew filmed while I participated in conducting the Count. It wasn't until I got into the edit studio the following week that I saw what they had done. Reviewing the footage, there it was, or more correctly, there she was - an interview my crew had done with Julie Garcia, who had been there that night serving a dinner of chili dogs to the guests. I watched and listened as she told about how her daughter was a heroin addict and lived on the streets, how she would come to places like Cannon in search of her daughter, and how those living on the street would help find her. As she talked, I began to weep. My project editor, DW Clark, was sitting next to me. "Are you okay?" he asked. "I'll be fine," I said, as I worked to regain something resembling a professional composure. But "fine" didn't cover what was happening.

When building a documentary, my process is to break it into topical "segments" with a basic plan for what I want to accomplish in each segment. Sitting in front of the edit screen and hearing Julie's story re-wrote any script I had for this segment. Going in, I thought the segment would be all about the Point-In-Time Count. But, now, I understood that it was about something a bit more human. It was about both the people experiencing homelessness and their stories, and about the people - like Julie and her daughter - who loved them. Yes, homelessness is a housing issue, a drug issue, a mental health issue, even a public health issue, and more. But at the end of the day, homelessness is a human issue involving those experiencing it, and those who love them and whose lives are part of the larger story.

Julie Garcia and I would collaborate for the next 5 years, through several shelters, numerous homeless camps, countless outreaches, and eventually the largest homeless camp in the State of Washington, to reveal and meaningfully address the all-too-human issue we commonly refer to as "homelessness." It would become our mutual task to help those experiencing unsheltered homelessness find the Shalom - the peace, wholeness, and restoration - that they had known so little of on their journey. And it would begin by restoring a long-lost sense of hope.

An Invitation And A Question

While producing *The Spokane Homeless Connect* in early 2019, I received an invitation from the Psychology Department at Washington State University in Pullman. Would I be willing to come to Pullman and speak to an evening class of roughly 30 Graduate students in Psychology on the topic of homelessness (nothing intimidating there, just 30 graduate psyche students analyzing everything I said!)? I accepted the invitation and traveled to Pullman where we spent an enjoyable evening talking about various aspects of homelessness. In the course of our conversation, I posed a question. "What do you think is the most important asset a homeless individual possesses, and the one asset they can't afford to lose?", I asked. This was a bright class, and they offered several tangible possibilities, things like dry clothes, personal possessions, debit cards, tents, etc.

"Those are all good," I responded, "but they aren't the most important, and you could even afford to lose them." They soon ran out of ideas, and it was time to offer mine:

"Hope," I said. "The most important asset any person experiencing homelessness possesses, and the one asset they can't afford to lose, is the great intangible of hope. Hope that this journey - this homeless nightmare - won't last forever; hope that tomorrow can be - and will be - better than today; hope that there are still people in the community who see what you're going through, who care, and who are willing to get involved, and help."

Writing to a struggling group of Christian believers in the 1st Century City of Rome, Paul of Tarsus encouraged them with words that are still relevant today, "Now hope that is seen is not hope. For who hopes for what he sees? But if we hope for what we do not see, we wait for it with patience" (Romans 8:24-25). It's the personal hope in a better future, one that they cannot yet see, that keeps the unsheltered homeless moving forward and enables them to survive until there is something better. Like my friend, Russ, whose *Bounder* RV we removed from Camp Hope when he moved from the Camp to the new Catalyst transitional living project. "Thank you," he said to me as we worked on his RV together, "You guys gave me hope again." Exactly.

That's why we named it *Camp Hope*. We peddle and deal in hope.

A Place to Exist

How The Martian Solved Homelessness

In the movie, *The Martian,* astronaut Mark Watney (played by Matt Damon) is marooned and left for dead on Mars. The problem, of course, was that he wasn't dead, just marooned. The movie is about his struggle to survive and make it back to earth. Spoiler alert: He survives and is rescued. Back on Earth and lecturing to a class of potential astronauts, he explains how he survived, "You get to work. You solve one problem, and then you solve another problem, and another problem, and if you solve enough problems, you get to go home."

Yes, there's a lesson for us here. Whether you're homeless on Mars, or homeless in a homeless camp in Spokane, the process for getting home is the same. Solve one problem after another. Solve enough problems and you get to go home. Interestingly, that's kinda how we build *shalom*, too, and that's where we'll start in Chapter 1.

Finding Common Ground

Mark Twain (a.k.a., Samuel Langhorne Clemens) once declared, "I don't vote for politicians. It only encourages them." I think we can all chuckle at his humorous poke at elected officials (of all stripes). And while this book is NOT a political treatise, I believe that the true role of politics and politicians in a civil and democratic society is to find and build on the common ground that unites us (or should unite us) as a community. I also believe that building the *shalom* (as I discuss in Chapter 1) of our community by serving and building the *shalom* of those experiencing homelessness and marginalization is an important place of "common ground" that we as a community need to occupy and build on together. I'm convinced that the defining values of any community are to be found in how that community treats "the least of these," the homeless, the hungry, the marginalized - those described by the Hebrew word *dal*. The insignificant poor.[4] We may yet discover that, in the balance scales of heaven, they outweigh our roads, our public buildings, our bloated municipal budgets, our impressive sports complexes, stadiums, arenas, skyscrapers, and universities. How we treat "the least of these" presents us with a disturbingly accurate window on the soul of any community.

Acknowledgments

No author works alone. When it comes to explaining homelessness in our Community, including the phenomenon now known as Camp Hope, many people have contributed to this book. It's only fair to acknowledge some of those amazing individuals whose contributions helped make it possible.

My profound thanks to those who contributed chapter-articles on specific issues where their expertise helps all of us better understand some of the issues that impacted our community, Camp Hope, and our homeless friends. I specifically asked Lisa Brown (and she graciously agreed) to explain the Right Of Way Initiative and her work at the Washington State Department of Commerce that brought over $24 million to Spokane for much-needed homeless services. I also asked former Spokane City Council President Ben Stuckart, now the Executive Director of the Spokane Low Income Housing Consortium, to address the issue of housing in Spokane, because - as he explains - homelessness is ultimately a housing problem. I asked my friend and co-worker, Sharyl Brown, to explain the work of Peer Navigators, amazing people who became our "secret weapons" in our fight to move the unsheltered homeless of Camp Hope forward toward better things. Without them, we could not have accomplished what we did. My friend, Jeffry Finer, represented Jewels Helping Hands (and the other plaintiffs) in the Federal suit against the City and County of Spokane to prevent local law enforcement from forcibly closing the Camp. I asked Jeffry to write a chapter that would help everyone better understand why a lawsuit was necessary, the legal basis for it, and the legal process that resulted in a Temporary Restraining Order (TRO) for the protection of Camp residents. I also asked my friend and co-laborer, Anwar Peace, Chair of the Spokane Human Rights Commission, to address the issue of utilizing law enforcement as a tool of homeless policy.

Many others deserve to be mentioned. My thanks to Ami Manning from the Spokane Low Income Housing Consortium who tracked Camp Hope data and helped me to understand it and include it in the book. My thanks to Ken Crary, Stefanie Damm, Regina Thompson, Jason Green, Sharyl Brown, Dan Babcox, Anwar Peace, and the entire Jewels team for all they did to make Camp Hope a success.

My thanks to the Empire Health Foundation for a grant to help bring this book into print.

Two additional people deserve special mention and thanks. My thanks to my friend, Julie Garcia, Founder and Executive Director of Jewels Helping Hands. Thank you for our 5-year journey together of filming, serving, and advocating for the homeless of our community. To say more would require another book, so you'll just have to settle for this one as my way of saying, "Thank you."

And last, but not least, my love and thanks to my wife, Gale, whose steadfast love and faith kept me moving forward during those times when I wondered if I could continue and considered giving up. You embody the grace and faith of Ruth, and the patience of Penelope awaiting Odysseus' return from his adventures. Thank you, for bearing all things, believing all things, hoping all things, and enduring all things (1 Corinthians 13:7).

A Place to Exist

1 - Not The Way Things Ought To Be

He was almost naked and dancing in the snow when we encountered him, dancing in a drug-induced reality that only he could see. I was on a nighttime outreach in late December with Julie Garcia and an outreach team from Jewels Helping Hands. Their goal on that cold, snowy night was to find people experiencing unsheltered homelessness on the streets of Spokane and to make sure they had what they needed to survive such a difficult night. My goal was to film the outreach for a documentary I was developing around a temporary homeless warming shelter operated by the same non-profit in a building provided by City Church Spokane.

Once the outreach team saw him, as they passed the parking lot of a local business, they circled the block, came back, and approached him to see if they could help. For my part, I stopped filming. It simply wasn't fair to this person to film him in such a condition just so I could use his experience as footage in a documentary. He was obviously high and needed help, including warm clothes and shoes to avoid frostbite (all he was wearing was a pair of pants).

I watched the team assess his needs. Someone shouted, "He needs shoes. Does anyone have some ten-and-a-half shoes?" Crickets chirping. It was one of those moments when the Holy Spirit whispers in your ear and says, *You do.* I took off my very comfortable shoes and handed them to the team. They helped him put on some clean dry socks . . . and the shoes. I had more shoes at home. He didn't. I was in no

Yes, those are my shoes he's wearing in the snow.

danger of frostbite and losing toes. He was. Sometimes, even for a documentary filmmaker, serving *the least of these* and building the *shalom* of the homeless means putting down the camera, taking off your shoes, and helping someone high and dancing in the snow to survive the night with warm clothes, dry socks, and shoes. Welcome to the practical work of building the *shalom* of those experiencing homelessness, which is what Camp Hope, and this book, are ultimately all about.

Why Shalom?

If we're going to set out on a journey of meaningfully addressing homelessness, it might be a good idea to first identify the destination before we start planning the trip. To do otherwise is to run the risk of ending up at *The Bowery* in lower Manhattan rather than in *Pirates of the Caribbean* at Disney World in Orlando. There is a difference. This book is built on a thesis: That the destination of meaningfully addressing homelessness is not simply housing, but *shalom*. And that deserves an explanation.

Whether we realize it or not, you and I know something about *shalom*, even if we can't define it, explain it, or even if we've never actually heard about *shalom*. For example, when you and I drive through the downtown streets of our city and we see someone sleeping on a public sidewalk or in the doorway of a local business (or dancing almost naked in the snow), we may think or say to ourselves, *That's not right. That's NOT the way things ought to be!* But, then you and I see a news story about someone or some group in our community helping a struggling individual or family get on their feet through acts of generosity and kindness, helping them with housing or rent or food or medical expenses, or paying off the cafeteria lunch bill for an entire school located in a poor neighborhood. In that moment we say to ourselves, *That's the right thing to do. THAT's the way things ought to be!* [5]

Now you understand *shalom*. On the one hand, you understand what *broken shalom* looks like. Broken *shalom* causes us to respond by thinking (or saying), *That's not right. That's NOT the way things ought to be!* It makes us long for (and hopefully work for) better solutions. On the other hand, you also understand what true *shalom* looks like. True *shalom* causes us to look at acts of generosity, kindness, justice, or restoration and to say, *That's the right thing to do! That's the way things OUGHT to be!* True *shalom* motivates us to say, *I want to be part of something like that!* It motivates us to get involved, to help someone in need to better their situation, to bring cosmos (order) out of the chaos of life, and to make a difference in the lives of those around us. And in the process, the pursuit of genuine *shalom* changes us, and changes the way we see people.

Let's Define Shalom

Shalom is an old and rich Hebrew word encompassing five basic ideas: 1) peace, 2) well-being or welfare, 3) prosperity or good fortune, 4) physical health and healing, and 5) restoration. The verbal form of *shalom* (*shalam*) meant to make something or someone whole by restoring an overall sense of wholeness in mind, body, and possessions.[6] This concept of restoration and wholeness lies at the heart of *shalom* in all of its various uses.

In his book, *Walking With the Poor*, author Bryant Myer applies the concept of *shalom* to the issue of poverty, defining poverty as "the absence of shalom in all of its meaning."[7] Building on Myer's thought, if poverty represents the head-waters of homelessness in our community, then it's appropriate to say that homelessness, too, is a manifestation of the absence of *shalom* in all of its meaning. My friend, Marchauna Rodgers, is an International Development Specialist who has spent considerable time studying the biblical concept of poverty both domestically and abroad. In late 2021 I interviewed Marchauna for my documentary, *The Night of the Unsheltered Homeless*.[8] I found her observations on poverty, homelessness, and *shalom* helpful.

"So, I went to school and studied developmental justice, got a graduate degree, and in the process of doing that I studied poverty and homelessness and shalom and where it comes from. And the thing that just blew me away is how we misdefine poverty. We think of poverty as the absence of material resources. It's defined that way functionally in all of our programs. Ask anybody and they'll tell you, 'Oh, it's not having money, it's not having money and stuff you can look at.' But poverty is not primarily about the absence of material resources. So, the assumption that we've made that it is about the absence of material resources, we've replaced the resources, but that's a symptom. It hasn't solved the problem, just like with somebody who's experiencing homelessness. You think that the problem is not having a home, but not having a home is a symptom of a deeper issue and you have to look past the obvious symptoms to be able to deal with the root causes. A comprehensive or more robust definition of poverty is the absence of shalom characterized by broken and unjust relationships and, back to how you define shalom, shalom is a result of just relationships."

In an unpublished 2021 paper submitted to Multnomah Seminary as part of her doctoral studies, Marchauna went on to suggest that, when we look beyond the rhetoric of the various social justice movements, "what you find is the desperate cry of broken people, longing for shalom."[9] Combining these perspectives, we begin to see how the restorative nature of *shalom-building* speaks to the needs of those mired in personal brokenness, poverty, and homelessness. The work of *shalom-building* in the homeless community is the process of restoring to those experiencing homelessness an overall sense of wholeness in mind, body, and possessions. Do they need appropriate housing and a home? Of course they do. But that's the beginning, not the ending, of our work to build *shalom*.

This process of restoration will look different for each individual. There are no cookie-cutter solutions to poverty or homelessness. Joe Ader, Executive Director at Family Promise of Spokane, suggests that there are two common denominators of homelessness - deep personal trauma and loss of community. If true, any restorative process that fails to address these issues in the life of the individual will ultimately fail long-term. For many of those experiencing homelessness, this process may need to begin in a low-barrier shelter that meets their immediate needs for food, sanitation & hygiene, and a safe bed, while providing them with an important first step toward stability. Some will be ready for a transitional living arrangement as their intermediate step toward more permanent housing. Others will need treatment for substance abuse or mental health issues, while still others may be ready for life-skills recovery or job-training programs. Meaningfully addressing homelessness must take into account the diversity of personal issues and needs as part of the *shalom-building* process of peace, well-being, wholeness, and restoration. To do otherwise is to court failure, both for them and for us as a Community.

A Place to Exist

Shalom Is About Who We See

On this particular morning, I was having coffee with my friend Mark Terrell at The Gathering House in north Spokane. Mark (along with his wife Rachel) is the founder and Director Emeritus of Cup of Cool Water, a ministry to youth on the streets of Spokane. I was in the process of launching my documentary work on

> "Remember, Maurice, how we see people is the beginning of how we treat people."

homelessness in Spokane. Little did I know that our visit on this particular morning would have a profound impact on my work moving forward. Mark's simple words penetrated deep into my thinking and touched my soul. Gazing at me he simply said, "Remember, Maurice, how we see people is the beginning of how we treat people." It was a simple - even self-evident - statement, but one that had the impact of a personal earthquake with aftershocks that have rolled on during the intervening years, even today. *How we see people is the beginning of how we treat people.* And when we begin to see people differently, we begin to understand their need for *shalom* - peace, restoration, healing, and well-being. They need the same things - tangible and intangible - that you and I need. Their journey to finding them is just different from yours or mine.

One of my favorite scenes from the movie *The Hobbit: The Battle of the Five Armies* features a brief interaction between Bilbo Baggins and Bard (who killed the dragon Smaug and is now leading the refugees from Laketown) the night before the looming battle between the Elves and the Dwarves. Bilbo tries to prevent the battle and save the dwarves by offering a precious compromise, The Arkenstone:

Bard: "Why would you do this? You owe us no loyalty."

Bilbo: "I'm not doing it for you. I know that dwarves can be obstinate, pig-headed, and difficult. Suspicious and secretive, with the worst manners you can possibly imagine. But they are also brave, and kind, and loyal to a fault. I've grown very fond of them, and I would save them if I can."

Bilbo understood. He saw the Dwarves differently than others did, because he had shared their journey and had gotten to know them. As I learned from Mark Terrell, and have repeated in my documentary work, when it comes to working with those experiencing homelessness, "*How we see people is the beginning of how we treat people.*" How do we do that? It begins by sharing their journey, walking alongside them and getting to know them.

During the months of Camp Hope's existence, but with roots going back much further, our community was exposed to an ugly perspective that sees people experiencing homelessness as something less than ourselves, even less

> . . . history has unkind and painful lessons to teach us about the tragedies born from treating people as less than human . . .

than human; nuisances, drug addicts, criminals, even "garbage." If that is how we as a community see them and talk about them, it won't be long before that is how we will treat them - as garbage to be swept away and disposed of. The homeless, particularly the unsheltered homeless, have become the expendables and disposables of our community. And history has unkind and painful lessons to teach us about the tragedies born from treating people as less than human, less than ourselves, and less than how we would want to be treated if our situations were reversed.

For nearly a year, it was my job to oversee the organizing and cleaning of Camp Hope. We used to joke that my title was "Director of Water, Garbage, and Sanitation." In other words, I was the chief garbage collector and overseer of water tanks and porta potties. In my work of cleaning the Camp and hauling out garbage, I saw many needles and burnt foils (both signs of intense drug use). Too many to count. But what do you see when you see a spent needle or a burnt piece of foil in a homeless camp? Do you see a drug addict who deserves to be treated as a nuisance, or a criminal, or as garbage to be swept out? Let's be truthful. Isn't that how most of us have responded at some time in our lives? It's taken time, but I've learned to see needles and foils as representing people trapped in a cycle of substance abuse that's out of their control (which is why it's called an addiction); a person, created in the image of God, in desperate need of redemption, treatment, and restoration, but trapped in a chemical bondage from which they can't break free without help. Your help. And my help.

> **What I learned from Camp Hope. . .**
>
> Generous hospitality and empathy go a long way towards supporting people in overcoming their lived traumas and returning to full productive participation in our community. It is not a guarantee of success, but without it, there is no chance of success.
>
> Breean Beggs, Attorney
> Spokane City Council President

Epilogue

Building genuine *shalom* - peace, restoration, well-being - among this challenging population begins when we see people differently, when we see the homeless and marginalized as human beings struggling through a difficult phase of their life. How we see them is the beginning of how we treat them. Are you willing to see them differently? Are you willing to help? Or are you as stuck in your opinion as they are in their addiction? Make a decision about who and what you see. If you're ready to be a *shalom-builder*, then it's time to get involved and to make a difference. Someone's life and future well-being depends on it.

A Place to Exist

2 - A Small Town On One City Block

By the Summer of 2022, what had begun as a peaceful protest on the steps of Spokane City Hall, protesting the lack of adequate low-barrier shelter beds and involving a few dozen tented protesters, had grown into the largest homeless encampment in the State of Washington. Situated on one city block of Washington Department of Transportation (WSDOT)

Camp Hope in the Summer of 2022

property on the edge of town along I-90, the Camp at its peak was home to 689 unsheltered homeless individuals, representing 84% of the then known-and-counted 823 individuals experiencing unsheltered homeless in Spokane.[10] At its peak that Summer, the population of Camp Hope was greater than the population of

- Sprague, WA (511 residents)
- Reardan, WA (471 residents)
- Edwall, WA (470 residents)
- Harrington, WA (433 residents)

At its peak, Camp Hope was the size of a small Eastern Washington town, crammed onto one city block; a town populated solely by those experiencing unsheltered homelessness. Camp Hope alone could have filled 96% of all the shelter beds in the city-side shelter system, had they been open and available, which they weren't. [11]

Whether large or small, homeless camps aren't anyone's favorite alternative homeless service. But they do represent an integral part of the homeless community. They make for an engaging optic for local news outlets, and for great social fodder for people who don't understand why they exist. How do they get started? Why is a homeless camp even necessary? Why don't these people just go to a shelter and access all the services that might be available there? Homeless camps like Camp Hope embody a visual illustration of poverty in the heart of a middle class urban landscape and offer visual testimony to the failure of homeless policy over a period of years. And like the proverbial canary in the mine, Camp Hope signaled a housing crisis that had pushed a growing number of people from housing to homelessness.

The Perfect Storm That Became Camp Hope

By the Summer of 2022, Camp Hope had reached its maximum size and had become the *perfect storm*. When it comes to storms, there are storms, and then there are great storms. We call those great storms *perfect storms*. Another perfect storm was recorded 21 centuries ago by the writer Matthew in the New Testament book that bears his name. He records a storm that engulfed Jesus and his twelve disciples on a trip across the Sea of Galilee in a 26-foot fishing sloop. Matthew tells us that *"there arose a great storm upon the sea"* (ESV). While that makes for good English prose, the Greek text is a bit more descriptive, *"a great shaking came about in the sea."* The word "shaking" (*seismos*, from which we get our English earthquake words like *seismic* and *seismology*) occurs fourteen times in the New Testament describing literal earthquakes. How violent was this perfect storm? It was like *"a great earthquake in the sea."* Welcome to Camp Hope, the perfect storm, and great earthquake, that shook Spokane in the Summer of 2022.

Every perfect storm has some inauspicious beginning. That includes the perfect storm that became Camp Hope, the largest homeless encampment in the State of Washington. Approaching storms tend to send out warning signs; gathering clouds, increasing winds, changes in atmospheric pressure, signs that are obvious to those who know what they're seeing, but not to those who don't. At the end of the day (or the beginning of the storm) we all see what our worldview allows us to see. In the pages that follow, worldviews regarding the homeless will be challenged as we tell the story of how that storm came

What I learned from Camp Hope. . .

Even the extraordinary number of over 600 people living in the one square city block of Camp Hope turned out to be only the tip of the iceberg of the total number of unsheltered people currently living in Spokane.

Breean Beggs, Attorney
Spokane City Council President

about, the challenges of managing the Camp it created, how the Camp shook the Spokane community, and how it changed homeless services and what it meant to fulfill the call to serve the unsheltered and chronically homeless who, for over a year, called Camp Hope home. And this story would be woefully incomplete without serious reflection on the lessons we learned along the way, lessons that we hope others who serve the unsheltered homeless can embrace without the challenge and pain of learning them from scratch as we did. Let the story, and the lessons, begin.

3 - How It All Got Started

The issues underlying the eventual genesis of Camp Hope in December of 2021 had existed for years. They included a serious underestimation by policymakers of the true size of homelessness in greater Spokane, and a glaring shortage of available low-barrier shelter beds where those experiencing homelessness could find appropriate shelter (compounded by a more recent historically tight rental market with a vacancy rate of under 1%). In addition, street homelessness was complicated yearly during the winter months when temperatures plummeted below freezing with no meaningful provision being made by City leaders for warming centers where the unsheltered homeless could escape both the cold temperatures and the ever present threat of such serious issues as hypothermia or frostbite.

Let's Go Back to 2018

In the Fall of 2018, under pressure from homeless advocates who understood the problem, the City of Spokane temporarily suspended the enforcement of its "No Sit & Lie" ordinance, promising that the suspension would remain in place until an additional 200 beds were added to the City-wide shelter system.[12] But with Winter weather approaching and no firm plan for additional beds, in late November homeless

Camp Hope at City Hall, 2018

activists - led by Alfredo Llamedo - staged a homeless tent city in front of City Hall to focus public and political attention on the lack of either permanent shelter beds or even temporary warming beds. By late December, under pressure from the tent city protest, the City of Spokane had arranged for 40 temporary warming center beds at a newly leased building located at 527 S. Cannon Street, and an additional 60 temporary warming center beds at Salem Lutheran Church, both to be operated by the Guardians Foundation. Later, in early January, the City arranged a third temporary warming center with 50-to-120 beds at the recently closed National Furniture building on East Ermina Avenue, to be operated by the Salvation Army.[13] But early on Sunday morning, December 9 of 2018, as snow fell and Spokane slept, Spokane City Code Enforcement and Police, claiming the availability of warming center beds, removed the Camp, illegally disposing of campers' personal property.

A Lawsuit And A Settlement

Seven months later, in July of 2019, several former residents of the Camp sued the City of Spokane in U. S. District Court for the Eastern District of Washington (Case 2:19-cv-00236-TOR), claiming that the City of Spokane had failed to provide basic due process protections required by law without any plan to store the plaintiff's property as promised in the 48-hour notices issued by the City to the camp residents.[14] The Plaintiffs' suit came ten months after a similar case out of Boise, Idaho in which a 9th Circuit U.S. District Court had ruled that the removal of homeless campers was unconstitutional when there were insufficient low-barrier shelter beds available for the known and counted homeless in the community.[15] In November of 2020, the Plaintiffs in the 2019 Spokane case stemming from the original 2018 Camp Hope agreed

CITY OF SPOKANE
EXECUTIVE ORDER

EO 2020-00_17_
LGL 2020-00_08_

TITLE: **DIRECTIVE OF THE MAYOR REGARDING ADOPTION OF AN ADMINISTRATIVE POLICY**

RECEIVED

EFFECTIVE DATE: November _13_th, 2020
REVISION DATE IF APPLICABLE:

NOV 1 3 2020
CITY CLERK'S OFFICE

Pursuant to the City of Spokane (the "City") Administrative Policy and Procedure Number 0325-18-1, Section 5.2.1, the Mayor hereby issues this Directive:

AUTHORITY:

Section 5.2.1 provides in part as follows:

Copies of proposed policies and procedures shall be provided to all affected departments for review and comment for at least a two week period prior to final adoption, *unless* (emphasis added), directed otherwise by the Mayor or City Administrator.

ACTION:

In this instance the undersigned Mayor of the City directs that the Encampment Removal and Cleanup Policy, attached hereto as Exhibit "A", is to become effective immediately upon signature, for the reasons set forth herein.

1)   The effective date of the application of this Policy is necessary in order to resolve litigation filed in the United States District Court for the Eastern District of Washington captioned David Ham vs. City of Spokane, case No. 2:19-cv-00238-TOR; and

2)   The potential enforcement of the City Municipal Code provisions that prohibit camping on public lands may create the need for additional camp site clean ups and this policy and procedure will provide rules and guidelines for certain property found in any encampments

Dated this _13_ day of November, 2020.

Mayor Nadine Woodward

Mayor's Executive Order required to settle lawsuit.

to a settlement and dismissal of the case in exchange for a revision and clarification of the City of Spokane's *Encampment Removal and Clean Up Policy*.[16]

A Lesson Not Learned

A rational person might conclude that the City of Spokane had learned its legal lesson regarding the pitfalls of using law enforcement to resolve homeless encampments, the importance of adequate shelter beds for the known and counted homeless population in the Community prior to enforcing local "No Sit & Lie" and "No Camping" ordinances, and the importance of due process. But such a rational person would be wrong. On the one-year anniversary of the original peaceful protest named Camp Hope, a local news outlet aired a story declaring, *Last winter, Spokane city council temporarily suspended its "sit and lie" ordinance. But it is still enforced today*.[17] And nearly two years after that original Camp Hope at City Hall to protest police sweeps and a lack of adequate shelter beds, an article in *The Inlander* declared, "Despite a lack of shelter space, records show Spokane police still enforce laws targeting homeless people."[18] The City of Spokane was back to business as usual, enforcing "No Sit & Lie" and "No Camping" ordinances, using law enforcement as a tool of homeless policy, and forcing the street homeless to move with no where to go due to a lack of sufficient shelter beds to accommodate them or their needs.

Our Annual Greek Homeless Tragedy

Fast forward two years to the Summer of 2021. It was hot that Summer, hot as ... well, you know. For several years leading up to that Summer, Spokane homeless policymakers had performed an annual homeless play that I've described as *Our*

Annual Greek Homeless Tragedy in a documentary short piece I produced to focus attention on our annual lack of planning for winter weather warming centers for the unsheltered homelessness.[19] It was, in fact, a two act play featuring political anti-heroes whose lack of foresight combined annually with their lack of understanding of poverty and homelessness to create a Greek tragedy complete with a chorus of homeless advocates warning policymakers of the dire consequences that lie ahead for both them and the homeless as a result of their failure to act. Act One would unfold annually in the late Fall and early Winter months when temperatures plunge below freezing with insufficient shelter space where the unsheltered homeless could find warmth and refuge. Act Two of this annual performance would be acted out each Summer when temperatures rose into the 90s or above with nowhere for the unsheltered homeless to go to escape the heat.

What I learned from Camp Hope . . .

"Even the least influential members of our community can sometimes command the stage of public attention by displaying their raw humanity and vulnerability-especially with the support of strategic activists. By gathering together visibly, previously unsheltered people garnered public attention and millions of dollars in support that manifested meals, permanent shelter and much needed services that would never have been provided if they had remained solo or in small groups."

Breean Beggs, Attorney
Spokane City Council President

In June of 2021, I was filming our 7th documentary on homelessness in Spokane, *The Night of The Unsheltered Homeless*.[20] The morning of June 29th found me filming a law enforcement sweep of homeless campers trying to stay cool and beat the heat along the Spokane River, across from Mission Park. It was already 100 degrees when I was filming in late morning. The temperature that day would peak at 109, and the campers - whose lives were being turned upside-down - were told by law enforcement that they could walk 2 miles downtown (yes, in the heat) to an official City-sponsored public cooling center.

In about the same time frame, Spokane City Council was preparing to amend the Spokane Municipal Ordinance on homelessness to require the City Administration to make provision for summer cooling centers and winter warming centers. Columnist Shawn Vestal summed things up in a column that appeared in the *Spokesman-Review* on Friday, July 9th:

A Place to Exist

"The council proposal is simple and humane and overdue. It is a sad sign, if not surprising, that it rouses such passionate opposition from the mayor, her major funders and those who want to treat the chronically homeless as weeds – to use the metaphor offered in a meeting Wednesday by Union Gospel Mission's executive director, Phil Altmeyer . . . . On Monday, the City Council will vote on a proposal to amend the city ordinance on homelessness offered by Council President Breean Beggs . . . . These proposals, and particularly that final one, fly in the face of the street-sweeping, weed-pulling approach favored by the mayor."[21]

Spokane City Council would go on to pass the Amendments, and the City Administration would go on to ignore them, or to find ways around them that satisfied no one, left homeless outreach workers frustrated, and left the unsheltered homeless with no realistic options. The stage was being set for events that would soon unfold on the steps of City Hall.

Trent & Waterworks

Illegal Camping Status List

Case Number	Open Date	Responsible Party	Site Address	Parcel	Inspection Type	Inspection Date	Inspection Result	Count of Occupants
					Hold			
E21-15097	11/9/2021	Parks	3450 W GOVERNMENT WAY	26231.0602	Illegal Camping - Abatement	02/01/2022	Safety Concern	6+
Additional Info: Camp Description: Camp is located by the river next to the Cemetery. Additional Information: Cars are parking on pacific and along Gov Way dropping off supplies etc								
					In Progress			
E21-07063	6/16/2021	Parks	2545 N PETTET DR	25123.0015	Illegal Camping - Abatement	03/03/2022	Partial Abatement	2-5
Additional Info: Camp Description: In the parking lot on the west side of the road there are people camping / using their vehicles as a base camp in this parking lot. Additional Information: In the parking lot on the west side of the road there are people camping / using their vehicles as a base camp in this parking lot.								
E21-08091	7/7/2021	Parks	2911 W WHISTALKS WAY	25116.0054	Illegal Camping - Abatement	11/04/2021	Partial Abatement	Unoccupied
Additional Info: Camp Description: At least 7 tents, garbage, clothing, pets. Caller did not see any people this time Additional Information: On bank of river north of new development								
E21-05143	5/6/2021	WSDOT	2335 W 26TH AVE	25253.0034				6+
Additional Info: Camp Description: 12 tents, unknown number of occupants, garbage, clothing spread around. Occupants have weapons. Additional Information: 12 tents, unknown number of occupants, garbage, clothing spread around. Occupants have weapons.								
E21-04181	4/14/2021	Private	2423 W 25TH AVE	25253.0212				6+
Additional Info: Camp Description: The homeless are turning this area owned by the railroad into a landfill. It looks disgusting from Fish Lake Trail. Additional Information:								
E21-11816	9/7/2021	Parks	2720 W ELLIOTT CT	25116.0054	Illegal Camping - Abatement	11/04/2021	Partial Abatement	2-5
Additional Info: Camp Description: Caller lives across the river from this encampment and said it has popped up over the weekend. It is on the river bank, there is a tent and a camo tarp over it. Various stuff and trash. At least 2 people. Additional Information: Caller lives across the river at 1627 N West Point Rd, please do not disclose address but can be useful in mapping where the encampment is on the opposite side of the river from them.								
E21-11155	8/25/2021	Parks	3303 S INLAND EMPIRE WAY	25361.0045				1

Spokane Law Enforcement publishes a regular
"Illegal Camping Status List"

During the last half of 2021, the immediate catalyst for what would become Camp Hope could be found in homeless encampments throughout Spokane County, including one along the Spokane River at a location known as Trent & Waterworks in the Spokane Valley. Local Law Enforcement was well aware of homeless camps like the one at Trent & Waterworks, maintaining and circulating a regular *Illegal*

Camping Status List.[22] I have several editions in my files. Spokane law enforcement conducted regular sweeps of such camps, forcing campers to move with no options but to set up a new camp in another location in what I described as a cruel game of "homeless whack-a-mole."

With that reality as background, fast forward from the Summer of 2021 to the second week of December, 2021, six months after the City Council passed those proposed Amendments. The annual Winter performance of *Our Annual Greek Homeless Tragedy* was once again underway with the City of Spokane offering no practical warming center options for the unsheltered homeless. According to the City's own *Shelter Capacity Report*, in the first two weeks of December, 2021, a nightly average of only 58 open low-barrier beds existed in the City-wide shelter system, available to the hundreds of individuals experiencing unsheltered homelessness in greater Spokane.

In the second week of December, 2021, homeless outreach workers with Jewels Helping Hands received word that Spokane law enforcement planned to sweep a large homeless encampment (roughly 30 camps and 50 people) at a location by the Spokane River known as Trent & Waterworks. Learning of the impending sweep, I showed up early at Trent & Waterworks on Tuesday morning, December 7th,

Trent & Waterworks Today in mid-2023

the day of the planned sweep, with my own plan to film whatever transpired. After all, I'm a documentary filmmaker on homelessness. By mid-morning, two things had transpired. First, after a flurry of phone calls between homeless outreach workers and the City, the planned sweep had been cancelled. Second, at a time of cold weather and no shelter beds or warming centers for those left out in the cold, the threatened sweep had pushed homeless outreach workers and activists over the threshold from pacifism to activism. I asked Julie Garcia, the Executive Director of Jewels Helping Hands, to talk me through the events that took things from a homeless encampment at Trent & Waterworks to a tent city at Spokane City Hall:

"We found out that Trent and Waterworks was getting ready to be raided. The police had literally told them that they were going to come in and move them and remove their things. There were no low barrier beds available for those folks to go to. Our question became, 'Where do they exist?' They can't go downtown. They can't go to a park. They can't go to public land. Where? Where's that space? We asked the city, 'Where would you like these folks to exist?' with no acknowledgment that there needed to be space. The only thing that was ever told to us was, 'There are shelter beds available,' which there aren't. I mean, there may be a handful on any given night spread between children, men and women, but none for that specific group of people. At that time in December, there were no women's beds available, and there were women out at this camp. Our only option was to do some kind of peaceful protest." [23]

To all appearances, Spokane's homeless policymakers had learned very little about the true size of unsheltered homelessness from the experience of Camp Hope at City Hall three years earlier. So, once again, it was time to take the issue of inadequate shelter beds and no warming centers directly to City leaders and homeless policymakers where they worked: City Hall. A plan was quickly launched to stage a peaceful protest by bringing a homeless encampment to the public area in front of Spokane City Hall. It was time for Camp Hope to return.

Like Falling Dominos

Like predictable falling dominoes, a threatened law enforcement sweep of a homeless camp on the Spokane River led to a peaceful protest on the sidewalk in front of City Hall. Another threatened law enforcement sweep of the camp at City Hall would turn that peaceful protest into a movement that would captivate the attention of a community and create the State's largest homeless camp on WSDOT property along I-90. Poorly thought-out political

Setting up Camp Hope at City Hall, December 10, 2021

decisions, combined with the failure of leaders to embrace the true size and nature of homelessness or to listen to the voices of those experiencing it or working to address it, would have practical consequences moving forward. 689 of those consequences would eventually reside at Camp Hope by the Summer of 2022, a visible, public testimony to failed policies and practices.

A Peaceful Protest That Launched A Movement

It's Friday, December 10, and "go time" for Camp Hope on the sidewalk in front of City Hall. In the early morning hour of 4 a.m., a team from Jewels Helping Hands meets to load up tents, sleeping bags, pallets, space heaters and other essentials for setting up the camp. Organization and speed are essential. The plan for the camp isn't a secret, and the team doesn't know if a law enforcement welcoming committee may be waiting for them. Once everything is loaded and ready to go, the team takes a quick break for rest and prayer before heading out.

Sitting in Julie Garcia's living room, seeing the exhaustion and stress written on her face, I ask her what's on her mind this morning. "I hope it works," comes the reply.

Ken Crary, Chief of Operations for Jewels, chimes in, "This is it. This is for our friends. It has to work." I've trudged through numerous homeless encampments with Ken while filming documentary footage. I've come to appreciate his genuine heart for those experiencing unsheltered homelessness, and I can sense his genuine concern as he leads the team in prayer this morning.

"Thank you dear Lord. Thank you for bringing us together for such a just cause. We pray dear Lord that you would guide us, protect us and strengthen us, as we carry out your word with love and compassion. We pray that the city of Spokane Municipal Government can see the love and compassion pouring out through the community. We pray for our friends out there freezing and suffering in this cold, dear Lord. We pray for a building, that everybody can come inside and get warm, where people can feel safe to live and be protected from the elements. We pray that the police department of Spokane, too Lord, sees what we're doing. We love you, Lord. Amen."

It's 24 degrees outside and the streets of downtown Spokane are quiet, with no official welcoming committee in sight, when the team arrives around 5 a.m. to begin setting up. Pallets are laid out to keep as many tents as possible off the cold concrete. There are sleeping bags for each tent. A central canopy will eventually be set up to serve as a hub with space heaters, food, water and other supplies. With the basic camp set up before City Hall employees arrive for work, a day of nonstop activity quickly picks up pace.

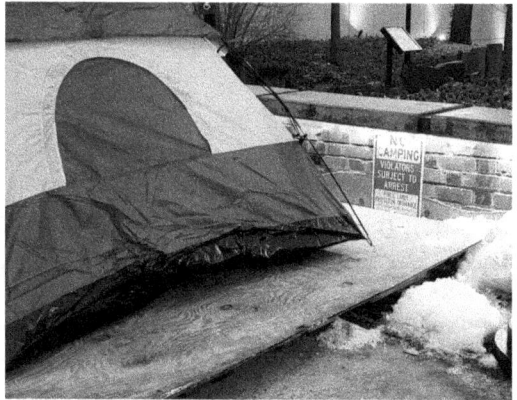

A "No Camping" sign behind a tent at Camp Hope in front of City Hall, December 10, 2021.

A group of students from nearby Gonzaga University arrives in the early morning darkness to help set up tents. As I film them, I ask why they feel it's so important to be down here helping.

"It's the right thing to do . . . . We want to help serve the unhoused, which is unacceptable and we're not going to stand for it in our city where we're living. And these are our friends too. And they deserve as much rights as everyone else. So that's why we're here. They deserve the basic needs that everyone should have."

As the morning unfolds, community members stop by, asking what they can do to support the protest. "We can use food support," Julie responds. "We need to be careful of the food. So if anybody wants to donate anything, food is going to be the number one thing. It's supposed to be ugly this weekend. So, food and tarps, because of our city's failure to attract any kind of low barrier beds for the people experiencing homelessness in our city."

More community members stop by, including local media. A local news reporter asks Julie why she picked today for this protest. Julie sums up the events that resulted in today's peaceful protest:

"Well, about three days ago, the police were set to move a camp of 50 people. Clearly, we have no beds for those 50 people, and it looks as though there's nothing planned in the city for them moving forward. They didn't move that camp, but it's a constant threat to them. That camp's been there for maybe a year. And there's 0% housing in our city. So we're not housing them fast enough. But they're participating in services. So they're doing

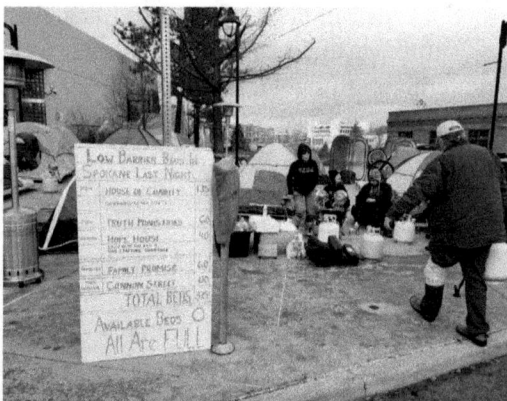
Camp Hope at City Hall, 2021

everything they can possibly do. And they still have no safe place to just exist. And that's all we're asking of the city, is, for them, a safe place for them to exist. Can there be a place that it is safe to be houseless without being criminalized, whatever that looks like? There's so many different kinds of solutions. This isn't the only one, but we need solutions."[24]

Asked how long she expects the Camp to stay in front of City Hall, Julie's answer is simple:

"We'll stay here until there's somewhere for these folks to go or until they move us . . . . At this point, these folks are exhausted. They've went through the summer with no added low barrier beds. They've been through two years of a global pandemic and no added beds. We've actually lost beds to them. It's been a long two years for them, and they just need somewhere to not die this winter. And Jewels is willing and ready to help them. If they have to be out here, so will we."

As the interview comes to a end, Julie points to a nearby banner that declares a peaceful protest.

"You can see our sign up here," she says, pointing to it. "So, you know, this is a peaceful protest. I know people think that it's a war for us. It's literally just keeping these folks alive. That's all we do is help people survive homelessness. And the only way for them to survive homelessness this winter is for them to have somewhere to exist."

48-Hour Notices

On Monday, December 13th, Day 4 of Camp Hope at City Hall, I received a call from a friend who works for a local shelter provider. After complimenting me on our documentary, *The Night of the Unsheltered Homeless* ("I felt like I was watching 60 Minutes." Wow. Thank you), he shared the following story. It seems that the previous Thursday (December the 9th), a city employee with the City of Spokane Valley was checking on the old White Elephant store on Sprague Avenue (then vacant and owned by the City of Spokane Valley) when he found a homeless individual sitting propped up against an outside wall of the building, surrounded by his belongings . . . and deceased. I found it sadly ironic that someone experiencing homelessness should pass away leaning against the wall of a building that could have been, and should have been, a shelter. I also found this to be a metaphor for how regional homeless policymakers were failing our homeless community. What was lacking in homeless policy wasn't buildings or locations, but the vision and the will necessary to make the hard decisions needed to save lives and to meaningfully address regional homelessness. No one deserves to die homeless, alone, and leaning against the wall of what could have been a life-saving shelter.

On Tuesday morning, December 14th, Day 5 of Camp Hope in front of City Hall, I was asked to participate in a meeting between the Spokane Homeless Coalition Leadership Team and a senior member of the City of Spokane's Community Housing and Human Services department. The purpose of the meeting was to discuss how the City and the Homeless Coalition could better communicate and collaborate on homeless policy issues and solutions

Spokane Code Enforcement issuing 48-Hour Notices To Remove Property

moving forward. I shared with the person from the City that on my drive to the

Camp at City Hall this morning to film, I noticed that the bridges were basically clear of homeless campers. Given a safe place to exist, they chose the tent camp at City Hall rather than a bridge. And it didn't require a police sweep to get them to move. It simply required a safe place to be.

My schedule required that I leave the meeting before it was over. Shortly after I left, Julie Garcia, a member of the Leadership Team, received a phone call from Camp Hope. Ken Crary, Jewels Chief of Operations, was calling with news. Spokane Code Enforcement, supported by SPD, was at the Camp handing out 48 Hour *Notice To Remove Property* by Thursday. The news came as a shock to everyone in the meeting, but it came as a gut-punch to the individual from the City who, apparently, had not been clued in as to the City's plan to sweep the Camp.[25] Whether intentional or unintentional, the City's left hand didn't know what its right hand was doing, which is no way to run homeless policy. In a conversation at the Camp later that morning, another member of the leadership team described what was happening as being "like Pearl Harbor." The historical analogy seemed appropriate. While the Japanese ambassador was cluelessly talking peace in Washington, D.C., the Japanese fleet was 250 nautical miles from Oahu and closing in for the attack.

The contrast between these two events (the meeting and the sweep) reinforced several perceptions at a time when perception was reality. *First*, it reinforced a perception among many homeless advocates and service providers that the City could not be trusted as a rational partner on addressing homelessness. The perception was that - contrary to what they knew to be true - City officials continued to offer public relations declarations about adequate shelter beds and the effectiveness of using the police-power of the City to solve

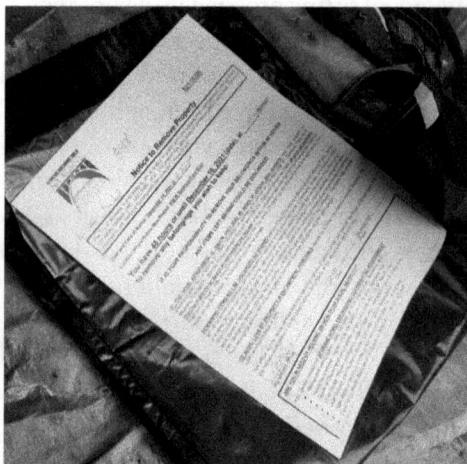

48 Hour Notice To Remove Property

homelessness. In reality, at the time that 48 Hour *Notice To Remove Property* were being handed out to the campers at City Hall, City policymakers were flying blind. They had no idea as to the size of unsheltered homelessness. As we will demonstrate in the next chapter, due to COVID restrictions, the 2021 Point In Time Count did not count the unsheltered homeless. The previous 2020 count had shown 541 individuals living unsheltered. 116 of those were now camping in front of City Hall at Camp Hope in 65 tents, while the City was proclaiming in local media that there were 78 open shelter beds in the city-wide shelter system. How the 116 people at Camp Hope (or the 541 unsheltered homeless from the 2020 PIT Count) were supposed to fit into those beds (most of which were not low-barrier), remained unexplained. The devil is often in the details, which is why people who insist on flying blind avoid discussing them.

Second, it reinforced the perception that the City Administration didn't want to meaningfully address homelessness (i.e., scaling resources up to match the scale of the problem); they simply didn't want to see it in parks, on sidewalks, under bridges, or on the sidewalk in front of City Hall. And if that meant using unverified "jello numbers" about non-existent shelter beds to justify a law enforcement sweep to clear the sidewalk in front of City Hall of peaceful protesters, well, so be it.[26]

Third, these events reinforced a perception regarding the City Administration's attitude toward peaceful protests against their broken and failed homeless policy. In the spirit of Hans Christian Anderson, and *The Emperor's New Clothes*, the Emperor simply could not tolerate anyone protesting his new clothes. Those new clothes might not exist, but how dare anyone be so rude and arrogant as to protest and point it out. Speaking truth to power is seldom received with appreciation by those on the receiving end.

The Chicken Coop

After the 48-Hour Notices were issued, Julie Garcia and Jewels Helping Hands met with the campers at City Hall to discuss their options and what they wanted to do. Reflecting on that day, Julie described the thinking process that resulted in the move to the WSDOT property.

"The campers decided that they were unwilling to allow the police to come in and take their things. They wanted to move somewhere else to avoid that from happening. We're talking about December in the snow and it was very cold. Losing their items would be sentencing them to death in freezing weather, and Jewels Helping hands had no ability to replace all of those items for those folks. Finding a spot to move to was very hard because homeless folks

"The Chicken Coop" on WSDOT property

are not allowed to exist anywhere in our county safely. So we thought about taking folks to already existing camps. But how unfair is that to the folks who were trying to maintain by themselves in independent encampments? We would be bringing people to an encampment that wasn't noticed by law enforcement yet. So we couldn't take them to encampments we already knew were there. We had been caring for the folks that were staying on that WSDOT property on Second and Ray for about three years. We called it the chicken coop because there was a man who lived there in a chicken coop, and it had just been referred to by outreach as the chicken coop area. So, there were already people experiencing homelessness staying and existing on that property. All we did was to move 68 people from City Hall to that WSDOT property."[27]

Preston

The move from City Hall to the WSDOT property known as "the chicken coop" began later the day of the 14th. Residents at the City Hall camp had to decide what they wanted to do, and everything had to be packed and moved. Breaking the camp down and moving residents to the new location took two days.

Two days before Christmas, 2021, I was filming at the nascent Camp Hope at 2nd & Ray when I saw an umbrella fighting to keep snow out of a tent. I decided the person holding it was someone I should meet. His name was Preston, one of the early residents of Camp Hope. I asked if he would talk with me and allow me to film our conversation for a documentary on the Camp, and he agreed.

Preston and his umbrella
days before Christmas of 2021

"So, what started your homeless journey?" I asked. "This one?" he asked, and continued,

"Thinking that I was actually getting into a home, and then not being able to actually get into that home, and leaving the home to get into the home. The confusion of it all just piled up and it didn't all fit together. And so, I'm in this spot and it's a lot better than walking around with five bags on your shoulders. And every time you go to work, you have to bring your own house with you."

Preston was very open and honest about why he avoids local shelters. "Have you tried any of the local shelters?" I asked.

"No, because I'm native spiritual and a majority of the shelters make you do like a religious thing. Also, I have PTSD. And so, it's kind of like fight or flight. So if somebody else is in the room and starts screaming, yelling, I start screaming, yelling, or I sneak out the back door and leave and I don't want to ruin any resources that I had by just staying a night or two and doing that. So I stay away."

Preston ended our conversation by reflecting on his stay at Camp Hope, and the possibility of housing,

"This is a lot better because it actually it helps out others at home, if people see that you're homeless. I'm homeless because of my mental illness mostly. I know that. There's some people who are homeless for other reasons. You'll never get rid of homelessness, even if everybody gets a house. There's going to be still people out there who don't want to live in those houses."

Epilogue

Moving Camp Hope to the new location at 2nd & Ray took two days. But Preston's story reminds us that resolving the issues that created Camp Hope would take much longer. Meaningfully addressing issues of chronic homelessness usually does. But in order to do this and to move forward as a Community with a coherent and effective homeless policy, we need to come to terms with the true size and nature of the problem: Homelessness is much larger than you think. And that's where we need to go next.

A Place to Exist

4 - Homelessness Is Larger Than You Think

The winter of 2021-2022 saw two events that would significantly impact the shape of homelessness and homeless services moving forward. The first event, of course, was the creation of Camp Hope. Starting as a peaceful protest on the sidewalk in front of City Hall with a few dozen tents and campers drawing attention to the lack of sufficient shelter beds, it would become a movement and grow into the largest single homeless camp in the State of Washington, re-located to WSDOT property along I-90. But a second event also unfolded that has since been overshadowed by Camp Hope.

In late December of 2021, the National Weather Service predicted bone-chilling single-digit temperatures. In spite of the peaceful protest of Camp Hope in front of City Hall, the City of Spokane had made no provision for warming centers to keep the unsheltered homeless warm and safe. On Wednesday, December 22, 3 days before Christmas, I received a call from my long-time friend Marty McKinney at Truth Ministries.

The Convention Center Warming Shelter on opening day.

"Dude," he said, "I just got off the phone with (person from the City of Spokane). They want to open a warming shelter for around 150 people at the Convention Center by Noon on Sunday. And they want to know if I'd be willing to operate it."

I was surprised, but not as surprised as I was about to be.

"If I say yes," Marty continued, "would you be willing to be my Shelter Director and run it?"

Wow. Didn't see that coming. I was both stunned and flattered. Marty and I go back nearly 20 years. I had served on his board for many years, had worked with the men in the shelter, and done just about everything a shelter director could or should do. And there had been others. This wouldn't be my first rodeo.

"You know me," I responded, "I want to be part of the solution, so I can't say no. But I need to talk it over with my wife and get her perspective."

Marty chuckled, "Yeah, I know. I haven't told Julie (Marty's wife) yet either!"

We both laughed, but we knew it was serious business. Opening a shelter for 150 chronically unsheltered people with only 3 days to prepare was a cross between a fool's errand and a Herculean task.

"The City will provide everything," he said. *Always famous last words*, I thought to myself, as Marty continued, "We'll need to provide the staff and run the daily operations."

We talked a little longer about the challenges we would realistically face, and concluded our talk with a deadline. "I'll call you tomorrow," Marty concluded, "The

City wants an answer by then."

As events turned out, both our families (yes, it was a family decision in both our houses) decided against operating the Convention Center Warming Shelter and the contract went to the Guardians Foundation. The Warming Shelter opened with 150 mats on the floor of a large ballroom, initiating a two-week existence fraught with problems. The first night saw all 150 mats filled with unsheltered homeless individuals. The second night, the number rose to 250. According to the shelter operator, with whom I had an extensive personal conversation about the shelter, the number of unsheltered homeless in the Convention Center Warming Shelter peaked at more than 450, or 3 times the number the City of Spokane had originally expected or planned for.[28] According to the Shelter operator, on a guided tour of the Shelter at its peak, he took the Mayor of Spokane from room to room filled with unsheltered individuals. "Every time we entered another room filled with people, the Mayor would say, 'I can't believe this.'"

Welcome to the intersection of reality and denial.

This event, and the Mayor's response, accurately illustrates a historic problem - a lack of understanding among local political leaders and homeless policymakers regarding the true extent of homelessness. They were unable to believe what they saw with their own eyes: homelessness is a much bigger issue than leadership had been willing to acknowledge. And the best way to not solve any problem, including meaningfully addressing homelessness, is to underestimate its size and to build your plans accordingly. Building a new shelter to house 350 chronically homeless people and declaring it the solution for the 689 residents of Camp Hope, or for the 955 known-and-counted unsheltered homeless (from the 2023 Point-In-Time Count), or for general homelessness in Spokane, would be like Captain John Smith of Titanic fame cutting off the infamous iceberg at eye level and declaring, *Problem solved! No more iceberg. Full speed ahead.*

This event also helps to explain both the existence of Camp Hope and our larger community's response to its existence. Camp Hope came into existence because Spokane's political and business leaders had spent years underestimating or denying the true size of homelessness in our Community. The community response, summarized in a series of front-page ads in the *Spokesman-Review* newspaper declaring *Camp Hope Must Close!*, embodied the response of a community roused from its slumber of denial and forced to look daily at the reality of what they had been told didn't exist: homelessness on a large scale.

The Challenge of Data And Definitions

Understanding the world of unsheltered homelessness and the phenomenon of Camp Hope has to begin with a better understanding of homelessness. To do that, let's start with some simple questions. How many people are experiencing homelessness in America today? How about your community? How about in Spokane? Answering these simple questions is no simple task, and that's where we need to start.

Current discussions around homelessness tend to focus on the importance of data and data-driven solutions, and rightfully so. Of course, the linchpin of any data-driven approach to homelessness is, well, good data. And that's where the challenges begin, starting with counting the homeless. The Point-In-Time Count is an annual census of people experiencing homelessness in the shelters and on the streets of communities across America. The PIT Count (as it's commonly referred to) is required by the Federal Department of Housing and Urban Development (and has been since 2007) for any community receiving Federal financial assistance to address homelessness.[29]

How we define homelessness determines how many homeless people we actually count. The PIT Count defines homelessness in narrow terms of "sheltered" and "unsheltered." In other words, you're homeless if you're staying in a homeless shelter (or some form of transitional housing), or if you're sleeping unsheltered under a bridge or in a homeless camp somewhere. But the McKinney-Vento Act, which falls under the Department of Education and tracks homeless school students, defines being homeless as not living in your own permanent residence, including being "doubled up" or "couch surfing" with family or friends. Two different definitions, two different counts, resulting in two very different tallies of those experiencing homelessness.

In my documentary filmmaking on homelessness during the three years leading up to Camp Hope, I maintained that the City of Spokane, along with other regional leaders, consistently underestimated the true size of homelessness in our Community, and built its plans accordingly. In my second documentary, *The Hidden Homeless: Families Experiencing Homelessness*, I devoted the opening segment to describing *A River of Homelessness* that flows through our community.[30] For that segment, I conducted an original survey of homelessness in greater Spokane over a 3 year period. I asked local homeless shelters to provide their unduplicated numbers of people who passed through their shelter systems during each of 3 years (2016, 2017, 2018).

By unduplicated I meant that we're making a serious effort NOT to inflate the numbers by counting the same people multiple times. And, trust me, an accurate unduplicated count is a bigger challenge than you might think. Next, we included numbers for local area school students experiencing

Original Unduplicated Homeless Numbers			
	2016	2017	2018
Shelters	6,521	8,459	5,503
School Students	3,659	3,137	3,263
School Families	1,830	1,269	1,246
Totals	11,832	11,471	11,319

homelessness as tracked by local school districts under the McKinney-Vento Act and reported to the Washington State Office of the Superintendent of Public Instruction. We also made allowances for their families. After all, if the kids are homeless, chances are good that the whole family is homeless.

Finally, we compared our revised numbers with those recorded by each year's official Point-In-Time Count. The results caught our attention. For 2016 our numbers showed a total of 11,832 individuals experiencing homelessness in Greater Spokane. But the Point In Time Count recorded only 981 or about 8% of our numbers. For 2017 our numbers showed 11,471 while the Point In Time Count recorded only 1,090. For 2018, our numbers were 11,319 against a Point-In-Time count of 1,245. When we averaged our annual totals into a 3-year average, we found a 3-year average of 11,541 individuals experiencing homelessness against a Point-In-Time count average of 1,105.

Here's the disturbing take-away: In an average year, relying only on the results of the Point-In-Time Count, we may only be

Point-In-Time Count As % of Original Unduplicated Count				
	2016	2017	2018	Average
Unduplicated Count	11,832	11,471	11,319	11,541
Point-In-Time Count	981	1,090	1,245	1,105
Percentage	8%	10%	11%	10%

counting 1-in-10 people experiencing homelessness in the Greater Spokane area. We can only wonder if similar results would be found in other communities. These numbers suggest a compelling reason why we're having such a difficult time moving the needle when it comes to meaningfully addressing homelessness in our Community. Our needle is broken. The issue is larger than we understand. Much larger.

But, How Much Larger?

In August of 2022 I received a copy of *Snapshot of Homelessness In Washington State for January 2022*, a report compiled and published by the Washington State Department of Commerce. And the story it tells regarding the true size of homelessness in Washington State borders on being breathtaking.

While producing our documentary, *The Night of the Unsheltered Homeless,* I had received an earlier copy of the same report, *Snapshot of Homelessness In Washington State for January 2020.* Table 3 of that earlier report ("Unstably Housed or Homeless Persons") showed 12,920 individuals in Spokane County living either in unstable housing or homeless (numbers that closely mirrored what we had found a year earlier). Table 4 of that report ("Homeless Persons") showed 5,483 individuals experiencing homelessness in Spokane County.

Comparison of 2020 & 2022 Shapshot of Homelessness In Washington State			
2020 Table 3 Unstably Housed or Homeless Persons (Spokane)	2022 Table 3 Unstably Housed or Homeless Persons (Spokane)	Net Change	Percentage Change
12,920	16,459	+ 3,539	27%
2020 Table 4 Homeless Persons (Spokane)	2022 Table 4 Homeless Persons (Spokane)	Net Change	Percentage Change
5,483	14,282	+ 8,799	160%

But the *2022 Snapshot of Homelessness* report did a deeper dive into homeless data from a variety of sources and found a noticeable - even breathtaking - change in the numbers of those individuals and families experiencing homelessness (the authors explain their revised methodology that resulted in the increases). The table above compares the two reports for 2020 and 2022.

Homelessness: A Pond or A River

As we can see from the above graphic, the 2022 report showed a 160% increase in "Table 4 Homeless Persons" compared to the 2020 report. This does NOT mean that the number of homeless persons actually increased by 160%, but that the improved methodology used for the 2022 report potentially identified more individuals who met the criteria to be classified as homeless. They

Homelessness in Spokane is a River, not a pond. From our documentary, *The Hidden Homeless*.

were always there, part of the unseen River of Homelessness. We simply chose not to count them or to see them. And there is none so blind as the one who will not see. Commenting on the 2022 report in the *Spokesman-Review*, Shawn Vestal noted,

"While it includes the chronically homeless street population, it also captures many other unhoused people who are less noticeable on the sidewalks: living with friends and relatives, sleeping in cars and cheap motel rooms, doubling up and tripling up with others. And here's something truly sobering: For as large as it is, the latest figure doesn't include homeless people who are not in the public-assistance system in some fashion."[31]

Yes, the River of Homelessness that flows for the most part unseen through our Community is much deeper and wider than we have been willing to acknowledge.

For more years than I can remember, regional homeless policymakers have unconsciously (but very genuinely) treated homelessness as a pond. Once a year we count all the "fish" in the pond (last time 2,390). We then proceed to build a plan to catch all the fish and drain the pond. We talk about shelter beds and capacity because if we're going to drain the pond we'll need beds for everyone in the pond. After all, if we can do that and squeeze them into enough shelter beds, then we can "solve" homelessness. Right? Every 5-Year or 10-Year plan to end homelessness (and I've seen several) rests on this assumption.

But homelessness isn't a pond, in Spokane or anywhere else. Homelessness is a river. The Greek Philosopher Heraclitus once observed, "No man ever steps in the same river twice, for it's not the same river and he's not the same man . . . . everything flows, nothing stands still." Heraclitus had a way with words, and his insight is relevant to our discussion of homelessness. It's easy to count the fish in a pond, because it's relatively static. But the *River of Homelessness* is much more dynamic, always flowing, never standing still. You never step into the same *River of Homelessness* twice, because it isn't the same river the next time you step into it. It's a river fed by families in crisis, losing their housing, staying with friends and relatives until the welcome wears out, then sleeping in their car in a local Walmart parking lot. It's a river fed by tributaries of poverty, often generational and extremely difficult to escape, that leave individuals and families living on a financial bubble, one paycheck or emergency away from losing their housing. It's fed by single moms with kids, a very high-risk group for homelessness. According to the MIT Living Wage Project, a single mother of 2 needs to earn $38.02 an hour to have a living wage in Spokane County.[32] That's like working 2 shifts at the Amazon fulfillment center, and still falling short. Good luck with that. And, yes, it's a river fed by a chronic lack of affordable housing (as Ben Stuckart will explain later in detail in Chapter 20).[33]

On a Saturday in December of 2022, I was at the Flying J "truck town" at Broadway & I-90 filling 20 propane tanks for Camp Hope. I struck up a conversation with the customer behind me who was patiently waiting for me to get done. We talked about the Camp and about homelessness. In the process, he shared that his rent had just been raised from $750/month to (take a deep breath) $1,750!! He openly wondered how long it would be before he, too, was homeless. And, yes, homelessness is a river fed by a tributary of mental health and substance abuse challenges with no options or resources for those whose mental health or substance abuse issues have left them homeless and vulnerable, and without any viable options for moving forward.

Epilogue

Welcome to the *River of Homelessness* that flows through our community (and many other communities). Not a pond to be counted and drained, but a river that is deeper and wider and more inclusive than we understand or have embraced. Many of the tributaries that contribute to this *River of Homelessness* are explored in a recent (and excellent) article in *The Atlantic* magazine, "The Obvious Answer To Homelessness."[34] It's time for us as a community to embrace the reality that meaningfully addressing homelessness isn't about Spokane meeting the legal requirements of *Martin v Boise* or *Johnson v City of Grants Pass* (or any other court ruling, for that matter). Yes, those requirements need to be met when it comes to emergency shelter capacity and criminalizing the homeless for existing. But meaningfully addressing homelessness is going to require us to go "upstream" to address and divert the tributaries that feed this river. Any homeless plan that fails to do so is little more than smoke-and-mirrors, an exercise in arguing over the makeup of the pond, and an exercise destined to eventual failure. It's time for us as a community to embrace the reality of the River of Homelessness that affects us all, not just those experiencing it.

A Place to Exist

2022 saw a burst of activity in the homeless services and shelter community. A new "Homeless Plan 2.0," political wrangling over, and eventual approval and opening of, a new City-sponsored shelter, and the creation and growth of the State's largest homeless encampment.

In early 2022, the Washington State Legislature passed *The Right of Way Initiative* that provided $144 million in new funds, administered by the Department of Commerce, intended to resolve homeless encampments on WSDOT properties across the State of Washington. $24.3 million was specifically allocated by the Department of Commerce to fund housing solutions for the residents of Camp Hope. In other words, the existence of Camp Hope brought over $24 million of *new* funding into the Spokane homeless services community to address chronic unsheltered homelessness.

But Camp Hope itself was brought into existence by Spokane's poorly kept secret.

Although well known among homeless advocates and service providers, it's a poorly kept secret (among the general public, at least) that, in the years preceding Camp Hope, the Spokane city-wide homeless shelter system did not have sufficient shelter beds for its known and counted homeless population. Prior to November of 2019, the City of Spokane's Community Housing and Human Services department published no official count of shelter bed capacity. In November of that year, the CHHS department began keeping a *Shelter Capacity Report* spreadsheet to track how many beds existed in the City-wide shelter system, and how they were being used.[35] Up to that time, no one knew exactly how many beds actually existed, or how they were being used or not used. In other words, there was no accessible shelter bed data, and without past data it's impossible to build realistic future plans. In the absence of such data, you're flying blind. In order to build realistic and effective plans for meaningfully addressing homelessness (or to at least accommodate those experiencing homelessness), you need at least two sets of data (you actually need more than two, but we'll start with these):

1. You need to know the total number of known-and-counted individuals experiencing homelessness (total, sheltered, and unsheltered) vis-a-vis the annual Point In Time Count, and
2. You need to know the total number of shelter beds in the City-Wide System.

Using numbers from the annual Point In Time Count and the City of Spokane's *Shelter Capacity Report*, lets try to understand this poorly kept secret. We'll summarize what follows in a graphic below.[36]

The 2019 Point In Time Count [37]

- Total Homeless - 1,309 individuals experiencing homelessness in our community.
- Total Sheltered - 994 were classified as "Sheltered"[38]
- Total Unsheltered - 315 were classified as "Unsheltered"
- Total Shelter Beds - 722 total shelter beds[39]

- Total Shelter Beds As % of Total Homeless - 55%

In 2019, at the time of the Point In Time Count, there were shelter beds for only 55 out of every 100 people experiencing homelessness in Spokane, and shelters were operating at 108% of capacity, with an additional 315 individuals living "unsheltered." These numbers beg the question, *Where were the 315 unsheltered individuals supposed to go?*

The 2020 Point In Time Count (conducted in January, prior to the outbreak of COVID)[40]

- Total Homeless - 1,559 individuals experiencing homelessness in our community.
- Total Sheltered - 1,018 were classified as "Sheltered" [41]
- Total Unsheltered - 541 were classified as "Unsheltered"
- Total Shelter Beds - 805 total shelter beds
- Total Shelter Beds As % of Total Homeless - 52%

In 2020, at the time of the Point In Time Count, there were emergency shelter beds for only 52 out of every 100 people experiencing homelessness in Spokane, and shelters were operating at 99% of capacity, with an additional 541 individuals living Unsheltered. These numbers beg the question, *Where were the 541 unsheltered individuals supposed to go?*

The 2021 Point In Time Count 2021 was a COVID year that saw a drastically truncated homeless count of only those living in shelters. The Unsheltered were either estimated or altogether ignored, resulting in unreliable numbers.

- Total Homeless - 992 individuals experiencing homelessness in our community.
- Total Sheltered - 992 were classified as "Sheltered"[42]
- Total Unsheltered - Unknown
- Total Shelter Beds - 713 total shelter beds
- Total Shelter Beds As % of Total Homeless - Unknown

In 2021, at the time of the Point In Time Count, there were 713 shelter beds in the City-wide shelter system, and 763 individuals staying at those shelters (which means shelters were operating at 107% of capacity). And the unsheltered homeless hadn't even been counted, which begs the question, *Where were the unsheltered homeless supposed to go?*

The 2022 Point In Time Count

- Total Homeless - 1,757 individuals experiencing homelessness in our community.
- Total Sheltered - 934 were classified as "Sheltered" [43]
- Total Unsheltered - 823 were classified as "Unsheltered"
- Total Shelter Beds - 710 total shelter beds
- Total Shelter Beds As % of Total Homeless - 40%

In 2022, at the time of the Point In Time Count, there were emergency shelter beds for only 40 out of every 100 people experiencing homelessness in Spokane, and shelters were operating at 102% of capacity, with an additional 823 individuals living Unsheltered. These numbers beg the question, *Where were the 823 unsheltered individuals supposed to go?* Part of the answer to that question is, *689 of them went to Camp Hope.*

	Point In Time Count vs Total Shelter Beds				
	Total PIT Count	Sheltered Count	Unsheltered Count	Total Shelter Beds	Shelter Beds As % Of Total Homeless
2017	1,090	952	138	Unknown	Unknown
2018	1,245	935	310	Unknown	Unknown
2019	1,309	994	315	722	55%
2020	1,559	1,017	541	805	52%
2021	992	992	Unknown	713	Unknown
2022	1,757	934	823	710	40%
2023	2,390	1,435	955	1,095	46%

The 2023 Point In Time Count
- Total Homeless - 2,390 individuals experiencing homelessness in our community.
- Total Sheltered - 1,435 were classified as "Sheltered" [44]
- Total Unsheltered - 955 were classified as "Unsheltered"
- Total Shelter Beds - 1,095 total shelter beds
- Total Shelter Beds As % of Total Homeless - 46%

In 2023, at the time of the Point In Time Count, there were emergency shelter beds for only 46 out of every 100 people experiencing homelessness in Spokane, and shelters were operating at 101% of capacity, with an additional 955 individuals living "Unsheltered." According to the 2023 PIT Count, overall homelessness increased by 633 individuals (or 36%) over the 2022 Count. Just the increase in overall homelessness alone would fill two(2) additional TRAC shelters. These numbers beg the question, *Where were the 955 unsheltered individuals supposed to go?* That question would take on renewed significance after Camp Hope closed and the unsheltered homeless were left with no options. [45]

A Summary of Shelter Bed Capacity
Referring to the graphic on the next page, *Shelter Bed Capacity By Shelter (as of*

Shelter Bed Capacity By Shelter (as of June 2023)		
Shelter	Beds	Low Barrier
Cannon Street Shelter (CLOSED)	0	0
Crosswalk Youth Shelter (VOA)	18	18
Family Promise (Households w/ Minor Children)	80	80
House of Charity (Adult Men)	135	135
Trent Shelter (Adult Co-Ed)	350	350
Truth Ministries (Adult Men)	64	64
UGM Men's Shelter (Adult Men)	125	0
UGM Crisis Shelter for Women & Children	80	0
VOA Young Adult Shelter (18-24 Years)	44	44
VOA Hope House (Adult Women)	80	80
YWCA Domestic Violence Shelter	39	39
Totals	1,015	810

June 2023), the City-wide emergency shelter system in Spokane remained in flux throughout 2023. In May of 2023, the City of Spokane closed the Cannon Street Shelter due to budget constraints, moving the 80 residents to the TRAC shelter, but without increasing the bed capacity at TRAC. The only way to move 80 people into a shelter without increasing capacity is by displacing existing residents. In simple terms, it appears that as many residents left the TRAC shelter as entered from the Cannon Shelter.

Prior to May of 2023, the city-wide shelter system had 1,095 total beds (890 of which were low-barrier). After May of 2023, the city-wide shelter capacity fell to 1,015. Again, to place this in perspective, that's enough beds for 43 out of 100 (or 43%) of the 2,390 known and counted homeless population recorded by the 2023 Point In Time Count.

Why All This Hand-Wringing Over Shelter Bed Availability?

By this point you may be experiencing information overload and asking yourself why all of this hand-wringing over shelter bed availability is even important in the greater scheme of things. Good question, and the answer is two-fold.

First, welcome to Spokane's historical and perennial homeless policy shortfall.

A lack of sufficient shelter beds for the known and counted homeless population. Consider 2,390 individuals experiencing homelessness in January of 2023 and only 1,095 shelter beds at that time. The shortfall of 1,214 beds alone in 2023 could explain the existence of Camp Hope, or the potential creation of a future Camp Hope if nothing changes.[46]

Second, welcome to the Federal 9th Circuit. It's important to note that recent Federal court decisions in the 9th Circuit have focused on 1) the number of known and counted homeless individuals according to the local Point In Time Count, and 2) the number of permanent, year-round shelter beds available to those experiencing homelessness. In Spokane, the number of city-wide shelter beds (1,095) equaled 46% of the known and counted homeless population from the 2023 Point In Time Count (2,390). [47]

In September of 2018, the United States Court of Appeals For the Ninth Circuit handed down a ruling in a case known as *Martin v. City of Boise* that involved public

FOR PUBLICATION

UNITED STATES COURT OF APPEALS
FOR THE NINTH CIRCUIT

ROBERT MARTIN; LAWRENCE LEE SMITH; ROBERT ANDERSON; JANET F. BELL; PAMELA S. HAWKES; and BASIL E. HUMPHREY,
Plaintiffs-Appellants,

v.

CITY OF BOISE,
Defendant-Appellee.

No. 15-35845

D.C. No.
1:09-cv-00540-REB

OPINION

Appeal from the United States District Court
for the District of Idaho
Ronald E. Bush, Chief Magistrate Judge, Presiding

Argued and Submitted July 13, 2017
Portland, Oregon

Filed September 4, 2018

Before: Marsha S. Berzon, Paul J. Watford, and John B. Owens, Circuit Judges.

camping by six homeless individuals in Boise, Idaho. The Court of Appeals ruled that "so long as there is a greater number of homeless individuals in [a jurisdiction] than the number of available beds [in shelters], the jurisdiction cannot prosecute homeless individuals for involuntarily sitting, lying, and sleeping in public."[48] Note the formula used by the Court: more homeless individuals than the number of available beds in shelters. This formula established by *Martin v. City of Boise* was acknowledged and followed by the United States Court of Appeals For the Ninth Circuit in *Johnson v. City of Grants Pass,*

"The formula established in Martin is that the government cannot prosecute homeless people for sleeping in public if there 'is a greater number of homeless individuals in [a jurisdiction] than the number of available' shelter spaces. Id. (alteration in original)." [49]

The City of Spokane has consistently maintained a position that as long as they have sufficient open beds somewhere in the system for the particular group of homeless individuals they are attempting to remove (e.g., 65 residents of Camp

Hope, and 65 open beds at the City's TRAC shelter), then the City is in compliance with the requirements of *Martin v. City of Boise*. But the formula laid out by *Martin v. City of Boise*, and followed in *Johnson v. City of Grants Pass*, appears much broader in scope than a single group of x-number of individuals versus x-number of available shelter beds. And that's the heart of the practical and legal argument over Spokane homeless policy, shelter beds, and Camp Hope.

Epilogue

Now you know Spokane's poorly kept secret, that, in the years leading up to Camp Hope, the Spokane city-wide shelter system never had the sufficient shelter beds (low-barrier or otherwise) to accommodate the known-and-counted number of those experiencing homelessness in Spokane, as required by the two Federal Court decisions cited above. You also know the secret of why Camp Hope came into being in the first place, and why it was so fiercely resisted by local homeless policymakers: it represented the tangible and visible embodiment of the broken and failed homeless policy of those who had consistently denied the true size of homelessness in Spokane and had built their plans accordingly, while publicly promoting the existence of shelter beds best described as *The Emperor's New Clothes*.

6 - From A Peaceful Protest To An Earthquake

Someone once observed that "History is prelude."[50] Three years after the original Camp Hope, the same issue that brought the original Camp Hope to City Hall - the absence of any plan to provide adequate shelter/warming space and beds during the winter months - raised its head again on Friday, December 10th with the formation of another homeless tent camp on the steps of City Hall as a peaceful protest. Camp Hope was back. And duplicating its response from three years earlier, the City issued 48 Hour *Notice to Remove Property* to the residents of Camp Hope with nowhere for them to go. In a peaceful response, and with no alternatives, the Camp residents moved from City Hall to the WSDOT property located north of I-90 at 2nd & Ray.

In the waning days of December, 2021, the camp at 2nd & Ray that started with roughly a dozen tents and 20 residents had grown to approximately 68 people. But neither winter nor homelessness had disappeared. The City Administration, embarrassed by the Camp Hope episode and under pressure from pending single-digit weather and public outcry, announced plans to open a temporary warming center at the Spokane Convention Center with an initial capacity for 150 guests. The original capacity was quickly reached and the City was forced to increase capacity by adding additional rooms, thanks to the efforts of outreach workers who visited camps and overpasses to encourage all who were able to come to the Convention Center. The Convention Center Warming Shelter would operate from Monday, December 27 until Sunday, January 9th, peaking at 486 people (a number that never appeared in any media reports, which is why we told more of that story in the opening of the previous chapter).

Number of Camp Residents Total Unsheltered Homeless Average Nightly Open Beds	December 2021
Number of Residents @ Camp Hope (City Hall)	116
Total Unsheltered Homeless (2020 PIT Count)	541
Average of Nightly Open Low-Barrier Shelter Beds	58

But it's important to underscore that the Convention Center Warming Shelter would not have come about had it not been for the existence of Camp Hope on the steps of City Hall. A large winter warming shelter simply hadn't been part of any coherent City plan to keep people safe during the winter months. Throughout the episode, the City of Spokane's official and public position was that no need existed for any additional shelters or warming centers, and certainly no reason to scale things up to match the scale of the challenge. Their position was based on the supposed availability of a handful of shelter beds that were not being utilized in the city-wide shelter system. This repeated mantra permeated local media unchallenged, and clouded public perception of homelessness in general, and of Camp Hope in particular. The graphic on the previous page shows the reality regarding available shelter beds at the end of December, 2021.[51]

Throughout the Camp Hope episode at City Hall, the City of Spokane's basic narrative was that homelessness in Spokane would be solved if all those 'shelter resistant' people would just go to a local shelter and get a bed. The eventual reality of 486 people at the Convention Center demonstrated for all to see that the City's basic narrative was not just wrong but fatally flawed, and that the number of those experiencing homelessness was much larger than policymakers were willing to admit, much less plan for. As I said in Segment 2 of my documentary,

> "If you want to see first-hand what a failed homeless policy and acute program failure look like, they're staying warm and spending the week at the Convention Center."

The Night of the Unsheltered Homeless, "One sure-fire way to not solve a problem is to underestimate its size and to make your plans accordingly. Any plan created on such bad data will be smaller than the problem we're trying to solve and will doom us to eventual program failure." As I shared with the 1,700 members of the Spokane Homeless Coalition in my December 29, 2021 email, "If you want to see first-hand what a failed homeless policy and acute program failure look like, they're staying warm and spending the week at the Convention Center."

Camp Hope In The Winter of 2022

During the winter months of 2022, from January through March, the number of campers living at Camp Hope at 2nd & Ray remained around 68. Soon after the Camp established itself there, the Washington State Department of Transportation (WSDOT) put up *No Trespassing* signage and posted its own *Notice And Order To Remove* with a deadline of Friday, January 14. But in a statement released that Friday afternoon, WSDOT announced that it was temporarily rescinding those notices because Spokane simply didn't have an adequate number of available shelter beds.[52] Camp Hope on WSDOT property had now become a safe place for

State of Washington
Notice And Order To Remove

the unsheltered homeless to exist, setting the stage to become the largest homeless encampment in the State of Washington.

Camp Hope, whether at City Hall or on the WSDOT property at 2nd & Ray, didn't exist in a vacuum. It existed within the context of a larger dispute over homeless policy. Two years earlier, a 2020 article in the *Spokesman-Review* newspaper expressed the question that had yet to be answered, but that lies at the center of Camp Hope: *Spokane City Leaders Ask: when shelter isn't an option, where do the homeless turn?*[53] Homeless camps large and small are home to people who, for a wide variety of reasons, cannot stay (or "maintain") in traditional shelters, even low-barrier shelters. Mental health, social anxiety, PTSD, substance abuse, and chronic medical conditions are just a few of the reasons why many of the unsheltered and chronically homeless avoid shelters (yes, even those with open beds) and choose to live in homeless camps, or under downtown city viaducts.

Shelters, Not Fences

In February of 2022, the dispute over homeless policy included building fences under downtown viaducts to prevent homeless camping. During the week of February 8, 2022, the City of Spokane began installing chain link fencing along the sidewalks under the Browne Street viaduct. The goal was to deter people experiencing homelessness downtown from seeking refuge from the elements by camping under the viaduct. This issue had become particularly chronic under the Browne Street viaduct, located roughly a block north of the House of Charity homeless shelter. The City admitted a lack of

"Shelters, Not Fences" posting the names of 140 individuals who died while homeless. This one honored the author's friend, Jeremy.

sufficient shelter space to accommodate the homeless camping under city viaducts, but offered no alternative solution, and no places for the unsheltered homeless to go. City Council President Breean Beggs agreed with the need to clean up the downtown viaducts, but questioned the new fencing policy, "It's kind of cruel to say we're going to make it impossible for you to camp even though you don't have another place to go." Commenting on the fence policy, Barry Barfield, administrator for the Spokane Homeless Coalition, described the new policy as "basically make life as hard and miserable as possible for homeless people sleeping on our sidewalks."[54]

On Saturday, March 5th, peaceful protesters gathered in downtown Spokane to protest the City's fencing policy. The event featured speakers and attendees having the opportunity to attach cards (like the one featured here) to the fences bearing the names of more than 140 individuals who had died while homeless over the past two years. I produced a documentary short piece on the event that's available for viewing on our YouTube Channel.[55] In an irony not missed by those of us working to manage Camp Hope at 2nd & Ray, the City's new plan to fence off downtown viaducts and reduce downtown homeless camping had the net effect of forcing those downtown campers to find a new place to camp, and they did . . . at Camp Hope!

One of those downtown campers who made the early transition from downtown to 2nd & Ray was Cindy, whom I've followed and filmed through three low-barrier shelters, and now a homeless camp. If you could look Cindy up in the CMIS homeless tracking system,[56] you'd find that she's had and lost housing more than once. Why? Because meaningfully addressing homelessness isn't simply about more shelter space, or giving people housing. It's about working with them to address all of the other issues that have kept them under city viaducts or in shelters or in homeless camps, and have prevented them from keeping the housing they worked long and hard to get. The reality is that none of us foresaw that, in the months ahead, 689 more "Cindy's" would call Camp Hope their home.

On February 10, I posted my thoughts on the new fences in an email, *Shelters, Not Fences*, to the Spokane Homeless Coalition as follows: [57]

"Something there is that doesn't love a wall," wrote Robert Frost, in one of my favorite poems, *Mending Wall*. The 45-line poem is a masterful reflection on the annual meeting of two neighbors who share a common property border, separated by a wall that requires annual repair. The poem is also a reflective metaphor on why we build walls (and fences) and why keep them in place rather than rethinking their purpose . . . and their need. The apex of the poem, at least for me, is found in these words:

> "Before I built a wall I'd ask to know
> What I was walling in or walling out,
> And to whom I was like to give offense."

There are many kinds of fences, and many types of walls, but they all exist for one of two basic purposes. We build them - or let others build them - to either keep something (or someone) in, or to keep them out. We're either walling in, or walling out. If only our City leaders read more and better poetry, starting with Frost. Perhaps they would think twice about building fences as part of some ill-conceived policy to address downtown homelessness, all the while repeating the mantra of Frost's neighbor, "He only says, 'Good fences make good neighbors.'"

No, they don't.

It's time to openly ask and answer the two questions Frost posed: What are we walling (or fencing) in, and what are we walling (or fencing) out?

What are we fencing out? We're fencing out the homeless under excuses of public safety and ease of cleaning. In other words, we're getting rid of those dirty and dangerous homeless people. Welcome to the first two steps in dehumanizing those experiencing homelessness: unlike you and me, they're dirty and dangerous. In the process, we're fencing out any hope of humanizing homelessness and those experiencing it. We're fencing out kindness, compassion, understanding, engagement, and human empathy. We're fencing out what Lincoln described as "the better angels of our nature."

What are we fencing in? We're fencing in stereotypes. We're fencing in prejudice. We're fencing in an "us-against-them" narrative and tone that has haunted Spokane across years and administrations, reinforcing tones of anger and attitudes of "they're getting what they deserve." We're fencing in the unspoken but underlying attitude that quietly whispers, "We don't want to solve homelessness. We simply don't want to see it anywhere downtown."

Whatever lessons the Convention Center Warming Shelter offered us had been forgotten. The City had returned to the pre-Convention Center mantra of "We have sufficient open beds for those people." That was their mantra before 486 people descended on the Convention Center, several times the number of supposedly open shelter beds. Those of us who serve this challenging population had hoped that the City had learned an important lesson as a result of the Convention Center, but apparently not. Building shelters is expensive. Building fences is cheap. The City opted for cheap. Meaningfully addressing homelessness in its diversity is going to require something different. Frost's poem ends with a neighborly caution that we would do well to reflect on:

"Bringing a stone grasped firmly by the top
In each hand, like an old-stone savage armed.
He moves in darkness as it seems to me,
Not of woods only and the shade of trees.
He will not go behind his father's saying,
And he likes having thought of it so well
He says again, 'Good fences make good neighbors.'"[58]

No, they don't.

A Conversation With Chancey

It's now late February at Camp Hope, and mild winter weather (that would soon change into snow and single digit cold in the week ahead) gave me another chance to connect with people at the Camp. Winter thaws can be deceptive that way. When you've been filming documentaries among the homeless for several years as I have, you're going to run across some familiar faces. That's what happened when I found Chancey at Camp Hope. I had met and filmed Chancey six months earlier in the Summer of 2021 as I was building a Segment on law enforcement sweeps of the homeless for my documentary, *The Night of the Unsheltered Homeless*. And now we're connecting again at Camp Hope. Our conversation went like this:

MAURICE: "So, you and I talked last summer down in Coeur d'Alene Park, and now here we are at the tent camp. What's been going on in the past six months?"

CHANCEY: "About pretty much the same, one day at a time. Can't get no housing. Been approved. Got the money. But there ain't none out

MAURICE:"	"So where were you staying before you came down here?"
CHANCEY:	"I move my truck every two days, just wherever I can find that's quiet. Yeah. I just move every two days. Down around HOC (*Editor: House of Charity*) they want you to move every 24 hours."
MAURICE:	"Now, you said you've got money for housing?"
CHANCEY:	"Yeah. Section Eight, $920 a month I got toward housing. I can't find an efficiency apartment. They got them all over the place. When I first got here, she (his caseworker) said, sure, you can sign up. You only got a two-and-a-half to three year wait. I thought she was joking. She was not joking. I talked to a lot of people on the street. Oh, yeah, that's about right. I mean, that's a long time wait for one of those little apartments."

Chancey's experience highlights a fundamental cause of homelessness. A lack of affordable housing. You can resolve all of the other issues holding someone in homelessness, but if there is no affordable and appropriate housing available for them to access, then they have no exit ramp out of homelessness. And a homeless camp becomes a seemingly permanent detour on a never-ending journey.

Spring Growth Brings Challenges

Throughout the winter months of 2022, the number of campers living at Camp Hope at 2nd & Ray remained around 68. No one enjoys winter camping in the snow and freezing temperatures (I did it as a Boy Scout and didn't much enjoy it then!). But as Winter gave way to Spring weather, numbers at the camp began to grow. By late March, Camp Hope was home to 60 tents, 26 RVs and camper-trailers, and 120 residents (up 76% from the winter numbers). In a month's time, by late April, those numbers had grown to 172 tents and 401 residents (an increase of

Camp Population Growth By Month		
Month	Population	% Growth
January	68	0
February	68	0
March	120	76%
April	401	234%
May	468	17%

234% in a month!), with more arriving every day, including people being sent, and even dropped off, by local law enforcement. That's right. City law enforcement was unofficially using the Camp as an overflow shelter! Such numbers raised a serious question: *If the City of Spokane succeeded in convincing WSDOT to close the camp, where were those 401 people supposed to go?* The opening of the City's new TRAC (Trent Resource and Assistance Center) shelter on Trent was still five months away with a planned initial capacity of 250, leaving 151 individuals with no place to go. And that didn't include other unsheltered homeless individuals we were aware of, staying in other camps.

As Camp Hope was growing in the Spring of 2022, I took some time to film and talk with residents of the homeless encampment where the Camp Hope movement began (see Chapter 3, "Trent & Waterworks"). I had filmed that camp back in December of 2021 and wanted to see what had changed. The camp appeared to be about half the size it was back then, but with several dozen people still camping there. And that was just one of many homeless encampments tracked by local law enforcement via their regularly published *Illegal Camping Status List*. Many of those campers would eventually migrate to Camp Hope as law enforcement forced them to move on.

The month of April brought the release of the preliminary results from the 2022 Point In Time Count. The results were eye-catching. The "Unsheltered" part of the count showed 823 unsheltered individuals experiencing homelessness, up 52% from the 2020 PIT count of 541. With area shelters at-or-near capacity, where were those 823 individuals supposed to go?

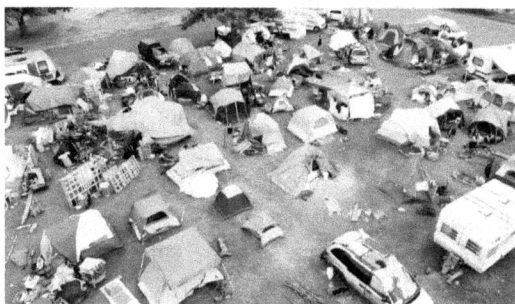

One quarter of Camp Hope
in late Spring of 2022 (and growing).

Roughly half of them found their way to Camp Hope by the Spring of 2022, with others scattered in smaller camps around Spokane County. As other encampments emptied, Camp Hope grew, because it had become the only safe place for them to exist.

That Spring, while most public attention was focused on Camp Hope, the City of Spokane announced the proposed location for a new shelter to accommodate up to 250 people.[59] The building, located at 4320 E. Trent Avenue, was a 33,000 square foot industrial warehouse with one bathroom and no other running water. According to the City, the size and location of the building, in and industrial area, outside of downtown, and close to a bus stop, made the building an ideal candidate. Time and events would prove otherwise. As City Councilman Zack Zappone noted during early discussions, "A shelter on Trent is not going to solve homelessness in Spokane. It is not even going to allow us to clear a camp because it doesn't have enough capacity."[60]

The growth of Camp Hope in the Spring of 2022 brought new challenges, both to the Camp and to local homeless policymakers and City leaders. One of the lessons I've discovered over the years, by both instruction and example, is that good leaders set people up for success, while poor leaders set people up for failure. This soon became a lesson on display in the City's response to Camp Hope. As Spring blended into summer, Camp Hope was very much a self-managed homeless encampment. The eventual funding from the Department of Commerce and the Right of Way Initiative was still months away, while Camp Hope was growing daily to the size of a small eastern Washington town on one residential city block. With that growth came all of the practical problems of a small town but with none of the supporting infrastructure, such as garbage collection, sanitation (sewer), and water. The City of Spokane provided three medium-size trash dumpsters, but consistently denied repeated requests by Jewels Helping Hands for water and electricity service, although connections were readily available on the property, to prevent giving the Camp the appearance of permanency. Simply put, by its actions and inactions, the City of Spokane had set the camp up to fail. Had it not been for the resiliency of the residents, and the diligent work of Jewels Helping Hands to meet the challenges the City created, the Camp might well have imploded under the weight of all those challenges.

Over time, both in documentary interviews and in personal conversations, I asked Julie Garcia to talk to me about the early challenges she and Jewels Helping Hands faced in managing Camp Hope with minimal outside help and in the face of City opposition. What follows is my digest of those conversations and Julie's thoughts on several of those challenges.

People. First, the sheer amount of people; just finding space for the people who showed up every day with no place to exist. Dealing with RV's and cars, because that's a big population of folks who live unsheltered, people who live in RVs and cars. Getting them onto this small piece of property with all the tents as well. So just the space first of all.

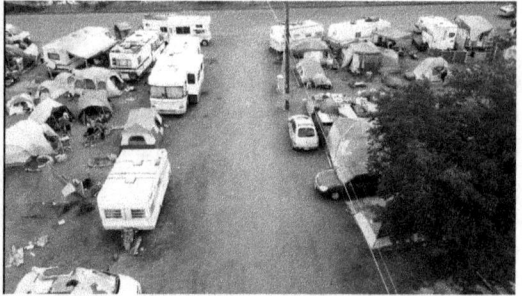

Just a few of the RVs and people at Camp Hope in late Spring of 2022.

Secondly, we're dealing with people with immense trauma, all trying to coexist together. And were doing this with no funding at all. There was no funding to have security, employees, or peer support. We didn't have any money for that. So we had to teach the camp to pick up the slack from what we couldn't do. We still supported the camp. We taught them how to create government. They had their own security team. At Jewels Helping Hands we didn't have a staff member that stayed on site 24/7. We didn't even have a staff member on site for half of the day. We just came in and out of the camp and talked regularly with the campers there. The City provided two private security guards (employees of Crowd Management Services or CMS) 24 hours a day, but they weren't allowed to engage with our clients.

Food. So, meals. First of all, how do we feed 500 people? We all know and we hear the same stories about will they get food stamps? Okay. So for a single individual, the max amount of food stamp benefits is $191 a month. That will feed one person with no way to cook. They pooled together some of their money to cook together. But Jewels has a food bank, so we just started bringing things that they could cook. We set up a meal train, and a meal train is just a Google

Community partners delivering
fresh food boxes

document where community members sign up and say, "Yeah, I'm going to feed some members of the camp today. I'm going to feed them at lunch. I'm going to feed them at dinner. I'm going to bring them some breakfast." And organizations that have feeding sites started to come out and feed these folks because our folks were no longer downtown and not utilizing all of the food at those feeding sites anymore. That should show people that these are the things that are needed. If there is a feeding site close to a homeless encampment, it will be utilized. If we just put feeding sites anywhere and expect people to show up and go there, they won't. Where they're at is where they have to be served.

Sanitation And Porta Potties. We eventually had 12 porta potties. There was supposed to be 16, but we deal with what we can get. We actually started with only six. A lady named Barb Brock, a supporter of Jewels Helping Hands, gave us six porta potties for a month. We didn't know how long this encampment was going to last or if it was. We had no idea what was going to happen. There was no plan ahead of time. So the six porta potties got there and the camp began to grow and we couldn't keep up with only six porta potties. American On-Site,

Porta Potties being delivered and serviced

our porta potty company, was going to pull out because they literally had to come out every day and dump them. We asked the city, in fact, we spent a couple months begging the city, to give us more porta potties to put out there. At least it keeps the public health and safety under control. And the City refused. So Empire Health Foundation decided to help us out and pay for more porta potties to come out. And we worked out a really good agreement with American On-Site. We would clean the porta potties if they would just dump them.

Garbage. People generate trash. Most of us generate trash, but we have a garage to hide it, and we're not using everything disposable. Remember, there was no electricity or water service at the Camp. There was no access to those things. So every single thing that they used had to be disposable. They lived in the weather. So, when rain comes in, it destroys a lot of things, especially clothes and bedding. There was no laundry service there. So, what do you do

The challenge of managing garbage for a small town on one city block

with a tent full of your wet stuff? Well, you throw it away and we start all over again every single time that we have a downpour of rain. The City of Spokane provided three trash dumpsters. We could have used a lot more, but we were allotted three, so we used those to the best of our ability. Once the Right of Way Initiative kicked in, WSDOT helped us with excess trash. WSDOT also helped us remove the shopping carts. Shopping carts are gigantic for homeless people. As much as we stress that they should not take shopping carts, they still carry their things in shopping carts and WSDOT agreed to come out and take them back to the stores they came from.

Public Health And Safety. Public health and safety were huge. That was a lot of people in one area. So, we reached out to the Spokane Fire Department and the Spokane Regional Health Department for some guidance on what we could do to at least mitigate their safety concerns. Everyone would prefer no open burning. But, if these folks were going to burn, which they were, because they have to stay warm, what could we do to make it safer? So, we asked the fire department to come out and give us some guidance on safe burning. Same thing with the Spokane Regional Health Department. If they're going to be on this property, what can we do to keep them safe and healthy? So, what

Two of three large water tanks for clean drinking & washing water

both the Fire Department and the Health District did was they came out, walked through the camp, and gave us some ideas on what was acceptable and what wasn't acceptable and what needed to change moving forward.

Water. The Camp existed on a water desert. City water connections were available, but the City of Spokane refused to authorize water service. We purchased and set up three water tanks holding 900 gallons of water. A local neighbor of the camp authorized us to extend a hose from their house to provide the water to fill those tanks three times a week.

Assessments and Resources

By early July of 2022, the Camp had grown to 623 residents, with more arriving almost every day, making it the size of a small eastern Washington town. One of the big challenges confronting outreach workers was how to discover and meet the needs of so many people without having a basic understanding of their individual situations. Why were they

Julie Garcia doing an assessment with a Camp resident.

homeless? How many of them were housing ready, should housing come available? How many were struggling with substance abuse issues? What about mental health issues? Did they have the "core documents" needed for identification? And how do you get that information from chronically homeless and unsheltered individuals who don't trust traditional systems set up to help them? The answer came on Tuesday and Wednesday, July 6th and 7th when staff and volunteers from Jewels Helping Hands conducted more than six hundred individual assessments of camp residents. We'll analyze the results of those assessments in Chapter 7.

But assessments alone don't solve problems. To begin the process of turning assessments into solutions, the two days of assessments were followed by a two-day resource fair on adjacent WSDOT property.[61] The location allowed camp residents to walk across the street from the camp and talk with service providers about things ranging from getting a new phone to signing up for drug treatment. The resource fair served to reinforce a growing principle that would not only impact Camp residents moving forward, but

Resource Fair at Camp Hope following assessments.

would signal a significant change in homeless services, at least for those willing to listen and learn: to be effective, homeless services need to be delivered on site where those experiencing homelessness exist, rather than off site in an office. Moving forward, outreach, rather than "in-reach" would define effective homeless services and the providers offering them.

The Cooling Tent

In late July of 2022, as temperatures rose into the high 90s and above, and with nowhere for the unsheltered homeless to go to escape the heat, Act Two of *"Our Annual Greek Homeless Tragedy"* began to unfold. The City Administration refused to open designated cooling centers and simply urged those needing to escape the sweltering heat to go to a

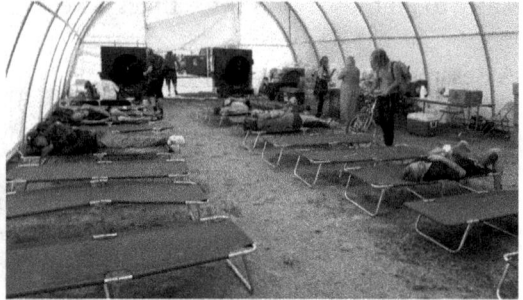
Cooling Tent showing industrial coolers and residents.

local library to cool off. For the 689 residents of Camp Hope, that would have meant walking (in the heat) a mile to the Liberty Park Library and leaving their personal property unattended at the Camp. It was an unrealistic plan (by just the shear numbers, if for no other reason), created by upper middle-class policy makers in cubicles for people living in abject poverty and homelessness in homeless camps.

Fortunately, the organizers and overseers of Camp Hope had a more practical idea. Set up a cooling tent on WSDOT property across the street from the Camp, easily accessible by Camp residents. And that's what community volunteers, including a local construction crew, pitched in to make happen.[62] The tent was erected over two days, and large industrial-size swamp coolers (run on portable generators) were installed to cool it down. The idea of the cooling tent was so practical, reasonable, and effective that the Spokane City Council unanimously approved funding to reimburse Empire Health for the cost of operating the cooling center,[63] while community groups pitched in to supply water, ice, and even ice cream. Julie Garcia, the Camp organizer and overseer, reflected on the importance of the tent and the struggle - from money to permits - to get it up and running.

Julie Garcia reflecting on the importance of the cooling tent.

"The cooling tent was the most important thing we did to keep people alive. There were no deaths in the camp over this stretch of heat wave, which is so different compared to the deaths last year with the same kind of heat. So, this saved lives. I know it was an issue with the city, but for Jewels Helping Hands, once this cooling center was up, it wasn't coming down. So, Empire Health stepped up and gave us a grant for the full amount so that we could get it going and running. City Council has now allocated money to pay Empire Health back for getting this up and running because traditionally the government takes too long to do anything. And these folks would have been dead by Monday when they decided to bring it to the attention of everybody else. Everything in it is donated ice, water, Gatorade, food, clothing, staff. The community's really stepping up to make this happen. I hope that the city figures out how we can permit it. I hope that everybody figures out how we can work together to keep it running."

In spite of strong opposition to the tent by the City Administration,[64] including a refusal to permit it and the threat of a $536-per-day fine, WSDOT refused to remove the tent.[65] The tent would remain up for the duration of Camp Hope, transitioning into a Resource/Access Tent for Camp residents and serving as a winter warming tent during the winter months of 2022-2023.

Growth And Activity In The Fading Days of Summer

It's now late summer. The pace of activity in and around the Camp is increasing, as so is the public scrutiny of the Camp. As I said earlier, Camp Hope did not exist in a vacuum. It existed within the context of a burgeoning homeless crisis (with unsheltered homelessness up by 52%), an inadequate and failed homeless policy going back years, and grudging attempts to "right the boat" with the opening of a new shelter whenever the homeless spilled out onto the sidewalk in front of City Hall or filled Convention Center ballrooms to overflowing.

The early July headcount at the Camp had shown 623 residents. In late July/early August, Jewels Helping Hands conducted the last physical headcount of Camp residents before WSDOT assumed direct oversight of the Camp and began fencing, badging, and counting residents in September. That final headcount showed 689 residents in the Camp.

Camp Population Growth By Month		
Month	Population	% Growth
February	68	0
March	120	76%
April	401	234%
May	468	17%
June	500	3%
July	623	24%
August	689	11%

A Place to Exist

WSDOT Assumes Oversight Of Camp Hope

In early 2022, the Washington State Legislature had passed the *Right of Way Initiative* designed to move people off state right of way properties and into better living situations, including the residents of Camp Hope. The ROW Initiative (as it came to be called) appropriated $144 million to be managed by the State Department of Commerce and allocated to five specific counties in the state, including King, Pierce, Snohomish, Thurston, and Spokane (see Chapter 18 for more details on the ROW Initiative). In June, the Department of Commerce announced that approximately $24.3 million would go to Spokane County to provide housing alternatives for Camp residents, and to eventually close the Camp (for a breakdown of how those funds were allocated, see *Spokane Funding Allocation From The Right of Way Initiative* in Chapter 11). By late summer, early funding from the ROW initiative began to be felt. In August, the Department of Commerce released the first installment ($500,000) of the $3.4 million allotted to Empire Health Foundation to manage Camp Hope through the end of June, 2023.[66] EHF, in turn, contracted with Jewels Helping Hands to implement that task. Up until this time, there had been no outside funding to manage or operate the Camp.

With funding becoming available, Julie Garcia came to me with a question: Would I be willing to join the Jewels staff as a Camp Manager. "Maurice," she said, "I need someone who knows and understands our people, and who I can trust, to clean and organize the Camp." Up until now, I had been involved, just not in an official capacity. I had helped set the camp up back in December of 2021. I had filmed it from the very beginning with a plan for producing a documentary on the Camp for Community Minded Television

The author sitting atop his office, a dumpster!

(Comcast 14), where I served as a community producer. Saying yes would mean laying down my documentary plan and camera for the foreseeable future and taking up the job description of "chief garbage collector" for the very camp I had helped set up nine months earlier. "Yes," I said, "Of course I would. I'm all in." I simply couldn't reconcile my own message of building the *shalom* of our homeless friends with the idea of saying "No" to an opportunity to personally do what I had so often encouraged others to do. Get involved, and become part of the solution. And that's how I became Camp Manager for Water, Sanitation, and Garbage.

The Transition Month of September

As Summer gave way to Fall in the Inland Northwest, a September 4th opinion piece by columnist Shawn Vestal at the *Spokesman-Review* accurately summed up the situation at Camp Hope: *"A quick end to camp hope is probably not on the horizon."* His observations would prove almost prophetic.

> "The odds are beyond long that Camp Hope will be gone, and the 650 or so residents housed, by the time the snow flies . . . . If you could move every single human being out of Camp Hope tomorrow, there would be nowhere for hundreds of them to go." [67]

Politicians wanted a quick resolution to the problem of unsheltered homelessness represented by the Camp. Homeless advocates and service providers knew better, but few people were listening. The work to clear and close Camp Hope would be a marathon for better housing options, not a sprint to a handful of available shelter beds.

The month of September became a busy transition month for the Camp, and for the larger Spokane Community. The Camp itself transitioned from being a Camp managed by the residents, with help from Jewels Helping Hands, to one actively managed by Jewels Helping Hands in cooperation with Empire Health and WSDOT under the ROW initiative. The Camp also transitioned to finding itself placed under a growing public and media spotlight, along with a growing tone of *us-against-them* including threats by the City and County officials to close the Camp.

On Thursday, September 8th, the City of Spokane sent a letter to State officials (WSDOT and the Department of Commerce) threatening legal action if the State did not begin removing the Camp by September 23, with the removal to be completed by October 14th. [68] In other words, the City gave WSDOT and the State three weeks to solve the problem of chronic unsheltered homelessness, embodied at Camp Hope, a problem the City had not been able to solve in three years. In the weeks ahead, such public official demand-threats would prove counter-productive with unintended - but predictable - consequences for the Camp and the Community.

An Open Letter To The Spokane City Administration

On Monday, September 19, I sent an email to the 1,700+ members of the Spokane Homeless Coalition titled *"An Open Letter To The Spokane City Administration."* In it I touched on several recent events at and around the Camp that occurred following the City of Spokane's announcement of its plan to have the property declared a "nuisance" property. In the process I addressed what I saw as the "cancerous" tone the City Administration was setting for our larger Community toward those experiencing homelessness. That letter is reproduced below without alteration.

Mr. Johnnie Perkins
Administrator, City of Spokane

A Place to Exist

Nadine Woodward
Mayor, City of Spokane

Mr. Perkins and Madame Mayor,

Another Incident

As I am sure you are now aware, on Thursday, September 15th, a Dodge Caravan belonging to the City of Spokane Water Department (license plate XMT39245D) visited a private home next to Camp Hope where a City employee disconnected a water hose that was supplying water to the Camp. This individual also proceeded to take two of the hoses that had been connected to the water supply, effectively stealing private property. A police report for the theft was filed (Incident Number 2022-20163829, taken by Officer Mead, Badge 1314). I would expect this kind of stupid behavior from a couple of "bored & beered-up" college sophomores, not City of Spokane employees. This incident represents the second effort by City of Spokane employees to cut off water to the Camp, the first being the visit of two uniformed SPD officers to the home supplying the water and asking the homeowner to please stop supplying water. This second time, the homeowner was livid that the City would come on her property, turn off water, and disconnect hoses without her permission or any legal authority to do so. Again, the City of Spokane should be ashamed of its behavior in these incidents. But there is a growing reason why such incidents are occurring ever more frequently.

A Growing Cancer

Over the past year, I have successfully fought off two rounds of cancer. While I'll spare you the details, the aftereffects and scars left over from those two fights present me with daily reminders of how insidious, dangerous, and life-changing cancer can be, and how long-lasting those scars and aftereffects are. But now I and my community, beginning with the homeless community, are being confronted with one of the most insidious and dangerous cancers any individual or community can face. It is the cancer of anger and bigotry leveled toward those experiencing homelessness. It is the cancer of marginalization and dehumanization that declares 600(+) homeless individuals to be nothing more than "nuisances" to be "abated," removed by whatever means might work, including cutting off their water supply.

The Wisdom of Simon & Garfunkel

Simon & Garfunkel famously sang *"Fools," said I, "You do not know, Silence like a cancer grows."* To remain silent about this growing cancer would be to acquiesce and allow it to grow unchecked and unopposed, eventually destroying the Shalom of our entire community and falsely placing the blame upon "those homeless nuisances." The blame for this broken Shalom must fall on the doorstep of those who broke it: on the steps of City Hall. Dehumanize 600(+) individuals experiencing homeless by declaring them to be nothing more than public nuisances, then force them into the new prize shelter project that can't accommodate more than 250 (when fully ramped up). Forget the impossible math of forcing 600(+) people into 250 beds. Forget individual stories of people trying to work their way out of homelessness. Forget the vulnerable elderly and disabled in the Camp who have NOWHERE to go. Forget the terminally ill cancer patients who live there because they have no other options. Forget basic human compassion and simply label everyone on that city block as drug addicted, mentally ill, criminal derelicts, and "nuisances" to be "abated."

From A Peaceful Protest To An Earthquake

Forget that "How we see people is the beginning of how we treat people." Forget that this spreading cancer threatens the Shalom of our entire community, not just Camp Hope. *"Fools," said I, "You do not know, Silence like a cancer grows."*

This Cancer Is Metastasizing And Spreading

This spreading cancer is metastasizing to the larger community. Two weeks ago we had an incident at the Camp when an individual from Idaho showed up ostensibly to help a camp resident retrieve a stolen laptop. This vigilante from outside the Camp came armed with a GoPro video camera and a semi-automatic pistol sidearm! I confronted him and told him he could not be on Camp property wearing a sidearm, and if he wanted to remain on the property he would need to secure the weapon in his car. He tried to argue with me about his Second Amendment rights. I politely but firmly told him I didn't care, and that he either had to leave or remove the weapon. He reluctantly complied and a more serious confrontation was averted. I reported the incident to the SPD officer assigned to watch the Camp, but the officer (whose name I'm withholding) said, *"There's nothing we can do about it."* Right. A local news outlet later ran a story about the stolen property and the laptop at the Camp and was given the GoPro footage. But no mention in the story about an armed vigilante, only rampant property crime and a stolen laptop that was recovered later that day off Camp property.
"Fools," said I, "You do not know, Silence like a cancer grows."

It Is Spreading To Local Media

This cancer of anger, bigotry, marginalization, and dehumanization leveled toward those experiencing homelessness is metastasizing and spreading, even into the local media. People who should know better and should be discerning are now manifesting the symptoms of this disease. A local news outlet recently ran a story describing the Camp as "worse than Lord of the Flies" and featuring an anonymous interview with someone describing alleged incidents of rape and "branding" in the Camp. No such incident was ever reported to Camp managers (I'm one of the managers and am in the Camp daily) or to the police (who will tell you that there's nothing they can do without a police report being filed). As Julie Garcia, the founder of Jewels Helping Hands, is a rape survivor herself, we take such accusations VERY seriously. The day after the story aired (without ANY requested input from Jewels Helping Hands), we scoured the Camp, asking residents for ANY information they might have regarding the alleged rape incident. The result? Neither a victim nor a perpetrator, nor a time, nor a location, could be identified. Only unsubstantiated rumor that gets reported as "news." And the "branding" incident? We found the individual involved, who confessed that he had been involved in a drug deal gone bad, and the "branding" was the consequence (that doesn't make it good or right, just very painful). He wouldn't say if the incident occurred on Camp property or elsewhere. But, yes, he was the victim of a pissed-off drug dealer. Being stupid has consequences, whether in a homeless camp or anywhere else life takes you. Lesson learned . . . hopefully.
"Fools," said I, "You do not know, Silence like a cancer grows."

An Abnormal Atmosphere

Under any normal conditions, journalistic integrity would have rejected both of the above stories as nothing more than anonymous and unsubstantiated accusations. But this spreading cancer has created an environment where stories that should have been scrutinized and rejected as anonymous rumors and gossip become believable and printable stories. By publishing them, news outlets become a megaphone and a vehicle for spreading this cancer into our larger community; this cancer of anger, bigotry, rumor, gossip, marginalization, and dehumanization leveled toward those experiencing homelessness who have no way to defend themselves and no voice with which to tell their stories. As a result, don't waste time wondering why the residents of the West Hills Neighborhood (or ANY neighborhood, for that matter) don't want a shelter or transitional housing facility filled with those "nuisances" in their neighborhood. The cancer this Administration has created and fostered has spread and metastasized into the very neighborhoods the City needs for any homeless plan to succeed.

"Fools," said I, "You do not know, Silence like a cancer grows."

A Financial Cancer
This spreading cancer has financial implications. A story published by a local news outlet declared, "Camp Hope Costs Taxpayers Hundreds of Thousands, City Files Nuisance Order." That's right. Those homeless people are a nuisance that's costing Spokane big money. According to the story, the City of Spokane has spent more than $400,000 on garbage dumpsters and police overtime. Here's what's missing from the story. How does that expense (if accurate) compare with the more than $400,000 the City of Spokane overpaid for two weeks of operating a warming center at the Convention Center? That would be $200,000 per week at the Convention Center, compared with providing sanitation services at Camp Hope for more than 24 weeks, at a per week cost of less than $17,000. In comparison, the City has gotten one hell of a good deal for their expenses at Camp Hope but got royally ripped off at the Convention Center. Why was such a per week waste a justifiable expense at the Convention Center, but a per week cost of less than 1/10th (actually 8.5%) of that expense a terrible thing at Camp Hope? Answer: This spreading and metastasizing cancer can't do math, or re-interprets math to support the narrative of "nuisances," people who aren't worth the cost or effort of keeping them safe. And the City wants to be reimbursed for having to waste money on those "nuisances."

"Fools," said I, "You do not know, Silence like a cancer grows."

"She's Going To Be Okay, Mom"
Last Sunday, the 11th, I was picking up garbage on the perimeter of Camp Hope when a woman approached me. She told me her daughter (whom I met later) is in the Camp and has been homeless for a year. She lives two hours away and had driven to Spokane to check on her daughter. As we talked she began to weep. I held her as she sobbed, trying to comfort her saying, *"She's going to be okay, mom. She's going to be okay."* Perhaps what I should have told this distraught mother was the cancerous truth: *"Your daughter's going to be okay as long as some fool from the City doesn't cut off our water supply. She'll be okay as long as the City doesn't fine us for helping her, or the Mayor doesn't have her declared a nuisance and swept off this property with nowhere to go."* Let me know which truth I should be sharing with the moms, dads, and families that come to the Camp, concerned for the well-being of their loved ones and hearing from local media that they are all about to be swept off the property by a City that regards their loved ones as nothing more than nuisances.

"Fools, said I, You do not know, Silence like a cancer grows." [69]

From A Peaceful Protest To An Earthquake

On Tuesday, September 20, the State of Washington responded to the City with a letter signed by officials from the Washington State Patrol, the Washington State Department of Commerce and the Washington State Department of Transportation, declaring the City's deadline for clearing the camp to be "completely unrealistic given the scope of the issue and current lack of housing capacity."[70] There was more, and City Hall observers in the media described the tone and scope of the State's response as "scathing" in its rebuke of City leaders and their failure to meaningfully address homelessness.[71]

Director of Commerce Lisa Brown, front & second from left visiting Camp Hope, September 2022

Official threats against the Camp continued when, on Tuesday the 20th, the Spokane Fire Department demanded that Jewels Helping Hands remove the Resource/Access Tent (erected back in July) no later than Thursday the 22nd or face a $536 per-day fine. The next official threat came on Thursday, September 22nd when County Sheriff Knezovich announced his own plan to clear the Camp by mid-October.[72]

This week-long parade of threats and responses was best summed up in a Shawn Vestal column in the *Spokesman-Review* for Friday, September 23: "If dumb, angry responses to homelessness worked, we'd have solved it already." Cutting to the heart of the week's activities, Vestal wrote,

> "The community is desperate for effective, unified leadership on homelessness. Instead, we're being treated to "The Ozzie and Nadine Show" – a hacky farce of grandiose proportions, in which local officials who could make a real difference instead lash out, politicize, undermine, threaten and obstruct progress in bringing an end to Camp Hope." [73]

Despite the distraction of both the City and the County threatening lawsuits, issuing ultimatums for the Camp's closure, and generally promoting a negative tone of NIMBYism toward people experiencing homelessness in our Community, progress was being made toward organizing the Camp and preparing for the delivery of promised services. In late September, Washington State Department of Commerce Director Lisa Brown, paid a visit to the Camp to check on the status of the Camp as the impact of funding from the Right of Way Initiative began being felt.

Under the direction of Ken Crary (Jewels Chief of Operations) and myself, Jewels Helping Hands staff, along with Camp residents, began clearing and pushing back the perimeter of the Camp by 3-to-6 feet in order to create space for new fences to be installed. Trash was cleared while RVs and camper-trailers were rearranged. We all agreed that fencing was an important step for addressing safety and security challenges both

Security fences being installed around Camp Hope

inside and outside of the encampment. The fences, installed by a WSDOT contractor on Thursday, September 29th, gave camp management better access control over people entering and leaving the Camp while helping to protect Camp residents from outside harassment.

October's Unprecedented Events

October of 2022 became the first full month of Camp Hope functioning as a managed Camp, overseen by WSDOT and managed daily by Jewels Helping Hands with the assistance of service providers for housing, substance abuse counseling, peer navigation, and more. As a result, the Camp experienced a dramatic up-tick of activity.

In the first week of October, a WSDOT contractor installed privacy screening to the fence around Camp Hope's perimeter. The privacy screening offered an additional buffer between residents and the Community. The fence, along with the new front and rear gates, was inspected by the Spokane City Fire Marshal. The fence became an important step toward addressing safety and

Spokane Homeless Coalition meeting at Camp Hope, October 2022

security challenges felt both within and outside the Camp. WSDOT also hired a private security firm (Security Services Northwest) to provide 24/7 Camp security, to provide 24/7 perimeter patrol, and to work alongside Camp staff to control access to the Camp.

But the first week of October also witnessed an unprecedented event at the Camp. On Thursday, October 6th, the Spokane Homeless Coalition held its monthly meeting at Camp Hope. I'd been involved with the Coalition for over 15 years, and in all that time the Coalition had never met on the site of a homeless camp. The meeting attracted community attention with more than 150 people in attendance, including service providers, homeless policymakers, politicians, homeless advocates, media representatives, and community members. The presenters included a combination of homeless service providers and Camp residents sharing their perspectives and experiences. Attendees got to hear directly from Camp residents about their personal journeys through homelessness and what the existence of the Camp had meant to them. The event was a genuine community conversation about homelessness and the Camp, followed by tours through the Camp. I filmed the event and made it available on our YouTube Channel.[74]

The Identification Connection

Back in July, when Jewels Helping Hands conducted 601 written assessments of Camp residents, those assessments revealed that 98% of Camp residents needed help restoring lost or stolen identification. The need revealed by those assessments launched a project that became one of the highlights of Camp activity in the month of October.

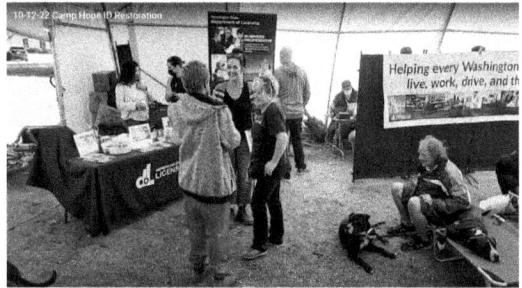

The "Identification Connection" helping Camp residents restore lost IDs

Officially known as *The Identification Connection,* on Wednesday, October 12, the project sponsored the first in a series of "ID Restoration Fests" at Camp Hope. Tammy Meyers, a homeless outreach worker and identification restoration specialist, worked behind the scene to coordinate the involvement of the Departments of Licensing and Health, convincing them to come and work on site and issue State IDs, driver's licenses, and birth certificates to residents who had previously had IDs or licenses in Washington but no longer had the cards in their possession (lost, stolen, etc.). Starting with the July assessments and with on-going assessments over several weeks, service providers at the Camp had learned that many Camp residents previously had their "core documents" (birth certificate, SS Card, State ID or Driver's License) but no longer had them in their possession. Lost or missing ID documentation was a major hurdle for Camp residents who wanted to take steps toward stabilization and long-term housing. Possessing valid and current identification is critical to employment, medical care, housing, and many other services. By prior arrangement through *The Identification Connection,* DOL employees would be onsite at Camp Hope every Wednesday for several weeks to continue the process of ID restoration with the practical goal of connecting those at the Camp to services and housing.

Badging, Tent Tagging, And Assessing

On Monday, Oct 17 Camp Management began implementing a Camp Hope Identification Badge system to monitor and control access to the Camp while giving Camp Management an accurate census of how many individuals resided in the Camp. Before receiving their badge, residents had to sign a Good Neighbor Agreement & Rules, designed to begin holding Camp Residents accountable for their behavior both inside and outside of the Camp. These Camp Hope Identification Badges served as a security tool to help determine who should or shouldn't be at the Camp, to identify who wanted to take a positive next step toward stabilization, and to help create a sense of order and engagement at the Camp. The badges became an important tool for service providers to know exactly how many individuals were living homeless at the Camp and who needed safe housing options and additional services. The badges also enabled Camp Management to effectively close the Camp to new

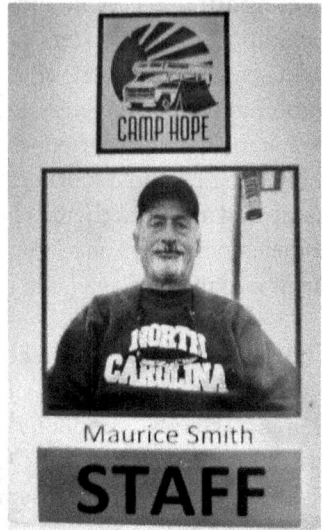

Author's Camp STAFF ID Badge. Resident badges showed resident's name and badge number.

residents once badging of all the residents was completed. Through this process, 467 badges were issued to Camp residents. By late October, with badging completed, the Camp was closed to new residents.

In addition to badging the residents, the Camp was divided into four quadrants (A, B, C, & D). Every tent in each quadrant was tagged and assigned a quadrant letter and a number. The residents of each tent were identified by name, badge number, tent number, and quadrant. This enabled caseworkers and Peer Navigators to more easily locate and work with each resident on their personalized exit plan.

As part of the process to receive a Camp Hope ID badge, Camp residents also completed another individual needs assessment. With the help of service providers, caseworkers, and peer support staff, this assessment collected more detailed and necessary data on the demographics of the Camp residents and looked more closely at what services each person needed. The assessments included questions about needs for such things as bus passes, health insurance, mental health counseling, substance use treatment, medical & first aid, and other items. The assessments also collected more details about each person's specific individual history and story. Those more in-depth assessments were critical to developing individual plans that would move residents onto a successful exit-ramp out of homelessness.

Official Threats And Lawsuits

From the very beginning, the City of Spokane's displeasure with Camp Hope, and its desire to close the Camp by any means possible, were no secret. Veiled attempts to harass the Camp and cause it to implode under its own weight included such things as denying water and electrical services requested by Camp managers, law enforcement refusal to respond to calls for help from Camp managers (documented in an article in the *Inlander*),[75] attempts by City employees to cut off the water being supplied by a sympathetic neighbor, and refusal to permit the Resource-Access tent where service providers worked with residents. But the Fall of 2022 saw official displeasure turn into official threats to close the Camp and to force residents into local shelters.

On Thursday, September 9th, Spokane City Administrator, Johnnie Perkins, sent an official letter to WSDOT demanding that the agency begin clearing Camp Hope from the 2nd & Ray property by 23 September, with the removal to be completed no later than October 14th.[76] That letter became the first in a stream of demands-threats made by the City and County of Spokane to remove the Camp. Later that same month, on the 22nd, Spokane County Sheriff Ozzie Knezovich announced his plan to clear the Camp by mid-October.[77] On Wednesday, October 5th, Spokane Police Chief Craig Meidl sent a letter to WSDOT and Jewels Helping Hands informing them that he was planning to pursue a Chronic Nuisance Notice for the 2nd & Ray property and declaring that the property and the Camp must be cleared by October 31st.[78] On Thursday, October 13th, Spokane Police Chief Craig Meidl and Spokane County Sheriff Ozzie Knezovich met to re-affirm their plans to clear the Camp by no later than mid-November.[79] And on Monday October 24th, the Sheriff announced his plan to set up an Emergency Operations Center to co-ordinate the removal of the Camp.[80]

A month of growing threats by law enforcement and local officials to forcibly remove the Camp culminated on Friday, October 28th when three Camp residents, along with Jewels Helping Hands, and Disability Rights Washington filed a Federal lawsuit in United States District Court for the Eastern District of Washington against the City of Spokane, Spokane County, Spokane County Sheriff Ozzie Knezovich, and Spokane Police Chief Craig Meidl.[81] The suit asked a Federal Court to declare that plans by local law enforcement to remove Camp residents and their property violated their constitutional rights, and to grant a Temporary Restraining Order (TRO) to prevent local law enforcement from arresting and removing Camp residents without probable cause of a criminal offense.

Adding to the anxiety and confusion of Camp residents regarding law enforcement's intentions were night-time helicopter surveillance flights conducted by Spokane County Sheriff's Department using search lights and infrared surveillance equipment to peer inside the Camp. These flights took place for three successive nights, Thursday, Friday, and Saturday, November 17, 18, and 19. Spokane County Sheriff Ozzie Knesovich claimed that the surveillance flights, used to count the number of residents in the Camp, were legal without a warrant. Attorney Jeffry Finer, representing Jewels Helping Hands and others in the Federal lawsuit filed at the end of October, disagreed. "You can use (IR imaging) if you're chasing someone who's running away, or a camper who's stranded, but can't use it to peer into someone's home to figure out how many people there are," Finer told the Spokesman-Review.[82]

Law Enforcement As A Tool Of Homeless Policy

In my four years of making documentaries on homelessness in Spokane, I've seen and filmed several law enforcement sweeps of homeless camps in a variety of locations, ranging from the sidewalk in front of City Hall to downtown sidewalks to city viaducts to camps along the Spokane River. Segment 3 ("Sweeps & Collateral Damage") of our documentary *The Night of the Unsheltered Homeless* focused on this issue in particular with footage of sweeps and interviews with those being swept. Civil Rights attorney Andrew Biviano was one of the attorneys representing the Camp residents in the Federal lawsuit.[83] He also sat for an interview with me for our documentary where he shared his perspective on the use of law enforcement as a tool of homeless policy, just as Spokane City and County officials were threatening to do against Camp Hope.

"Our current policy in Spokane of conducting police sweeps of homeless really fits into a very long historical narrative throughout the country of using the police power of the state to try to rid us of undesirables, whoever they might be, whether it was day laborers, or migrant workers, the poor, minorities, whether they be racial, or sexual, or otherwise, we have a long history of trying to solve that problem as we see with force, with criminal sanctions, with police, with jail, and judges, and punishment. And our history is very clear that it just doesn't work to meet the goals that we might have, and it's inhumane, and never goes to the root of the problem. Maybe it's the easiest fix that one can reach for. We have these police already here and they can use force and we can get an immediate response . . . by morning this area will be clear, but it doesn't do anything for the long run. It doesn't solve the root cause. If you remove someone from the street for a day, where do they go tomorrow? And then it just shows a lack of . . . empathy. I think the problem solving that we need, if we really want to solve this problem for our sake, if not for the other person's sake who we're frustrated with, we need to figure out what the root cause is. It's really unfortunate, I think, that there's so many better tools available. They are usually less expensive, more humane, and more long-term. The thing is, we need to have all of us invested in that. The other tools we might need, like funding, like places to go, community support, programs, treatment, housing, require political will, community will, financial commitment, all the things that are a little bit harder to do and take more time and attention, whereas, if you give it to the police, that's their problem. They'll take care of it. Don't think about it anymore. Out of sight, out of mind. And I think that's where the main disconnect is."[84]

The real-world impact of utilizing law enforcement as a primary tool in homeless policy - and its impact on the residents of Camp Hope - would soon become painfully evident.

November - A Month of Ramping Up Services
The work to stabilize and close the Camp by transitioning residents to safe and secure housing, rather than just "sweeping" the Camp and dispersing the residents to other outdoor locations, continued in November as services ramped up. By November, the on-site services offered to Camp residents included:

❏ Individualized case management and housing navigation from housing caseworkers with SLIHC, Revive, and on-site Peer Navigators.
❏ Recovery services provided onsite through Compassionate Addiction Treatment (CAT) via their mobile outreach van and on-site caseworkers.
❏ Onsite medical services provided by Street Medical Teams from the CHAS Denny-Murphy Clinic.
❏ Spokane Regional Health District providing services including COVID testing and vaccinations.
❏ Health insurance agencies such as Molina meeting with residents regularly to enroll them in health plans
❏ Reunification services to reunify people experiencing homelessness with family members. We bought a lot of bus tickets for people to return home to family in other communities.
❏ Life-Skills building workshops to assist residents with recovering basic life-skills. It's how we help residents become housing-ready and set them up for success when they move into housing.
❏ Food boxes and regular meal donations by a variety of faith-based and volunteer programs.
❏ Assistance with legal and judicial processes and needs, including walking residents through Community Court.
❏ Connecting residents with employment opportunities and programs.

Goals And Timelines
There's an old joke about the airline pilot who addresses the passengers, saying, "Ladies and gentlemen, I have good news and bad news. The bad news is, we're lost. The good news is, we're making excellent time!" Feel free to chuckle, but it does no practical good to fly faster if you don't know where you're going. Some wise person once defined a "fanatic" as someone who redoubles his (or her) efforts, having lost sight of their goal. No one wants to fly with a fanatical pilot who's lost sight of the

destination and simply wants to fly faster and "make good time."

If the goal for Camp Hope was to simply clear the Camp and remove those "homeless nuisances," then a law enforcement sweep and a forcible removal of the residents could have made that happen sooner rather than later. But if the goal was to close the Camp, end the cycle of homelessness that created the Camp in the first place, and build the individual Shalom we discussed back in Chapter 1, then a more thoughtful, methodical, and long-term approach was required. The unsheltered homelessness of Camp Hope wasn't created in a month, nor could it be solved in a month.

Both State-wide and nation-wide, the most successful efforts to meaningfully address unsheltered homelessness have involved the availability of different housing options, including temporary rental assistance in private market units, leasing of hotel rooms, tiny houses, temporary shelters that could provide some level of privacy, and federal housing vouchers dedicated to people who are unsheltered. The availability (or lack of availability) of those housing options was the single greatest factor impacting the timeline for closing the Camp in the Fall of 2022. The timeline for closing the Camp could have been much faster if the City and County of Spokane had possessed more housing options for the 689 unsheltered homeless who called Camp Hope their home in the Summer of 2022. But those options, in the quantity needed, simply didn't exist. And the focus of regional homeless policymakers was on ramping up the large warehouse shelter on east Trent so that the Camp could be forcibly closed, sending the residents to a large congregate shelter where most of them could not maintain, even if they were willing to go (which most were not).

Eliminating Barriers And Accessing Services

One of the lessons Camp Hope taught us was that eliminating barriers by offering on-site services was key to moving people experiencing unsheltered homelessness forward. On-site services - even in a homeless camp - represented services offered on their terms (immediate and accessible) rather than on our terms ("Make an appointment and come to our office"). November saw several examples of this approach and its effectiveness. Camp Hope managers and the service providers who worked there understood the importance of eliminating barriers that traditionally kept those experiencing homelessness from accessing the services they needed to exit homelessness. And one of those barriers was the proximity of services to those who needed them. Camp Hope managers took a simple approach. Bring the services as close as possible to the people who need them. And the month of November witnessed examples of this principle being actively worked out.

DSHS Mobile Services Arrive At Camp Hope - On Tuesday, November 1st, the Washington State Department of Social and Human Services brought their Mobile Community Services Office van to Camp Hope to work with the residents. The 40-foot van and eight DSHS staff came to the Camp to connect Camp residents to a variety of services and programs, including Electronic Benefits Transfer (EBT) cards that are used like debit cards in stores for people receiving food or other financial assistance. DSHS staff also enrolled residents in other available programs (including the Medicaid Savings Program, which helps cover some Medicaid costs such as deductibles, co-pays, etc.), reviewed existing cases, and connected residents with other agencies and programs. The DSHS mobile unit was on-site four days a week for two weeks. During their two weeks of work at Camp Hope, DSHS staff were able to help 161 residents to access services. Eliminating barriers and connecting residents with needed services was crucial in helping residents to successfully transition out of the Camp and into housing options as staff worked to close the Camp.

The Identification Connection Returns - As we described earlier, *The Identification Connection* is a program created by outreach worker Tammy Meyers in collaboration with Jewels Helping Hands. For six consecutive Wednesdays, from October 12 through the middle of November, *The Identification Connection* brought the state Department of Health and the Department of Licensing from Olympia and Spokane to the Camp to work with Camp Hope residents to obtain or replace lost identification, such as birth certificates and state issued IDs. Current and valid IDs are required for accessing jobs, obtaining permanent housing, and applying for other assistance. By the end of October, 213 state identification cards and 78 birth certificates had been issued to Camp Hope residents. People like Joseph Vara, a Camp resident who hadn't had a valid ID in 15 years(!), got their IDs restored and issued on-site through *The Identification Connection*.[85] By the time the program ended in late November, the Department of Health had issued 106 birth certificates, and the Department of Licensing had issued 400 ID cards!

Preparing For Winter

Winter arrived early at the Camp, bringing snow and freezing temperatures. Camp managers turned their attention to making sure Camp residents had what they needed: warmth, shelter and water. To provide warmth, large diesel-burning commercial heaters were installed to warm the Resource/Access tent and provide a warm space for residents and service providers. Managers also set up warming tents in the Camp with propane heaters where residents could warm up when needed. After relying on water from a nearby neighbor (via a garden hose that was starting to freeze and crack), Camp managers hired a water service to bring 800 gallons of potable water to the Camp twice a week to ensure public health and safety. The existing potable water tanks on site were fitted with heaters to prevent drinking water from freezing. Because cold temperatures, snow, and cycles of freezing and thawing had begun creating muddy conditions, gravel was brought in to provide traction, especially for the fire lane which ran down the center of the Camp and provided the main path through the Camp for residents and service vehicles.

A Surprise Visit

One Sunday afternoon in late November I received a phone call from Julie Garcia. "Maurice, the Governor is going to be at the Camp at 3 o'clock," she said. "Can you be there?" We had been told that Governor Inslee was paying close attention to the Camp and had asked for regular status updates, but his visit was unexpected and unannounced. I arrived at the Camp around 2:30

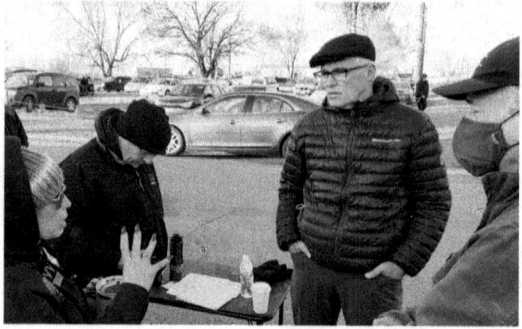

Governor Inslee visiting Camp Hope, November 2022

and hung out in the Resource/Access tent across from the main gate, expecting an "entourage." A little after 3pm, I looked toward the gate and saw two men, both casually dressed and chatting with the front gate security team. It took me a moment to realize it was Governor Inslee and his security person. No media. No entourage. Just him, visiting with the Jewels staff, expressing genuine interest, and asking how things were going. The unexpected visit was soon over, but its impact was longer lasting. The Governor's visit, along with the earlier visit of Commerce Secretary Lisa Brown, encouraged all of us that the Camp and its 467 residents weren't being ignored, but had the attention of government officials who could potentially make a difference and help everyone to move forward.

Better Demographics Helped Us Better Understand The Camp

Throughout the process of badging the Camp residents, on-going individual assessments gave Camp Managers a better understanding of the Camp and the changes that were taking place. The assessments were tracked and tabulated by the Spokane Low Income Housing Consortium (SLIHC), in partnership with the Empire Health Foundation and Jewels Helping Hands, working under contract with the state Department of Commerce. When the badging process was completed at the end of October, 467 resident badges had been issued and the camp was closed to new residents. By the end

Where Did They Come From?	
Number of Badged Residents	467
Greater Spokane (within 20 miles)	389 (83.3%)
City of Spokane	315 (70.7%)
Spokane County	9
Northeast Washington	16
Northern Idaho	22
Spokane Indian Reservation	4

of November (a period on 1 month), there were 433 Camp residents, a decrease of 34 people. 22 of those had gone to some form of housing: temporary housing (including a traditional shelter), or permanent supportive housing. The remaining 12 people had either left to reunite with family (both in Spokane and in other communities), or had received some other form of assistance to leave the Camp. Initial progress had been slow, but such results for a population of chronic and unsheltered homeless people were impressive. On more than one occasion local leaders publicly promoted the idea that most Camp Hope residents were from out of town, even from out of state, and that handing out bus tickets to send them back would solve much of Spokane's homeless problem.[86] But the on-the-ground data gathered from resident assessments painted a different picture of where those experiencing unsheltered homelessness at Camp Hope came from. Of the 467 badged residents of Camp Hope, 83% said they came for Greater Spokane (within 20 miles of the City), while 70.7% said they came from the City of Spokane.[87] The lesson was simple and clear: the overwhelming majority of Spokane's homeless (whether sheltered or unsheltered) are "home-grown."

Local Law Enforcement Visits Camp Hope

In spite of a Federal lawsuit to restrain law enforcement activity at Camp Hope that had been filed in late October, and in spite of the amazing progress Camp managers and service providers had made moving residents forward to better options, in early December the Camp was subjected to two days of law enforcement visits. For two days in a row, Tuesday and Wednesday, December 6th and 7th, Spokane law enforcement (both Spokane Police Department and Spokane County Sheriff's Department) sent a large

18 Law enforcement personnel gathering at the front gate of Camp Hope

contingent of officers to Camp Hope for the ostensible purpose of handing out "informational flyers" about available services. Camp Staff offered to distribute the flyers, but were told by the officers that they had to do it. Why so many officers were needed to distribute flyers is a mystery until you understand that their true reason for gaining access to the Camp was to engage in surveillance in preparation for something else. The flyers were an excuse, not a reason, for this exercise.

The flyer distributed on Tuesday displayed a NOTICE at the top declaring "This Camp Is To Be Closed" (no date given).[88] It appeared intended to frighten and intimidate, which it succeeded in doing to many Camp residents. The flyer was poorly produced and contained erroneous information. For example, the street address given for Compassionate Addiction Treatment (CAT's mobile outreach RV was parked at the Camp next to the Resource Tent) was the address for disgraced former State Representative Matt Shea's church (raising the interesting question of how that happened). On Wednesday, law enforcement returned with a revised flyer.[89] It seems that their surveillance operation wasn't as successful as they had hoped on the first visit and a second visit was needed.

At one point during Tuesday's exercise, I confronted a group of officers and told them that all of the "services" offered on their flyer were things Camp staff and service providers had been working with the residents on for the past four months, and that the very presence of Law Enforcement handing out the flyers represented an implicit declaration that no services have been offered to the residents prior to Tuesday's visit. Again, it's important to remember that the purpose of the exercise was NOT to hand out flyers but to engage in surveillance of the camp. I filmed both day's visits so that the Community could see for themselves what took place on these two days. [90]

Reflecting on those events in an email to the Spokane Homeless Coalition on December the 8th, I reminded Coalition members that,

"The role of every homeless advocate and service provider is to speak truth to power on behalf of the powerless, not to speak truth to the powerless on behalf of those in power. It is a calling that requires courage. But if we forget this calling - this responsibility that's been given to us - we will inevitably find ourselves serving the powerful, and oppressing the powerless. Beware."

Law Enforcement's "Disappointing and Harmful" Visit

In its "Camp Hope Update for December 7", WSDOT described the two-day episode of law enforcement invading the Camp as "Disappointing and Harmful." Plans were already underway to permanently close Camp Hope and to move people to substantially better housing when uniformed Spokane County Sheriff deputies and Spokane Police officers, and "mental health specialists" arrived unexpectedly to hand out fliers announcing that the camp was being closed. Why "mental health specialists" would participate in an event that seriously traumatized and injured the

NOTICE
THIS CAMP IS TO BE **CLOSED**
Shelter services and housing alternatives, including transportation, are available at:

Trent Resource & Assistance Center (TRAC)
4320 E Trent
509-280-6860

Additional Emergency Shelters

Cannon Street Shelter 527 S Cannon Street 509-624-7821	**The Way Out Shelter** 55 W Mission Avenue 509-866-5476
House of Charity 32 W Pacific 509-624-7821	**Hope House for Women** 318 S Adams 509-455-2886
The Salvation Army Shelter for Families 222 E Indiana Avenue 509-325-6821	**YWCA Shelter for Domestic Violence** 509-326-2255 509-326-1190
UGM for Men 1224 E Trent Avenue 509-535-8510	**Crosswalk for Teens** 525 W 2nd Avenue 509-624-2378
UGM for Women & Children 1515 E Illinois Avenue 509-535-0486	**Family Promise Emergency Shelter** 2002 E Mission Avenue 509-747-5487
Truth Ministries Shelter 1920 E Sprague Avenue 509-456-2576	**VOA Young Adult Shelter** 3104 E Augusta Avenue 509-624-2378

More Information
ShelterMeSpokane.org
Families without children
SNAP • 509-456-SNAP
Homeless Families Assessment
509-325-5005

mental health of Camp residents is hard to explain. As law enforcement worked their way through the Camp, they announced themselves as "outreach workers." No, they weren't. They were law enforcement officers, and the Camp residents understood that. And the use of such scare tactics as arbitrary closure notices riddled with incorrect information, hindered the resolution processes already underway to close the Camp safely and humanely, hindering it more than anyone knew.

The ripple effects local law enforcement's visit to Camp Hope were at least three-fold. The first ripple was confusion and fear among Camp residents who were confused and afraid about what to believe.[91] Confusion and fear produced the second ripple effect, causing a large number of Camp residents to leave the Camp for fear of being swept up by law enforcement closing the camp (more on this below). They quickly disbursed into new locations

Law Enforcement inside Camp Hope.

throughout the Community. The third ripple effect was the immediate filing of a request for a Temporary Restraining Order by the Plaintiffs in the Federal lawsuit filed back in late October, requesting the Federal District Court to prevent City and County law enforcement from making any attempt to clear or remove the Camp.[92] The requested Temporary Restraining Order was granted by U.S. District Court Judge Stanley A. Bastien on Monday, December 12th.[93]

They Simply Left The Camp
A funny thing happens when City officials begin demanding or threatening the removal of a homeless camp. People experiencing homelessness read and listen to the news, too. And when they hear City or County officials demanding the closure of a Camp by a certain deadline, they begin wondering if it's time to move on. Most of them have been swept by law enforcement before, and they prefer to avoid it. The population at Camp Hope peaked in late July of 2022 at 689, according to a physical head count performed by Jewels Helping Hands. That number stayed fairly steady for the months of August and September. The month of September saw the first public demands that the Camp be removed and closed. On Thursday, September 9th, City of Spokane City Administrator, Johnnie Perkins, sent an official letter to WSDOT demanding that the agency begin clearing Camp Hope from the 2nd & Ray property by 23 September, with the removal to be completed no later than October 14th. Later that same month, on the 22nd, Spokane County Sheriff Ozzie Knezovich

Time Line Of Events & Changes In Camp Hope Resident Numbers			
Month	Resident Count	Change	% Change
July/August/September	689	0	0
9/9/2022 - City of Spokane demands WSDOT close Camp by October 14th 9/22/2022 - Spokane County Sheriff announces plan to close Camp by mid-October.			
Late October Completed Count	467	**-222**	-32%
Mid-November Count 11-17-22	445	-22	-5%
Late November Count 11-25-22	433	-34	-7%
Early December Count 12-5-22	416	-17	-4%
December 6 & 7 - Law Enforcement teams visit Camp Hope and distribute flyers declaring the Camp is closing.			
Early December Count 12-09-22	377	-39	-9%
Late December Count 12-21-22	198	**-179**	-48%

publicly announced his intent to clear the Camp by mid-October.

During the months of July and August, leading up to these official demand-threats to close the camp and remove the residents, the number of Camp residents had remained fairly stable, hovering just under 700. But, in the weeks following these demand-threats, leading up to the completion of badging and counting Camp residents, 222 people left the camp. When the official badging was completed in late October, the official Camp census was 467, down 222 (or 32%) from the late July high of 689. But it wasn't over.

A month later, on December 5th (the day before law enforcement visited the Camp), another official count found 416 badged residents, a decline of only 51 people (or 11%) who had left the Camp over the course of the preceding 30 days. The official count on December 9th, two days after the last law enforcement visit, was 377, or a decline of 9%. But a physical headcount taken two weeks later by WSDOT and reported on December 21 showed that the Camp population had fallen to 198, a decline of 179 people, or 48% of the 377 Camp residents counted two weeks earlier.[94]

It is almost impossible to account for that many people leaving the Camp they called home without taking into consideration the impact of the two law enforcement visit on the Camp residents. The *Timeline Of Events & Change* graphic on the previous page shows the changes in Camp population from early September, and the beginning of public threats to close the Camp, until two weeks after the law enforcement visits of December 6th and 7th. During that four month period of time, some 400 residents left Camp Hope (222 in September and 179 in December) and were, for all practical purposes, unaccounted for.[95]

Epilogue

Our lives, both individually and as a Community, consist of our choices, our actions, and the consequences - both intended and unintended - of what we choose to do. The use of law enforcement - or the threat of its use - as a tool of homeless policy has consequences. It certainly did at Camp Hope. It is difficult to characterize what happened without coming to the conclusion that, as a consequence of official threats and actions to close the Camp between September and December, 2022, hundreds of individuals were potentially denied the services they needed (housing navigation, peer support, substance abuse treatment, and more), and might otherwise have received, to build an exit strategy out of their individual cycles of homelessness. This is the real-world impact of using - or threatening to use - law enforcement as a tool of homeless policy. For those impacted, it perpetuates the cycle of homelessness, re-traumatizes people already living with serious trauma (as Anwar Peace describes in Chapter 19), and creates new additional obstacles to building an effective exit-ramp out of homelessness. In simple terms, it doesn't work, and is even counter-productive.

As our story of Camp Hope closes out for December of 2022, I believe it's important to pause and reflect on recent events. Reflecting on the events of September and December, the only way to truly understand the impact of official threats and law enforcement actions to close Camp Hope is to understand the impact from the perspective of something known as "unintended consequences." So, that's what we're going to do in the following Chapter, before restarting our story in Chapter 8, "Fighting For The Finish Line."

A Place to Exist

7 - Homeless Policy And Unanticipated Consequences

For as long as I can remember, based on my 18-year involvement in serving the homeless and marginalized of Spokane, official Spokane homeless policy has embodied the unintended consequences of the actions - and inactions - of regional policymakers. Such a blanket declaration deserves an explanation . . . and some examples. And that brings us to Robert Merton of Columbia University. Buckle your seatbelt and take a deep breath, because this is important.

Robert K. Merton isn't a household name, but his research is legendary, and you're probably familiar with a well known by-product of his work: Murphy's Law, "What Can Go Wrong, Will Go Wrong."[96] Merton was a sociologist at Columbia University in 1936 when he published an essay, *"The Unanticipated Consequences of Social Action,"* which popularized the notion of "unanticipated consequences."[97]

In a nutshell, Merton formalized something you and I know to be true: our actions have both intended and unintended consequences. The intended consequences are what we were hoping for when we started. The unintended consequences are what we either feared could happen, or what we never imagined might happen (either positive or negative).

Five Causes

In his ground-breaking work, Merton identified what he saw as five principle causes of unanticipated consequences: 1) Ignorance, 2) Errors, 3) Immediate interests overriding long-term interests, 4) Basic values, and 5) Self-defeating prophecy.[98] From my perspective, based on 18 years of experience, Spokane homeless policy has suffered from all five causes. Allow me to explain.

Ignorance - I see a basic axiom here that is frequently ignored: *You can't fix what you don't know or understand.* Let me offer three examples.

First, as we discussed at length in Chapter 4, the true size and extent of homelessness has been denied by regional policymakers for years, with homelessness being treated as a pond to be drained, rather than a river to be explored and understood before policy is made.

Second, homeless policymakers have demonstrated an ignorance of the reality that homelessness is ultimately a housing issue, and that any meaningful homeless policy must include plans for sufficient and appropriate housing options. How do you meaningfully house people experiencing homelessness when you have a rental vacancy rate of 1% (a condition known as "statistical zero") and an overall housing shortfall of 25,000 units or more?

Third, the truth about homelessness, especially unsheltered homelessness, is found among those experiencing it under bridges, in public spaces, and in homeless camps, and as witnessed by the boots-on-the-ground service providers and outreach workers who work among them. Yet, these are the very people most frequently absent from (i.e., not invited to) homeless policymaking discussions and decisions. Such willful ignorance of the very people whom policy is intended to help makes it all but impossible to achieve intended consequences, or to anticipate potential unintended consequences. The inevitable result is an incomplete analysis and eventually policy failure, such as planning for 150 people at the Convention Center Warming Center and ending up with 469.

Errors - Ignorance is the fountainhead from which so many of our policy errors flow. Let's face reality. Our ignorance regarding the various realities of homelessness (housing, substance abuse, mental health, emotional/physical trauma, criminal history, family strife) inevitably produces mistakes in our analysis of the issue. Those mistakes in our analysis cause us to create plans that are either inappropriate to, or not as big as, the problem we're trying to solve. Our error-producing ignorance also causes us to fall back into habits (i.e., "policies") that may have worked at some point in the past, but are no longer effective. Warehousing people in large congregate shelters (a model that emerged out of the social upheaval of the Great Depression Era of the 1930s) may have worked for the homelessness of 50, 40, or 30 years ago, but is no longer seen as "best practices."

Immediate interests overriding long-term interests - Welcome to the expediency of politics. Politicians, under pressure from constituents who want "those homeless people" gone from City streets, parks, and neighborhoods, want quick and simple solutions to long-term intractable social problems. Install fences in downtown viaducts to prevent the homeless from sitting, camping, or sleeping there. Build a big shelter in a warehouse. Use law enforcement to enforce Sit & Lie, No Camping, and Nuisance Property ordinances to force those shelter resistant homeless people into the warehouse shelter. Simple. Easy, peasy! Problem solved. But it never does solve the problem. Short-term politically expedient solutions seldom work, except briefly in the short-term. But like a cruel game of homeless wack-a-mole, the unsheltered homeless seem to re-emerge somewhere else to start the cycle all over again. Why? Because the solution only satisfied a short-term interest (get "those people" off the street, so we can't see them) and was smaller than the problem it sought to address. And the cycle begins all over again.

Basic values - We all enter the discussion of homelessness - its causes and solutions - with a set of basic beliefs or values that shape our perspective and form the basis of our decision-making as we create policy. Our beliefs or values either require us to pursue, or prohibit us from pursuing, certain actions or solutions, regardless of the long-term consequences (even when the long-term consequences might eventually cause us to change our basic beliefs or values). The graphic on the next page illustrates how our Beliefs/Values might impact our treatment of those experiencing homelessness.

Self-defeating prophecy - A self-defeating prophecy starts with the fear of a negative consequence. Consider this starting fear: if we build more shelters and offer more services, it will draw more homeless people here from other places (in spite of consistent studies showing that 80% of Spokane's homeless come from within 20 miles of the City). This self-defeating prophecy discourages any expansion of either shelter capacity or available services. Consider another starting fear: If we provide

Our Beliefs/Values Guide Our Responses To Homelessness	
Belief: They're all addicts, criminals, lazy nuisances. *Response*: Practice an "us against them" policy, using law enforcement to force them into the criminal justice system to get help.	*Belief*: They're people just like you and me, on a journey through homelessness that we don't yet understand or appreciate. *Response*: Reach out, connect with them, show compassion, and learn their story before we try to "fix" them.
Belief: They need to be held accountable. *Response*: Force them into shelters to receive services where they'll be held accountable for what they receive.	*Belief*: Accountability comes with time through relationships. *Response*: We need to assess them and discover how they got here, and what they need to move forward.
Belief: They just need to get jobs. *Response*: None (How do bums, addicts, criminals, lazy nuisances get jobs?).	*Belief*: Employment is important. *Response*: Discover the barriers that keep them from working (disability, lost ID, training, legal issues).
Belief: They choose to be homeless. *Response*: They don't deserve our help. They chose this. They could choose to not be homeless if that's what they really wanted.	*Belief*: No one wakes up one morning and chooses to become homeless. *Response*: Discover what started their homeless journey, and what's keeping them homeless now. Offer appropriate help.
Belief: We make it too easy and comfortable for people to be homeless. *Response*: Deny them services and make them uncomfortable so they will go to shelters for help. Use law enforcement to force them into shelters by enforcing local ordinances.	*Belief*: There's nothing easy or comfortable about being homeless, whether under a bridge or in a homeless camp. *Response*: Meet them where they are. Use personal assessments to discover what they need to build an exit ramp out of homelessness.
Belief: They could all be housed. *Response*: Offer generalities, but no specific housing options.	*Belief*: Housing is the practical solution to homelessness, but not cookie-cutter housing options. *Response*: Offer better, more flexible, and appropriate housing options.
"How We See People Is The Beginning of How We Treat People"	

homeless people with more services, and make it easy for them to access those services (like offering them at a homeless camp), it will just enable their behavior and (again) may even attract more homeless people to our community. This fear creates a policy mind-set that says, *"We need to force them to go to a shelter to receive services. No shelter, no services."* Notice that the first self-defeating prophecy creates a shortage of shelter space and services which then feeds the second self-defeating prophecy by preventing the unsheltered homeless from finding either the appropriate shelter space or the services they might need.

Camp Hope, Threats, And Unintended Consequences

The official demand/threats made by Administration and law enforcement officials to close the Camp (the implied timeline being immediate, or very soon) embodied all five of Merton's causes for unintended consequences.

First, they embodied a collective *ignorance* regarding the psychological make-up of the Camp residents; their past encounters with law enforcement, their past trauma from those encounters, their fear of being forced to move (again) and perhaps losing all their possessions (again), and more. That psychology, based on past experience, would predictably produce both fear and a flight response.

Second, the ignorance of official policymakers regarding unsheltered homelessness led to the *error* of a policy decision to make public announcements, demands, and threats regarding closing the Camp without regard to the impact they might have upon the potential victims - the Camp residents. The public demand/threats made in September resulted in the mass exodus of 222 Camp residents who scattered out into the local neighborhood and larger Community. The same is true of the 218 Camp residents who left the Camp in the week following the December 6th and 7th law enforcement visits to the Camp. It's doubtful that such a mass exodus (two, actually) of unsheltered homeless individuals from the Camp and into the wider Community (and not to the City's flagship TRAC shelter) was what Administration and law enforcement officials intended when they made their official threats-announcements. Welcome to homeless policy, official threats, and unintended consequences.

Third, the *ignorance* and *errors* of Administration and law enforcement officials in these incidents coalesced around the *immediate interests* of local politics and over-rode the long-term interests of an effective homeless policy. In short, the desire to satisfy such immediate interests as taking a tough public stand against WSDOT, and a Camp filled with "bums, drug addicts, criminals, and nuisances," overrode the long-term goal of meaningfully addressing the issues that had brought 689 unsheltered homeless individuals to the Camp in the first place.

Fourth, their *basic beliefs*, as we outlined in the graphic above, required Administration and law enforcement officials to (in the words of Professor Merton) *"pursue . . . certain actions or solutions, regardless of the long-term consequences."*

Fifth, the *self-defeating prophecy* echoed by many in the Administration and law enforcement, dictated this course of action, *"We need to force them to go to a shelter to receive services. No shelter, no services."*

Epilogue

Reflecting on all that transpired, a coherent homeless policy should be built around a set of specific, quantifiable, and achievable goals, the consequences you intend, as well as around a set of unintended consequences which may not have been intended, but were predictable and should have been anticipated before moving forward.

January of 2022 marked roughly the 1 year anniversary of Camp Hope on the WSDOT property at 2nd & Ray in Spokane. What had begun as a peaceful protest on the sidewalk in front of City Hall had morphed into the largest homeless camp in the State of Washington. One year later, the Camp was down from it's July-August peak of 689 to 138 badged residents, a decline of 81% from the summer peak, and a decline of 70% from the 467 badged residents counted back in October. The graphic on this page shows the month-by-month change in Camp population over 17 months (Note that the two largest declines occurred in proximity to official threats to close the Camp).

But the month of January, 2023, also represented the beginning of the fight for a reasonable finish-line for resolving the Camp. Back in October, facing official threats to use law enforcement to close the Camp, a group of Plaintiffs had filed a lawsuit in Federal District Court to prevent City and County law enforcement from making good on its threats. Following the law enforcement visits to the Camp on December 5th and 6th (potentially signaling the City's intention to act on its threats), the Plaintiffs asked for a Temporary Restraining Order (TRO) which was granted on Monday, December 12th, preventing any and all official attempts to clear

Camp Population Change By Month		
Month	Population	Change
January (2022)	68	0
February	68	0
March	120	52
April	401	281
May	468	67
June	500	32
July	623	123
August	689	66
September	689	0
October	467	-222
Early November	445	-22
Late November	433	-12
December 1	416	-17
December 9	377	-39
December 21	198	-179
January (2023)	138	-60
February	124	-14
March	78	-46
April	52	-26
May	21	-31
June	Closed	Closed

and close the Camp. In granting the TRO, Judge Stanley Bastien cited the likelihood that the Plaintiffs would prevail at trial. The likelihood of losing in Federal Court motivated the City of Spokane to seek a settlement. As settlement talks proceeded I expressed my concern that the City Administration had not done anything to demonstrate that it could be trusted as a reasonable and rational partner in dealing with the Camp. Unfortunately, later events would only validate my concerns. The parties met in Federal District Court in Spokane on Friday, January 27th and a settlement was reached in which the City agreed that it would no longer engage in efforts to clear the Camp. Or, at least that's what everyone thought.

Back at the Camp, out of ear-shot of the legal wrangling over the future of the Camp, the daily work of moving residents out to better housing options, or to treatment and recovery, continued. Between December 21st and February 1st (encompassing the month of January), 42 tents/campsites were removed along with 10 RVs, while 60 residents moved on to better options (including 52 who moved into the Catalyst Project), thanks to the hard work of caseworkers and our network of Peer Navigators. A column by Shawn Vestal in the February 19th edition

Some of the JHH staff and other service providers who worked to close Camp Hope by getting the residents into housing and better situations. The author is second from the right in the back row.

of the *Spokesman-Review* summed up the differences between the City of Spokane and the Washington State Department of Commerce regarding two very different policies for resolving Camp Hope.

"The forking paths taken by the city and the state with regard to Camp Hope are more instructive and relevant than ever. One of them worked, and one didn't. Starting last fall, the city pushed to use police, code enforcement and the bully pulpit to sweep the camp, part of a devotion to wishful thinking predicated upon inflicting suffering to end homelessness. Commerce, on the other hand, deployed around $25 million in legislative funding to clear the camp gradually – operating on the principle that it would move people not just away, but into housing." [99]

On Monday, March 20, the concerns I had expressed in February concerning the City of Spokane's trustworthiness as a reasonable and rational partner when it came to Camp Hope were confirmed. Late on Monday afternoon, the City of Spokane filed a new suit against WSDOT in Spokane Superior Court. The new suit asked the Court to declare the Camp property at 2nd & Ray a "nuisance property," and to grant the City a "Writ of Abatement" that would grant the City and law enforcement the legal authority to clear the Camp, remove the residents, and dispose of their belongings.

From this author's perspective, it appeared clear that, having surmised they would lose in Federal Court regarding their efforts to close the Camp and overturn *Martin v Boise* (the prevailing case law in the 9th Circuit), the City chose to settle. Their legal calculus told them they stood a much better chance of winning a nuisance lawsuit in local court, hence, the new lawsuit in Spokane Superior Court (see a more in-depth look at the lawsuits by Attorney Jeffry Finer in Chapter 18).

At the time the new suit was filed, 85% of the 467 badged Camp residents had already left the Camp, and only 17% (78 individuals) remained. The work to find the appropriate housing needed to compassionately and effectively close the Camp and meet the needs of the residents, had been progressing well. Why the Administration would file a nuisance and abatement suit after 83% of the work to close the Camp had already been completed can only be understood as a political move designed to create a political optic and narrative that the Administration had successfully forced the closure of "that nuisance homeless camp."

On Thursday, March 23rd, a hearing was held before Spokane Superior Court Judge Marla Polin, who gave the City of Spokane a partial victory by granting the City's request to declare the 2nd & Ray property a "nuisance property." But Judge Polin denied the City's request for a "Writ of Abatement" that would have given the City and law enforcement the legal authority to forcibly close the Camp. Instead, Judge Polin ordered the parties to work together and come up with a plan for closing the Camp and to submit that plan to the Court at a later date.

A plan to close the Camp was eventually agreed to by the parties on Tuesday, May 30. [100] Among other things, the plan called for the Camp to close by Friday, June 30, 2023. Curiously, that was the date given by the Department of Commerce in a public document months earlier (dated 12/2/2022) showing that the financial allocation for managing and closing Camp Hope was scheduled to last through the end of June 2023.[101] In the memorable words of the King of Egypt to the King of Sparta, mocking his diminutive size, "A mountain was in labor, and Zeus was scared; but it gave birth to a mouse."[102]

> "A mountain was in labour, uttering immense groans, and on earth there was very great expectation. But it gave birth to a mouse. This has been written for you, who, though you threaten great things, accomplish nothing."
> - Phaedrus

A mountain of lawyers had labored and given birth to a mouse of a settlement that had no practical impact on the Camp or the ongoing work by staff and service providers to close the Camp. Convincing a judge to declare a homeless Camp to be a "nuisance" while requiring a negotiated date for its closure doesn't create more housing options, or more mental health treatment options, or more substance abuse treatment beds, or more of any of the missing resources needed to meaningfully address homelessness and close the Camp. It simply adds more fuel to the fire of an "us-against-them" NIMBYism and promotes a community narrative that everyone experiencing homelessness is a nuisance, a criminal, or a drug addict. And it does enable politicians and their acolytes, who have no actual plan for meaningfully addressing homelessness, to take credit after 85% of the work has been done by others.

Camp Hope Closes

Camp Hope officially closed on Friday, June 9, 2023 after the last remaining residents (Tracy and Justice Andino) left for housing the previous evening. The Camp closed 21 days ahead of the "official" Court-agreed-upon closing date of June 30. This is an important point. Neither attorneys, nor Courts, nor judges, nor law enforcement, nor the City Administration closed Camp Hope. The Camp was cleared and closed by Jewels Helping Hands staff, with Department of Commerce funding administered by Empire Health Foundation, in co-operation with WSDOT, service provider partners, caseworkers, peer support staff, housing navigators, community volunteers, and all those who had worked tirelessly for 10 months (since September of 2022) to move the Camp residents into better situations. Shalom-makers closed the Camp by finding or creating solutions that could build the Shalom of those who had

Service agencies celebrating the closing of Camp Hope. From left to right: Jewels Helping Hands, Compassionate Addiction Treatment, Empire Health, Revive Counseling, and SLIHC.

Closing Day celebrations at Camp Hope

taken refuge and sought help in the Camp over the 18 months of its existence. Below is the News Release from Jewels Helping Hands that announced the closing of the Camp.

Fighting For The Finish Line

FOR IMMEDIATE RELEASE
Camp Hope Closes

June 9, 2023, the last resident of Camp Hope 2.0 left camp for housing. Camp Hope, the largest Homeless encampment in the State of Washington, with the assistance of the Department of Commerce Right Away of Way funding, is officially decommissioned and closed.

Camp Hope was not closed by police sweeps, litigation, or political will. It was closed "in the spirit" of ROW funding, by providing housing, and better situations for the badged temporary residents of Camp Hope. It was closed in a trauma-informed, peer lead, intentional, collaborative, compassionate, and humane way.

Camp Hope started as a protest on the steps of City Hall highlighting the lack of low barrier shelter capacity in our community in the winter of 2021. As an imminent sweep was threatened, 68 of those people experiencing homelessness moved onto the lot on the corner of 2nd and Ray, in the City of Spokane, we today refer to formally as Camp Hope.

The population of Camp Hope, at its peak count of 689 people in the summer of 2022 has been slowly decreasing. When funding was granted, camp was closed to new residents, core documents obtained, barrier identified and removed, housing options identified/created and , and Sobering Center opened. Services provided on-site including but not limited to behavioral/mental health, medical access, sobriety services, harm reduction, criminal justice assistance, basic needs, peer/housing specialist/caseworkers.

A Federal lawsuit was filed allowing for a TRO to protect the rights of those experiencing homelessness under Martin V Boise and Blake V Grants Pass.

In the last 18 months 200+ people experiencing chronic homelessness have been housed through the ROW Housing options supported by Empire Health Foundation, Department of Commerce funds and on-site providers, Revive Counseling, Jewels Helping Hands, Compassionate Addiction Treatment and Spokane Low Income Housing Consortium.

In the last 18 months 150+ campers were employed. Programs teaching skilled trades were implemented, lived experience opportunities were implemented, employment specialists engaged, and second chance employment programs were utilized.

The data collected during the existence of Camp Hope will prove beneficial to other communities struggling to move the needle in their Chronic Homeless Populations. This data is a snapshot of chronic homelessness anywhere in our country. The Camp Hope model created can be replicated with successful outcomes and appropriate interventions. The successful closing and creation of the Camp Hope model, a model using people-centered methods proves that low-barrier, trauma-informed, peer-led, data driven solutions that honor the self-determination of the people experiencing homelessness, not only work but should be used in providing services to the members of our community experiencing chronic homelessness.

Many lessons learned from Camp Hope, but the five main ones are:
1. Politics has no place in homeless services.
2. Peers and workers with lived experience are the experts in the room.
3. Collaboration of Services and Service Providers are the keys to successful outcomes.

4.   600+ people in any neighborhood has a gigantic impact.
5.   We can move the needle in homeless services as a community.

There is still a lot of work to be done. 200+ badged Camp Hopers are still unaccounted for in our community. The re-engagement of that population is the next priority. JHH looks forward to continuing to follow our housed campers and assist in maintaining and sustaining their housing and re-engaging those that fell through the cracks.

Thank you to the residents of Camp Hope, The Department of Commerce, The Department of Transportation, Revive Counseling, Compassionate Addiction Treatment, Spokane Low Income Housing Consortium, Empire Health Foundation, on and off-site service providers, churches and community volunteers, Housing Navigators, Catalyst and Catalyst employees and all those who participated in aiding ROW funded providers to close this encampment successfully and compassionately.

Today, we will celebrate the hard work, hard won victories, the care and compassion, the community and collaboration, and the Camp closing. Media is allowed on site for questions from 12-3pm. Staff from Revive Counseling, Jewel's Helping Hands, Spokane Low Income Housing Consortium, Compassionate Addiction Treatment and Empire Health Foundation will be on site to answer questions.

Julie Garcia
Executive Director/Founder
Jewels Helping Hands

Epilogue

On Friday, June 30, (21 days after the Camp closed), Governor Jay Inslee visited the WSDOT property where Camp Hope had existed for 18 months. With local media and homeless service providers around him, the Governor acknowledged the closing of the Camp as a success story with lessons that could be applied across the State of Washington. "I would hope that everyone celebrates today as a success . . . that we have both closed Camp Hope and done it in a way that got hundreds of people housing." [103] In his remarks, the Governor noted several of the aspects of work done at Camp Hope that worked, including onsite services and re-purposing existing buildings (such as the Catalyst, which he later visited) for use as housing. But perhaps it's ironic that, as they celebrated the accomplishments and the closing of Camp Hope, observers at Friday's celebration also couldn't help but point back to where and how it all started, on the steps of City Hall and with policymakers who underestimated and failed to respond to the true size and nature of homelessness in our Community. "This problem started because the city could not deal with the number of people who were at City Hall. That's the reason Camp Hope started," noted Governor Inslee. "Then the state stepped in and we brought $24 million of state funds and we provided housing instead of just chasing people off." [104] At the conclusion of Camp Hope's 18 month journey, we can only wonder how much local policymakers have learned.

9 - Stories From Camp Hope

Our stories are our history, and the stories of Camp Hope embody the history of those who came to, lived in, passed through, and moved on from Camp Hope. In a very real sense, Camp Hope was a living, breathing organism made up of 689 people living in community, experiencing unsheltered homelessness together, while working to understand their individual journeys and trying to build their individual exit ramps out of the Camp and homelessness. It was messy. Sometimes it was

Our stories are our history that remind us of the real people who once lived or worked at Camp Hope.

cold, sometimes hot, sometimes dirty, sometimes challenging, sometimes rewarding and fulfilling, sometimes exciting, and sometimes frightening. But it was always very human. The history of Camp Hope is made up of their 689 unique stories, only a

few of which we were able to capture at the time. [105] Many people don't want to tell their stories, for a variety of reasons, ranging from personal privacy issues to not yet fully understanding their own journey and not being able to put it into words - like the Vietnam veteran with four purple hearts who stayed in the Camp and is now in housing, but simply doesn't want to talk about it right now. Sometimes life is like that. What follows in this Chapter is a variety of stories told

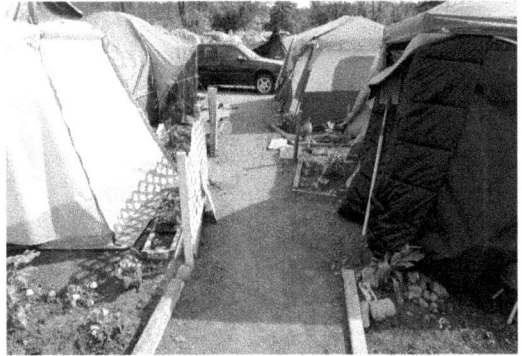

Someone once cared enough to call this place "home."

by former residents and those who worked with them. They range from the exciting to the touching to the sad. Sometimes, life is simply like that, too. As appropriate, I have tried to give a brief introduction (and occasionally an epilogue) to provide the reader with some context without altering or giving away the content.

I Just Get Overwhelmed Sometimes With Joy

Editor's Note. I met Brian, a 44-year old African-American man (who could easily pass for 20 years old) outside the Resource Trailer in the waning days of Camp Hope. We sat and talked as I recorded our conversation on my digital recorder. His enthusiasm over his new post-Camp life was infectious, and I don't know who left our conversation more encouraged, him or me. What follows is a lightly edited version of our conversation.

My name is Brian and I was at Camp Hope for about a year. Man, you guys are amazing for what you guys have done. You know what I mean? Like, you got to think about it, man. At one point in time, there's over 600 people here. And for there to be like no murders, nothing severe. Just maintain. And at first it was like everybody was close knit, you know what I mean? People took care of each other. That started to fade away towards the end, but for the most part, this place was a blessing for me. If I hadn't come here, I wouldn't have been able to make the changes that I made in life, you know what I mean?

I wasn't really ready to make a change, but I was like, I was tired of being gone from house to house and things like that. So I decided to come down and at first, man, I used to just stay in my tent. Even though I knew people, I just kind of maintained to myself and things like that. I had my tent set up in a way that I would forget that I was in a tent on a side of the road by highway, you know what I mean? And it was I remember one morning, I woke up, man, and I was like, *"You know what? You're in a tent on the side of the road, by the highway. Like, what are you going to do? What are you going to do with your life, man? Are you going to continue to progress with no progression, or are you going to take advantage of these things that are available for you to change your life?"*

And so I began doing that, you know what I mean? And, man, I just get overwhelmed sometimes with joy. I'm working. I'm going for custody of my son. I got my housing voucher, man. I'm just . . . I'm loving life again. I wake up and I smile and that's something I hadn't done for a long time. Like, I thoroughly enjoy life and it's thanks to you guys. It's thanks to you. It's thanks to Kenny. It's thanks to Cheryl. It's thanks to Sabrina. You know what I mean? Everybody played like a small part in that. Some people played a major role, but a lot of people played a role in this . . . this rejuvenation or whatever you want to call it, man oh man.

I try to spread the word, to try to, you know, motivate other people to try to go the same route. But you can't motivate everybody, man. And that's what I noticed here. After a while, I was like, "You can't help everybody," you know? And you got to want that. And that's the bottom line is you got to want it. If you don't want it, nothing is going to happen.

I'm 44 years old. I would say that the last time I had my own house was probably about 12 or 13 years ago. And before I got this job, this is the first time I had a job in 18 years. That's how long I've been doing my thing. Like, you know, hustling, just doing whatever. I just came to the point where I was just like, man, you know, I was just tired of the same thing, man.

I used drugs, but I've been sober four months. I'm with the Revive program. I came into the house clean. My UAs for the house every Monday and for CPS are clean. I got court on Thursday for my son. I'm trying to get custody of my son, man. That's my end goal - housing, reunification, and then life, you know what I mean? Housing, reunification, and then life.

I'm in a Revive house now. I've been there for going on three months. And I've been working for almost two years at the hotel. Yeah. And I love it, man. I love it. It's not boku bucks out the roof, but it's about the people, man. I didn't work for 18 years, and so I was nervous about getting back in the job was because I don't want to be overwhelmed with like 40 hours a week. But at the same time, I want to work, you know what I mean? And it's not that I don't want to work for anybody, but it's like I don't want somebody breathing down my neck kind of, you know what I mean? And so this job, it was perfect. They see that I work hard and everything like that. So they give me freedom as long as I take care of what I do. And for that, now they got me training people and it looks like I'm probably about to bump up a little bit. And we're talking in a matter of two months.

I can't I can't believe it, man. It's great, you know? I can't believe I was just living like this little small circle. That's it, man. This small circle. And I thought I was actually living life, but I've broken free of those people and things like that. And I'm not the type of person. I'm not going to shun anybody. But at the same time, if you're not on the same level, I don't want to sound like I'm above anybody, but I'm not the same person as I used to be. You know what I mean? And that's okay. I understand that, you know, it's okay to take care of yourself and then not be selfish, you know what I mean? And I'm understanding that now. It's okay. Take care of yourself and not be greedy. My mom told me a long time ago, she said, "Before you can take anybody, kids and all, Brian, you got to take care of yourself." And I didn't understand that. And to tell the truth, I didn't grow up until I came here. I really did not grow up, like mature, like a man, really, until I came here. I was a boy. I was a teenager. You know what I mean? I didn't look at life like the way I should, you know what I mean? And I came here and man, I grew up. I don't care what people say, the media, anybody else. Man, this place was a blessing. This place was a blessing, man.

A Father's Story

Editor's Note. It was on a Tuesday, as we were working to close the Camp, when this person handed me an envelope containing this note, addressed to Julie Garcia. This person had been a fixture at the Camp, coming every Tuesday morning to serve food (usually breakfast cereals and milk) to Camp Residents. Only after reading this note did I fully understand why. His son was one of our residents.

Julie,

First, I wanted to thank you for what you, the Lord (first and foremost), and your Board have done for our son (Name Withheld). Camp Hope was an opportunity for him to re-coup. He didn't have to carry all his belonging all the time. He was stationary. We knew where he was. We could find him. We'd pray before arriving and out of the tent he would come. He's in a group home now, on his meds, and doing well.

Thank you for the loss of stress for my wife and I. We didn't have to look for him in alleys or under freeway overpasses, under stair-ways or alongside of Coeur d'Alene City Hall in their bushes.

Finally, thank you for letting me come to do Bible study. It was more often a chance for me to talk, hand out doughnuts, or bowls of cereal. I learned more about myself, about people. For example, you can't know their needs unless you spend time to know them.

I saw miracles happen. One day a lady asked if I had a large print Bible she could have. I said, "I'm sorry, I don't, but I'll check at our church and I'll see what I can do." I asked her name. She said, "I'm Rebecca, but you can call me Becky." I left Camp Hope and went to pick up my wife from her Women's Bible study. A lady who also goes to it was standing with her. That lady had a bag of Bibles. She told me for several months the Lord told her to buy Bibles in Large Print. She wanted me to have them. I told her, "I know a lady who will be so pleased." I asked what her name was so I could tell the lady back at the Camp who it was that was being so nice and giving Bibles. She said, "I'm Rebecca, but you can call me Becky."

Thank you for allowing me to come to Camp Hope. If there's anything I can do to help, please call.

God bless you all.

(Name Withheld)

I Have Nothing to Look Forward To

Editor's Note: Gina was one of the early residents of Camp Hope. Gina had terminal breast cancer. As part of my early documentary work, I interviewed Gina in the Camp in July of 2022. This is Gina's story and her journey in her own words.

I've been here at Jewel's Camp Hope since the end of January. My mom said, "Get out and never to come back." Never see her again. She said that right here. Here. And she's 82. She's getting really old going through that dementia. I was taking care of her and I was just going through cancer myself, going through chemo every three weeks for a year and a half. And I was still taking care of my mom. I miss her and she's gone. I won't even know when she passes away. She told me to get out, that she's selling the house. She's been prepping me to take the house and now she's going to sell the house. I was planning on living in that house until the day I die. And now I'm out here.

I'm 52 now.

When I'm going through chemo, I had breast cancer. They thought I was stage two. And they were killing me with the chemo for a year and a half. I stopped. Just take it off. Take it off. So, they took it off. But I still had to be on chemo pills for ten years. I stopped treatment when I came out here because it's too painful. January when I came by here, I was driving to Mexico, actually. When she threw me out, I said, "Screw it". I'm going to Mexico and just find a little plot of sand by the ocean and I was just going to finish off my cancer there and just disappear. And I had to stop down here to repack my car so I could travel. And I looked and there's a bunch of tents, said, "Wow, I have a tent." I could just repack my car, and sit in a tent. I woke up to six inches of snow and I wasn't prepared for the snow in that tent. So they told me how to survive the snow.

And I just have been here ever since trying to leave, trying to figure out what to do, where I'm going to go. Since I've been out here since January, I came out here I was a size 13, which is probably 150 pounds. And now I'm a size four, which is about a hundred and ten. I've done nothing but lose weight. I have never been this thin, not even when I was going through chemo. So I feel I feel like I'm going to I'm going to die here. And that's okay with me. I'm okay with it. I'm ready. I have nothing to look forward to.

Editor's Epilogue - A few weeks after our interview, Gina was seriously burned when alcohol-based hand sanitizer and a cigarette caught her clothes on fire. After a stay in the hospital, Gina's family reconnected with her and she was able to exit the Camp.

I Need To Get Home

Editor's Note: Caleb was an early resident of Camp Hope, arriving in late April 2022. I interviewed him in the Camp and learned his story three months later in July when I spotted him helping rake and clean around the Camp dumpsters. This is Caleb's story in his own words.

I'm a Blackfeet from Browning, Montana. I came here (to Spokane) three years ago. I entered the Spokane Dream Center Men's Discipleship program, that was the reason I came over here. I did a year in the Men's Discipleship, which is a Bible treatment program. Basically, they transform your mind by the renewing of His word. It changed my heart.

I did a year in the Dream Center, in their transition program. And then I got pretty comfortable. I got a lot of money in my pocket, got a nice car. And I said, "All right, God, I think I got it from here." And, yeah, about a year later, here I am. And so this is where it's gotten me, kind of wanting to do my own thing, thinking I know what's best for me.

I got an RV from a job that I got. It didn't have any registration, so the only place I could park it was here. I just brought it down here and think I'm only gonna be here, like, a week, maybe, until I get it registered. And that turned into three months. I have a van right now, a 2004 Windstar, also from the job that I did. And I just need to get it running, get gas and head over to Missoula and get home to my two beautiful daughters. So, yeah, I need to get home.

This has just dragged out way longer and I just kind of, you know. . . yeah. Idle time, man, idle time is devil's playground. And, you know, I'm not working. I'm not busy. I'll find something to fill the spaces, you know? But I am a family man. I'm a father to two beautiful baby girls that, you know, melt me to pieces. So that's where I need to be.

I don't fit in here. You know, this is kind of cold, and it's kind of merciless, and love is seen as weakness, and it'll get you walked over pretty good. I don't like that, you know, it's not for me. It's for Him, you know? That's what keeps me going. I have something I could draw from. I stay connected. I talk to my dad every day, every morning. And that's the only thing keeping me going right now or I would have snapped weeks ago, brother. But really, there is good people here, though, there really is. There's good hearted people here I relate to.

I've learned that *"if you want to get to it, you got to go through it,"* and *"if you're going to be dumb, you've got to be tough"*! What I really learned here is, be the change you want to see. That's it. Be the change you want to see. Don't be overcome by evil, but overcome evil with good, because evil prevails when good men do nothing. So that's what I've learned.

Editor's Epilogue - In the Fall of 2022, Jewels Helping Hands arranged for a bus ticket so that Caleb could return home to his daughters and family in Missoula, Montana. He is now there and doing well. We wish him the best.

They Saved Me and Changed My Life

My name is Chris. I'm 52 years old. I'm an Army veteran. I'm also an addict. This is my story.

Born and raised in Spokane, Washington, I was adopted at birth. My adoptive parents divorced when I was two years old. My dad went to Alaska, while my mom stayed in Spokane and remarried when I was four.

I was raised right and had an amazing childhood. I never experienced any abuse and I never went without. I'm the youngest of 10 kids and the only adopted one in my adoptive family. Right out of high school, I joined the Army. I spent 15 years in the service, some on active duty and some in the Reserves, and was honorably discharged in 2002. I don't talk much about my service other than to say I proudly served and would do it again if I could.

In civilian life I became a printing press operator. In 2011, I moved to Idaho Falls for a printing job. Six years later, in 2017, my foot was crushed on the job by a forklift and I could no longer operate a printing press. I moved back to Spokane and started work painting houses. I eventually started my own painting business. But COVID hit, and no one would let me paint, due to fear of COVID. I eventually exhausted my savings, swallowed my pride, and went to work for someone else. But it was too late to stop my slide. They let me go when my car broke down and I couldn't get to work. I slowly lost everything and became homeless.

In March of 2022, homeless and without any options, I moved into Camp Hope. I had given up on myself and life, and had turned to drugs to numb my pain. I was now a homeless addict. I want to share this piece of my story in the hope that it will help just one person find their way. Through my addiction I destroyed my life, friends, family, and career. I don't blame my addiction. I take responsibility for it I did it. Because of my poor choices, I became homeless and moved into Camp Hope. I was lost, hurt, confused and didn't know what I was going to do. I continued using to numb myself.

I started volunteering as part of the Camp security team. One day I met Julie Garcia and Ken Crary, who oversaw the Camp. They saw something in me that I didn't and offered me a full time job on the internal Security Team. It was great for me because now I could afford my addiction. Shortly thereafter, I met my peer support angel, Sharyl Brown. Sharyl was there to help me get back into the "real" world.

I did my best to hide my addiction from everyone and I thought it was working until the night I got a call from Ken, *"I need you to come to Julie's house for dinner. We need to talk."* I could tell by his voice that something was wrong. After dinner we went out back and Ken dropped the bomb, *"We know you're getting high."* I knew I was caught. I was fully honest and said "yes." They immediately offered to help me get the help I needed. They showed me love and compassion. They didn't just give up on me when I'd given up on myself at that point. I accepted their help. Julie, Ken, and Sharyl immediately started the process of getting me into detox. They helped me find my way back to God and saved my life. I can never thank the Jewels Team enough for what they've done for me. They saved me and changed my life. As I write this, I've been clean and sober for six months. With the help of the Jewels Team, I've moved out of the Camp and into transitional housing at the Catalyst Project, and I'm working finding permanent housing.

I hope, through my sobriety and the work I do for and with them, they see how much I love, respect, and appreciate what they've done. With their help, I'm now training to be part of the Jewels peer support staff so that I can use my experience and my story to help others who are to lost find their way out of homelessness and addiction. Our work will never be done but we LOVE what we do.

Editor's Epilogue - Since this interview, Chris now has his own apartment and has been hired as a Peer Navigator with Jewels Helping Hands, using his life experience to help others find their path forward out of homelessness.

I Just Gave Up On Myself

Editor's Note: Chris R. was an early resident of Camp Hope, first at City Hall and then on the WSDOT property. During the 18 months of the Camp, 16 veterans stayed at the Camp, including Chris. In the Spring of 2022 I found Chris cooking breakfast outside of his tent and feeding other camp residents. That's where I interviewed him as part of my documentary work. The conversation below is a lightly edited transcript from that interview.

MAURICE: So tell me what life is like here in the camp right now.

CHRIS R. : What are we, about, two months in Seems like now that the police are telling everybody to come here, you know? So I'm hoping that that's a good thing. So if we get too many people, we're not going to get kicked out. So, I mean, but it stays quiet. We get a little bit of drama, but nothing much. Hasn't been any physical altercations, no drug paraphernalia, people are pretty much. cleaning up after themselves.

MAURICE: Tell me a little bit about the little Governing Council that you guys have set up.

CHRIS R. : That's still kind of like in the beginning stages. Back when our forefathers started getting I'm sure they had to work things out. Trying to figure out, you know, who's more going to be in control. And the thing that he's going to be in charge of, what areas. As far as me, I mean, I've got a seat on the council as far as when we vote on

Chris was cooking breakfast for the Camp
(like an Army cook on bivouac)
when I interviewed him in early Spring of 2022.

things or just get together and talk to everybody. But my job is basically cleaning up toilets.

MAURICE: You're a veteran, is that right? Yeah. So how long are you in the service?

CHRIS R. : I was in for five years. I got out in 91. So just three days before they bombed Iraq. So I was sitting on the couch watching at home Yeah, it was great. I was a cook. So we did a lot of a lot of field exercises, you know, training. Every time they'd go out to the field, I always called it camping.

MAURICE: So what happened resulting in you being homeless and in a homeless camp now?

CHRIS R. : I think a lot of it was I just gave up on myself, just thinking that I could do any better. I just I figured that seems like anymore, the way my thinking goes, it's like this is the best I could do. But I still. I'm not, like, really depressed. It's just kind of like how my thinking has gone on over the years. So it's just I've been homeless probably about the last five, six years. Traveling around Oregon, Washington, Idaho, Texas, Tennessee.

MAURICE: Now, I've seen some veterans workers from a Goodwill and a couple other agencies here. Have you talked to them and have they been able to help you any?

CHRIS R. : Yeah, I started talking to them when I first got into town, but then I just kind of got stuck into the camp. Just hanging out here and kind of seeing where it goes, you know? I know there's a lot of resources out there to get housing and all that, but I'd really like to be able to just, you know, get a place on my own without help, you know, to make me feel more like I've accomplish something. If I'm able, they'll just support and help keep it going. Keep up with the bills. And to me, that's like a normal person. You know, just kind of living life day to day. And just keep going.

Editor's Epilogue - Chris left Camp Hope soon after our interview. We've remained in touch and he is now living on his own and doing well.

A Requiem For Bigs And Mark

Editor's Note: The two events described below occurred in May of 2023 as we worked to close the Camp. What follows is a lightly edited version of an email I sent to the Spokane Homeless Coalition the day after these events occurred.

It was a tough 24-hours at Camp Hope. We lost two of our friends, both to unresolved homelessness, but for two different reasons. Here are their stories:

"Bigs" - We called him "Bigs" because, well, he was big. Sort of a gentle giant if you will. His tent was located in the "C" quadrant of Camp Hope. Bigs had been a resident of the Camp for about 9 months. The Camp was his community, and his tent in "C" quadrant was his home. He was quiet and kept to himself for the most part. He seldom (if ever) left the Camp. The last time I saw Bigs was last week when he was helping another Camp resident deal with the death of one of her puppies. *"You've got a big heart,"* was the last thing I remember saying to him.

Monday evening my phone rang and it was Ken Crary, Jewels Chief of Operations at the Camp. *"I wanted you to know before you heard it on the news,"* he said. *"Bigs committed suicide. He hung himself in his tent. S**** and I found him this afternoon."* Heartbreak is often a silent response to unforseen tragedy. It was for me at that moment.

We're not exactly sure when Bigs hung himself (sometime over the weekend). We're still filling in holes in our knowledge of events. It seems that he had told friends and staff that he would be gone for a couple of days (so no one would go looking for him), and that if he didn't see them again, he wanted to let them know that he loved them. Having covered his bases, he quietly slipped into his tent . . . and hung himself.

After learning the news (I was home since my shift as Camp Day Manager was over for the day), I took a long reflective walk on the Centennial Trail. It's one of the ways I work on my own personal Shalom . . . or to weep when someone I love loses theirs. I reflected on the reality that Bigs wasn't a "nuisance." He was simply another of our Campers working his way through the journey we call

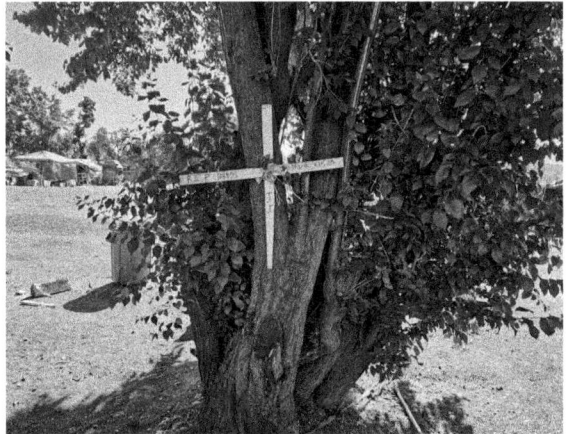

Camp Hope memorial for "Bigs"

homelessness. I reflected on how the eventual Coroners Report will probably say something like *Death From Asphyxiation By Hanging* or some other official wording for this type of event. But, on deeper reflection, I concluded that the Report won't list his true cause of death. The truth is that Bigs died of hopelessness. Camp Hope was his community. His tent was his home. We were his family. And all of these were being threatened by a City Administration that, having found a local judge who would declare the Camp a "nuisance" property (and its residents "nuisances"), was determined to close the Camp and force the residents to leave and go to a shelter, or back onto the street. If forced out of the Camp - his home for the past nine months - Bigs had nowhere to go. No community. No home. No hope. And that's a terrible darkness to stare into.

Let me be clear. Using the courts, law enforcement, and threats of sweeps with forcible removal as a tool of homeless policy has consequences. One of those consequences has a name. We called him "Bigs." And he deserved a better policy than the one being forced on him and so many others.

Mark - The other person we lost was Mark. He passed away at 2AM this morning at Holy Family Hospital. Mark was one of the original Camp Hope residents, going back over a year now. As the months passed, Mark came to the attention of Jewels Helping Hands staff and he was hired to work for JHH and run the mobile shower trailer. Five months ago, Mark got housing. Three months ago, he started chemo. And you can figure out the rest.

Camp Hope memorial for Mark

At the beginning of my documentary work 4 years ago I heard the Director of a homeless services agency say that the chronically homeless individuals they were placing into housing had been homeless for an average of 11 years, but that the majority of them would be dead within three years of getting housed. Why? Because homelessness is a journey that takes a heavy toll on people. Poor nutrition, poor health care, undiagnosed and untreated medical conditions, exposure to the elements, compromised immune system, and other co-occurring factors take a toll on the individual. Once they get housing, move from survival mode to maintenance mode, even get their substance abuse issues under control, their underlying medical conditions which have accumulated over the years now come to the surface. Think of homelessness like a cancer that, if found early, is very treatable, even curable. I know. My prostate cancer was found early, treated, and I'm now cancer free. But if left untreated, it grows and eventually proves fatal. Mark's journey through homelessness resulted in housing, but it also resulted in failing health and a cancer that took his life this morning at 2AM, but he didn't pass homeless or alone. He passed with JHH staff present to assure him that he was loved.

So, yes, it was a tough 24 hours at Camp Hope. If there are any lessons to be gained from the experience, they should include these.

First, we need a better homeless policy than using threats, courts, and law enforcement to enforce misguided policy that uproots people from the community they are in and forces them into options (like large congregate shelters) that are not appropriate for them.

Second, we need more and better mental health options for those who, like "Bigs," are struggling with both homelessness and mental health challenges (including, but not limited to, hopelessness).

Third, we need to get those experiencing homelessness (like Mark) housed, sooner rather than later, and provide them with the services they need (like health care) to prosper and grow. What we don't need is another 24-hours like the last 24.

Who Knew That I'd Be That Person

Editor's Note: It's time to meet one of my favorite homeless sages. I began following Suki's journey when she came to the City Church Warming Shelter in December of 2020. She continued with us to the Woman's Club Warming Shelter the following Spring. When Camp Hope popped up on the sidewalk in front of City Hall in December of 2021, Suki showed up again and volunteered to help keep things organized and running smoothly. When the Camp moved to the WSDOT property at 2nd & Ray, Suki helped coordinate the move and organized the resource/storage tent to make sure everyone had the basic supplies they needed during those crucial early winter months. I asked Suki to share her story.

My name is Suki. I grew up in Berkeley California, and I never imagined myself being homeless. I remember driving with my mother and her looking over at a homeless man who was digging through a dumpster and looking shocked and saying, "Oh my goodness, that's so and so. I used to date him. Who would imagine he'd be digging through a dumpster now. How embarrassing." Who knew that I'd be that person. I sure didn't! Homelessness has its pros and cons. One of the biggest cons is the social stigma attached to it. One of the pros is that you get to really discover who you are. I was homeless for almost 4 years, and it's not something I would wish on my worst enemy.

I know that a lot of people assume drug addiction with homelessness. Drugs are an issue, but drugs were not the reason for my homelessness. Basically, I had a very poor picker when it came to relationships, and I picked a really bad one. The year prior to my homelessness I was a single mother working to raise my son. I made a lot of bad choices in this relationship, and one of them was such a bad choice, allowing the boyfriend to move in with me and my son. Things went south from there. For the first time in my son's 10 years, I suddenly had CPS involved because a person

A Place to Exist

who was mad at the boyfriend reported me to CPS. They got involved and wanted to take my child away. Our family was in California. I asked my mom to take my son, because I believed it was very important for my son to be with his family. About that same time, my father died. I had not been getting any kind of child support since my son was about two years old, and my parents were supplementing my income by providing child support for me. After my father's death, my mother cut me off during the time of the CPS episode. Basically without that supplemental income, I couldn't support myself. To make a long story short, today my son's safe and happy, living with his father in Honolulu in a place where his skin color is the majority. I'm thankful that he's thriving, he's blossoming, he's happy, and he's got a life ahead of him.

I grew up in the upper middle class hills of Berkeley, California, and I had never dealt with the police up until being homeless. I don't do anything out of the ordinary for a homeless person, but we're made to move a lot. We're never allowed to sit down. I remember one time when there was a group of us at City Gate. It started snowing so we went into the tunnel under the train tracks below City Gate. Now, as homeless people, we have to carry everything that we own with us. You can't just leave it around because either a Geiger work crew will pick it up it will be thrown away, or it will be stolen. There's no leaving your things. We're like turtles except we don't get to have the hard shell and we're prodded to move constantly. So, all these people had taken all their belongings, picked them up, and moved them under the tunnel. They had finally settled in when the cops rolled in. It was snowing and we were told to get out of the tunnel and, that there's a shelter up the street at Garland and Monroe. Now, a lot of those people have carts with all their belongings, and you're asking them to go in a snowstorm from the tunnel at Madison down from City Gate, and all the way up to Garland and Monroe, and you don't know for sure if you can keep your cart or your belongings. As everyone knows, belongings are very important. They're just as important to housed people who get to leave their belongings in a nice little safe box as they are to homeless people. People are people, and we're attached to things, so it was kind of a laughable, ridiculous idea - almost a mockery - to ask these people to do that.

For me personally, my journey is about more than just being homelessness. I grew up in a house, okay? It isn't just about housing or getting housing because you can't just move into a house and everything is going to be okay. You still have your whole self. There are reasons why you were homeless, all the reasons that led up to this moment in time. You can't just fix that by moving into a box. So, I don't know personally that I'm necessarily looking to move into a box right away because there's a lot of things about myself that I need to work on. There's lots of programs that will provide the deposit, first and last month's rent. Okay, great! What about all those months in between? How am I going to pay for that? You know, just go find a job. Well, you know, surprisingly I've done the normal life. I tried the normal jobs. I've done everything from messengering to being a receptionist-slash-dispatcher. I've done that and it didn't work for me. And I think it's a lot about my mental health, my mindset, my maturity. So, in a lot of ways homelessness for me has been about growing up. Going back to my childhood, I'm adopted, and I was a very emotionally incorrect fit for my adoptive family, and I've got mental health issues. Being adopted, I've come to realize that I spent a lot of my life trying to please other people so they wouldn't throw me away. It was my survival mode. I realized that when somebody asked me what would make me happy, or what did I want to do, my answers were tailored to pleasing someone else, not to what I actually wanted. My whole life had been spent trying to make myself something that somebody wouldn't throw away. I didn't know what I wanted or who I was.

I don't mind waiting my time for a way out of homelessness because there is a self-discovery in this journey. I don't know that I want to be in a box, even though it would be wonderful to have a place where I can safely keep my things, because God knows how many backpacks and ID cards I've lost. I'm into beading and making jewelry. I've had huge amounts of things stolen from me, as has everyone out here on the street. But as much as I would like to have a safe place to have those things, I also like having social interaction on the street. You have to have social interaction with other people. You can't just haul away in a little closet and go out every once in a while. I personally get very reclusive - almost agoraphobic - so I'm not looking forward to that part, because I'm not sure that enough about me has been changed or discovered, however you want to put it, that I can move into an apartment and be comfortable. I don't want to go into the same behavioral patterns because that equals anxiety, depression, and all those things and that will eventually lead me back to ground zero, which is not where I want to be.

Editor's Epilogue - Suki is doing incredibly well. She and her husband (Rob) have an apartment and Suki has not only found her way out of homelessness, but she has found her niche, working for a local non-profit as a homeless service provider, caseworker, and peer navigator, using the lessons of her homeless journey to serve others.

They Appreciated Me For Just Keeping My Word

Editor's Note: Shanda is a service provider with Amerigroup and a member of the Spokane Homeless Coalition. We couldn't have helped all of the people at Camp Hope without our amazing service providers, most of whom are members of the Spokane Homeless Coalition. I invited Coalition members to submit stories about their work with residents at the Camp, and this is Shanda's story.

I would say I had many experiences at Camp Hope. However, this one sticks out to me. I was contacted by another agency to see a person there that had some barriers regarding their healthcare insurance. After some back and forth, this person and her boyfriend were available for me to meet them. I drive up in my Amerigroup car at the appointed spot and they both were wanting to get into treatment!

Their barriers were they did not have insurance cards, needed to change their

MCO to Amerigroup, needed case management, and wanted some of the additional benefits Amerigroup offered. They shared with me that people had taken advantage of them. They were not getting the help they needed, and were surprised that I would come there to help them when so many others had turned their nose up at them.

I got them all taken care of and even had another agency arrange for them to come and pick them up to go to treatment. I asked them if it was okay to get them lunch and they had this "wild, yet amazed" look on their face. I went to Subway and got exactly what they requested. When I returned with their food, they said thank you and they appreciated me for just keeping my word.

After they got into treatment, I got a text from the lady (she told me about both) saying she was 3 weeks into treatment, and so was he, and was starting to feel more like the person she remembered. She told me she really appreciated me and for the first time in years truly had hope that this time treatment would "stick." She said both of them were on their way to better! She just thanked me for being me and for being caring and kind.

I have so many stories of individuals and families I worked with that I pray I was able to do something for, but this one made me smile as it does not take anything to be kind to anyone regardless of where they are in life. Thank you so much for all of the work you do...there are not enough words to tell you that you are loved and appreciated...more than you know.

Editor's Epilogue - What stood out to me in this story was the importance of homeless service providers keeping their word with their clients. Broken promises frequently lead to broken trust, and repeated broken trust can lead to hopelessness among those who have experienced repeated disappointments. For us to meaningfully help them with their challenges, they must trust us. And trust must be repeatedly earned.

Camp Hope was created by a dramatic increase in unsheltered homelessness, combined with a city-wide shelter system that did not have enough shelter beds for its known and counted homeless population (all of which we discussed at length in Chapter 4). The Trent Resource and Assistance Center (or the TRAC Shelter, as it's known), was conceived and created as the City of Spokane's solution to the

The Trent Resource and Assistance Center or TRAC Shelter

problem of the 823 individuals experiencing unsheltered homelessness in greater Spokane (as counted by the 2022 Point-In-Time Count). Following the eye-popping experience of the Convention Center Warming Shelter in the Winter of 2022, when plans for 150 mats-on-the-floor encountered the reality of 486 unsheltered homeless individuals seeking refuge from freezing temperatures, the Woodward Administration vigorously pursued the idea of a large congregate low-barrier shelter with sufficient bed capacity to meet the standards set by *Martin v. Boise*. For City officials, it also offered the possibility of a solution to clearing Camp Hope. Build a large congregate shelter and then force the residents of Camp Hope into it.

As Camp Hope was silently growing toward its eventual peak of 689 residents in the Summer of 2022, the Spokane City Council approved the leasing of a 33,000sq/ft warehouse building on Trent Avenue for a new homeless shelter.[106] The initial approved capacity was for 150 beds. Capacity confusion soon ensued. On November 15, 2022, the Shelter was granted a Temporary Certificate of Occupancy for 250 beds (an increase of 100 beds). But a December 5 investigation by *Range Media* revealed that the TRAC Shelter had been "advertising a guest capacity of 275 for weeks" on the City's ShelterMeSpokane.org dashboard website, in violation of their authorized capacity.[107] Two days after that story broke, on December 7, TRAC received an updated Temporary Certificate of Occupancy for 350 beds.[108] The TRAC shelter officially opened on September 6, 2022, with 150 beds and 36 guests. By late September, the number of guests had risen to 97. Of those, 27 were reportedly from Camp Hope.[109]

Issues From The Outset

Homeless advocates and service providers had warned policymakers that such a large congregate shelter was contrary to current best practices and would result in the "warehousing" of the residents. It's very difficult to keep a straight face and say "we aren't going to warehouse people" when the very building chosen for the shelter was, in fact, an empty warehouse. The irony was (and continues to be) unavoidable. Service providers also warned that homeless individuals experiencing mental health and/or substance abuse issues would not be able to maintain in such an environment, and that the remote location would create problems for the accessibility of much-needed services.[110] And that placing large numbers of homeless individuals in a warehouse with nothing to do would result in them wandering the neighborhood and getting into trouble (we know our population very well). But no one listened. Data released by the Spokane Police Department in early February of 2023 revealed that SPD had received 890 "calls for service" within a 1/4-mile radius of the shelter in the time period from the day TRAC opened (Sept. 6, 2022) through February 6, 2023. Calls during the same time period of the previous year (2021-2022) totaled 154. In other words, SPD calls for service at TRAC were up 736 over the same time period of the previous year, an increase of 478%.[111]

The building had (and has) only one bathroom and no other indoor plumbing, forcing the use of porta potties and mobile showers, and no kitchen for food service.[112]

The original quoted cost to operate the TRAC shelter for the first year was $3.7 million. But by August, before the shelter even opened, the operational cost through December of 2023 had ballooned to $6.6 million (nearly doubling the original estimate), not including an additional $1.5 million the City would need to pay for a designated service provider.[113]

The shelter was bleeding red before it even opened, and it wasn't over yet. Accusations of embezzlement by an employee of the chosen shelter operator - the Guardians Foundation - forced the Spokane City Council to take the $6.6 million operator contract away from the Guardians and to offer it to The Salvation Army (the only other agency to submit a proposal during the original Request For Proposal process). But a surge in bed capacity to more than 250 beds (and eventually to 350 beds) resulted in a doubling of the contract (again) to $14 million through 2023.[114]

A projected shelter budget deficit of $4 million for the current year (2023), and $10 million projected for 2024, caused the Spokane City Council to announce the cost-saving closure of the Cannon Street Shelter (with the loss of 80 beds) by May of 2023. The 80 residents of the Cannon Shelter would be moved to the TRAC shelter, pushing its capacity to 350.[115] But it wasn't over yet.

In April of 2023, an investigation by *Range Media* reported wide-spread problems at the TRAC shelter ranging from accusations sexual assault, to unsafe working conditions, inadequate staffing (a 50-to-1 staff-to-guest ratio is more than double the standard of best practices and endangers both the staff and the guests), conflicts between the shelter operator (Salvation Army) and the service provider (Revive), and more.[116]

The Administration frequently referred to the TRAC shelter as a "navigation center," referencing a plan developed in Houston, Texas. But as columnist Shawn Vestal rightly pointed out in late December of 2022, the Houston navigation center, called *The Beacon*, offers much more than the TRAC shelter, including, "a commercial kitchen preparing three hot meals a day, served in a cafeteria; an on-site laundry service; computer and phone access; mail services; case management workers and robust on-site access to legal help, social services, medical care, treatment providers and housing navigators who work to move people quickly into permanent housing." [117]

The City's description of the TRAC shelter as a "navigation center" continues to be more aspirational than operational.

Epilogue

From its inception to its launch, the TRAC shelter and its promoters consistently over promised and under delivered regarding the services available to those experiencing unsheltered homelessness. As for its relationship to Camp Hope, neither the TRAC shelter operator nor the City of Spokane published any demographic information (and especially none that can be independently verified) regarding who passed through the shelter, or how many people actually received meaningful services, such as housing, while at the shelter. Three examples serve to highlight these issues.

First, news reports during the month of September when the TRAC shelter opened, stated that by the end of September, 27 Camp residents had gone to the TRAC shelter (before Camp residents became badged and tracked). Unfortunately, those numbers cannot be verified. Following the badging of all Camp residents in October, where badged Camp residents went when they left the Camp was tracked by our peer support staff who reported that no more than 15 badged Camp residents went to the TRAC shelter. The 27 Camp residents who supposedly left for TRAC in September, plus the additional 15 badged residents who went to TRAC in the following months, would suggest a total of 42 Camp residents who went to TRAC. That number would be consistent with what our July assessments had told us might happen when 51 residents surveyed indicated they would be willing to go to a shelter, depending on the operator. Service providers and caseworkers who have worked both at Camp Hope and at the TRAC shelter tell me that they have seen very few of their Camp Hope clients at the TRAC shelter.

Second, regarding housing. The ten (10) months from September of 2022 until June of 2023 provides us with a meaningful overlapping period of operation for both the TRAC shelter and Camp Hope. TRAC opened in September, about the same time Commerce/WSDOT assumed oversight and provided funding for the Camp. During that ten month period of time, the service providers and staff at Camp Hope successfully housed 216 Camp residents (see our housing data in the following chapter). According to information provided to me by service providers, during that same time period approximately 13 guests at the TRAC shelter were successfully housed. If the City or the TRAC operator have better data regarding the housing of guests during that period of time, it hasn't been made publicly available. [118]

A Place to Exist

Third, let's consider how money could have been better spent. As we mentioned above, the TRAC shelter is costing the City of Spokane roughly $14 million per year, or $40,000 per guest per year. For that amount of money, the 350 shelter guests could have been placed into very decent apartments while receiving a living stipend for an entire year. Or, the 467 badged residents of Camp Hope could have received $30,000 in assistance, again, enough for a decent apartment and a smaller stipend for an entire year. Instead, we have a shelter the City can't afford in a warehouse with no facilities, and 350 people who aren't being offered a meaningful exit ramp out of homelessness.

There are several versions of the story, but here's the gist. As the Bush Administration was planning to go to war with Iraq, then Secretary of State Colin Powell cautioned the President and his team that he would "own" Iraq following a victory. Secretary Powell, and adviser Richard Armitage, dubbed this the Pottery Barn rule, "You break it, you own it." [119] The idea of political leaders, particularly presidents, taking responsibility (ownership) for what happens during their administration was perhaps best summed up by President Harry Truman who had a plaque on his desk in the Oval Office which simply read, "The Buck Stops Here."

When the numbers for 2023 Point In Time Count were released in April of 2023, showing a 36% increase in overall homelessness and a 16% increase in unsheltered homelessness, Mayor Nadine Woodward's response was to blame her upcoming Mayoral opponent, Lisa Brown, for not solving homelessness while she was Secretary of Commerce. Not exactly a Harry Truman or Colin Powell moment in local politics. Blaming someone else for your failures, while taking credit for the successes of others, seems to be a time

> If the buck doesn't stop with you when things go wrong, then the credit doesn't go to you when things go right.

honored political tradition. Perhaps we need a new "Pottery Barn Rule" for politicians that simply says, *If the buck doesn't stop with you when things go wrong, then the credit doesn't go to you when things go right.* I'm not expecting a rush of politicians clamoring to embrace that one.

Perhaps the most disappointing line in the Mayor's Statement to local media was, "In Spokane alone, the Commerce Department has spent more than $25 million on Camp Hope and has only placed 20 people into permanent housing." [120] Such blatant misrepresentations regarding Camp Hope and the work of service providers, staff, and the Washington State Department of Commerce to serve the 689 residents of the Camp can only be adequately refuted with data, and the Mayor offered none. Again, I would refer the reader to what we noted in the previous chapter, that what the Administration is spending each year on the TRAC shelter could have provided 350 homeless individuals with decent apartments and a living stipend for a year. The purpose of this chapter is to briefly recount some of Camp Hope's "Data of Success." But before we can do that, we need to briefly address wrong data.

No, That's Not Correct

Let's begin by addressing the Mayor's allegation that "the Commerce Department has spent more than $25 million on Camp Hope and has only placed 20 people into permanent housing." No. Of the $25 million that Commerce designated for Camp Hope, the actual amount spent managing and closing Camp Hope was about $3.4 million over 9 months (through the end of June, 2023). It should be noted that $2 million was allocated by Commerce to the Mayor's flagship

Spokane Funding Allocation From The Right of Way Initiative			
		Amount	Beds
Catalyst capital acquisition, renovation	$	9,246,446	
Catalyst operating (through June 2023)	$	4,775,587	100
Empire Health Foundation			
(and subcontractors through June 2023)	$	3,474,659	
Spokane Management Information System	$	372,194	
TRAC (Trent Shelter)	$	2,000,000	42
Diversion (Spokane County United Way)	$	150,000	20
Shared Supported Housing	$	1,762,318	50
Outpatient 22-hour Detox	$	620,000	16
Hope House (Women's Shelter)	$	330,000	40
Hope House (Respite Beds)	$	490,000	8
Rapid Rehousing			
(City of Spokane and EHF)	$	1,313,250	50
Total	$	**24,534,454**	
Housing Choice Vouchers (HUD Funding)			50
		Total beds	376

TRAC shelter. $14 million went to the transitional housing project known as The Catalyst Project, operated by Catholic Charities (and supported by the Mayor) that was created specifically to provide a housing option for 100+ residents of the Camp. An additional $1.3 million went to Rapid Rehousing (also supported by the Administration) to find housing for another 50 Camp residents who were further along and ready for permanent housing (most were not). You can read the allocations for yourself in the above graphic, but note that most of the money was intended to create and fund up to 376 alternative beds targeted toward the residents of Camp Hope. So, of the $25 million that Director Brown and Commerce brought into Spokane to address Camp Hope, over $15 million went to projects the Mayor supported and advocated for.[121]

Another statement in the Mayor's response to the Point In Time Count needs a reality check,

"Throughout my first term in office we have increased mental health support, created needed shelter space for unhoused young adults, and added more than 500 beds to the regional shelter system, many of those shelters with wrap-around supportive services to prepare them to be successful in permanent housing."

That's not entirely accurate. When Mayor Woodward took office in January of 2020, there were 805 beds in the city-wide shelter system, according to the City's own *Shelter Capacity Report* (see Chapter 5, "Spokane's Poorly Kept Secret" for more detail). As of mid-2023, there were 1,015 beds in the city-wide emergency shelter system. That's 210 beds, not 500, for a net increase in shelter beds of 26%. But since the 2020 Point In Time Count of 1,559, overall homelessness in Spokane has increased by 53% to 2,390. In other words, since the beginning of the current Administration in 2020, *overall homelessness in Spokane has grown at twice the rate of growth in city-wide shelter capacity.*

Data Of Success

Let's begin our discussion of success at Camp Hope by reflecting on the steps required for those experiencing homelessness - especially unsheltered homelessness - to succeed, including finding permanent housing. Policymakers who talk about "permanent" housing for the homeless (both sheltered and unsheltered) frequently reveal a lack of understanding of both the meaning of permanent housing and the challenges the unsheltered homeless must overcome to achieve it. While I list some of them below, I talk about those challenges in detail in Chapter 22, "Lessons Camp Hope Taught Us." The unsheltered homeless often have numerous co-occurring challenges to overcome - steps they must take - in order to achieve the goal of finding some type of long-term, stable (a better and more accurate description than "permanent"), and appropriate housing that they can successfully maintain. These challenges often included:

✓ Lack of a current needs assessment by a caseworker,
✓ Lack of transportation to reach services (if not provided "on site"),
✓ Lack of required identification (you cannot get any form of housing, or a job, without proper identification),
✓ Struggles with resolved substance abuse,
✓ Need for mental/emotional health assistance,
✓ Legal issues (outstanding warrants, criminal record, court dates, etc),
✓ Lack of job skills needed for employment (resulting in no income),
✓ Lack of affordable and appropriate housing options,
✓ Loss of life skills needed to maintain housing once attained (as Camp Manager and garbage collector for Camp Hope, I know what a loss of basic life skills looks like),
✓ Lack of follow-up and wrap-around case management to keep the individual moving forward after acquiring housing.

Identification Restoration

As we described earlier, for a period of six weeks in the Fall of 2022, *The Identification Connection* brought together the state Departments of Health and Licensing from Olympia and Spokane at the Camp where they worked with Camp Hope residents to obtain or replace lost identification, including birth certificates, state issued IDs, and Social Security Cards (what we refer to as "core documents").

By the time the program ended in late November, the Department of Health had issued 106 birth certificates, and the Department of Licensing had issued 400 ID cards! The Spokane homeless community had never before experienced such a successful and productive agency collaboration toward the common goal of ID restoration. And, remember, you can't complete a job application or a housing application without valid and current ID.

Connecting DSHS Services

One of the common themes, and under-reported successes, of Camp Hope was the elimination of barriers between those experiencing unsheltered homelessness and the services they needed to build an exit ramp out of the Camp and out homelessness. Eliminating barriers and connecting residents with needed services was a crucial component of overall success as staff worked to close the Camp and transition the residents out of the Camp and into better housing options.

If identification restoration was the most frequently encountered barrier, the loss of DSHS services (and particularly EBT cards)may have been a close second. As we described earlier, in order to help Camp residents overcome this barrier, the Department of Social and Health Services (DSHS) brought their mobile outreach unit (an RV) on-site at the Camp four days a week for two weeks to help residents sign up for various services that they qualified for, or to restore services they may have lost when they lost their EBT cards. During those two weeks of work at Camp Hope, DSHS staff were able to help 161 Camp residents (35% of all 467 residents) to access services. In the chronic and unsheltered homeless community, such numbers qualify as a huge success.

A Bus Ticket Home

In September of 2022, Spokane Sheriff Ozzie Knezovich declared his intention to clear Camp Hope by mid-October. Part of his plan to clear the Camp included buying bus tickets to send people back to wherever they came from. But as we noted earlier, on-the-ground data gathered from resident assessments painted a different picture of where those experiencing unsheltered homelessness at Camp Hope came from. Of the 467 badged residents of Camp Hope, 83% said they came from Greater Spokane (within 20 miles of the City), while 70.7% said they came from the City of Spokane. These numbers were consistent with the 2022 Point-In-Time Count which found that 74% of those interviewed said they came from Spokane County, and 79% of those from Spokane County said they came from the City of Spokane.[122] The Sheriff's declaration was more of an anecdote intended for an uninformed public than a plan supported by actual data.

But for some residents of Camp Hope, helping them return to family outside of the Spokane area represented a genuine option for resolving their stay at Camp Hope and potentially for ending their journey through homelessness. During the life-span of Camp Hope, Jewels Helping Hands bought 12 bus tickets (not the hundreds imagined by the Sheriff) to help Camp Hope residents (like Caleb) return to families in other communities. In order to return someone to family, Jewels staff would contact the receiving family and verify that they were willing and able to receive and house the individual who would be coming. There was no point in sending someone to unwilling family elsewhere just so they could be homeless and traumatized in a different town. But reconnecting individuals with their core support community (family & friends) in another town can be a powerful step forward on their journey out of homelessness.

Successful Case Management And Peer Support
One of the "secret weapons" in the fight for better services and better results at Camp Hope was our staff and network of Peer Navigators, led by Sharyl Brown (you'll want to read her personal story in Chapter 14). These are people with lived experience who have faced many of the same challenges as the residents of the Camp and were able to successfully build their own exit ramps out of homelessness, drug addiction, the criminal justice system, and more. During the 10 months from September to June, as many as 30 Peer Navigators connected with Camp residents, conducted detailed assessments, took people to appointments, provided them with bus passes, arranged for bus tickets home to other cities, helped them complete required housing paperwork, recovered lost IDs, got them into substance abuse treatment, even sat at their bedside in the hospital to make certain they knew that they weren't alone. The work of successfully moving 216 people from the Camp and into better housing could not have been done without the tireless efforts of these dedicated and talented people.

Employing The Unemployable
Successful employment is one of the key building blocks for building a successful exit ramp out of homelessness. Unless you're disabled or retired, you're going to need income, which means a job. But getting a job is one of the challenges that many of the homeless face for reasons ranging from lack of basic job skills (such as showing up for work on time) or experience, to the lack of identification, to a lack of any recent employment history, to a criminal/legal history that creates significant barriers to employment.

To help residents of Camp Hope overcome these challenges and begin rebuilding an employment history, Jewels Helping Hands made it a priority to hire people from inside the Camp for a variety of jobs (internal camp security, grounds maintenance, support staff, and other tasks). During the 18-month life of the Camp, JHH hired 159 residents to work as part of the Camp Staff, providing them with an employment opportunity, basic job training, practical experience, and income. All residents who worked for JHH were required to pass a regular UA for drugs as one of the terms of their employment. This was intended to encourage their ongoing sobriety and to prepare them for similar requirements when they moved on to employment outside of JHH. Those who failed a UA were suspended and offered the opportunity to go to a sobering center for help and treatment. If they successfully completed their stay at the sobering center, they were allowed to return to work, followed by regular UA's. Refusal to go to treatment or to a sobering center resulted in termination.

In addition to hiring Camp residents, JHH also helped Camp residents enroll in a program sponsored by WSDOT (and taught by an independent contractor) called PEPP or the Pre-Employment Preparation Program.[123] Designed for individuals experiencing homelessness, including the residents of Camp Hope, PEPP was an intensive 4-week pre-apprentice course that combined in-class education and hands-on training. Individuals who graduated from the PEPP program earned certificates in OSHA 10, First Aid, and CPR with an AED, Traffic Control (flagging), and forklift qualification credentials. Graduation from the course enabled participants to connect with interviews, apprenticeships, and to begin using their traffic control certification for immediate flagging jobs. The course also provided case management services to address any employment barriers camp residents might have, including help accessing key documents, such as ID's, driver licenses and social security cards. The overall goal of the course was to connect Camp residents with jobs and to provide training that would hopefully empower them to earn a livable wage, improve their overall well-being, and set them up for long-term success. On Friday, March 24, ten residents of Camp Hope graduated from PEPP.[124] A second PEPP course held in late April and early May on site at the Catalyst resulted in seven more qualified graduates ready to find jobs. One of the graduates from the second PEPP class was Sam, a former Camp Hope resident who went to the Catalyst, graduated the PEPP class, became a dues-paying union member, and got a job as a Flagger making $40/hour! In the chronic and unsheltered homeless community, training 17 formerly unsheltered homeless individuals to find meaningful employment was a big deal.

Success And Struggles At The Catalyst Project

The Catalyst Project represents a microcosm of the challenges that caseworkers and peer support staff faced in placing the unsheltered homeless into stable housing. Operated by Catholic Charities of Eastern Washington, the Catalyst Project was created as a transitional housing facility for Camp Hope residents, funded with $15 million in state Right of Way Safety Initiative dollars. It was an

The Catalyst Project, operated by Catholic Charities for residents of Camp Hope.

important part of a larger plan to close Camp Hope by offering Camp residents better housing options than a tent in a homeless camp. Funds from the ROW Initiative paid for site acquisition (the Quality Inn and former Spokane House on Sunset Hill), building rehab, and the first year of operations. Detailed resident assessments regarding housing needs and potential barriers created a list of Camp residents who could be ready, and who might qualify, for a move to such a transitional living facility. In addition to transitional housing, Catalyst participants received meal and laundry services, on-site case management, employment and behavioral health services, on-site medical help, substance abuse recovery help, and more. The project goal was to help residents create better pathways to stable housing after their stay at Catalyst.

The Catalyst Project Transitional Housing For Camp Hope Residents		
Number of Badged Camp Residents	467	Percentages
Number of Camp Residents Referred To Catalyst	277	59%
Number of Camp Referrals Accepted/Housed	98	35%
Number of Referrals Declined or Ineligible	82	30%
Number of Catalyst Residents Removed	23	8%
Number of Referrals Who Went to Other Housing	9	3%

Designed to offer 87 remodeled hotel rooms that could accommodate roughly 100 Camp residents, the numbers in the graphic below illustrate the challenge of moving the chronic and unsheltered homeless into even low-barrier transitional housing, much less into what homeless policymakers would consider "permanent" housing. Let's take a quick look at the numbers. [125]

- Of the 467 badged Camp Residents, 277 (or 59%) met the initial requirements to be referred to the Catalyst.
- Of the 277 residents initially referred, 98 (or 35%) were eventually accepted and housed at Catalyst. This statistic alone should be an eye-opener for homeless policymakers regarding the challenges this population struggles with when it comes to acquiring meaningful and stable (i.e., "permanent") housing.
- Of the 277 initial referrals, 82 (or 30%) were declined/denied because of various barriers, including - but not limited to - a criminal history involving a violent offense (such as domestic violence, assault, or sexual offence) within the past 7 years.
- Another 23 individuals (or 8%) who were approved and housed at Catalyst were "exited" (asked to leave or "removed from the program") for various

infractions. In the parlance of the homeless services community, these individuals were unable to "maintain" what they had worked to gain.

- Of the 277 initial referrals 9 (or 3%) went to a different housing option.
- And 65 (or 24%) of the original initial referrals remained pending or unresolved for various reasons (unresolved barriers, on a waiting list due to no vacancy, incomplete background checks, unable to connect with applicant, etc).

Again, these numbers highlight the difficulty of moving the chronic and/or unsheltered homeless into stable housing, even low-barrier transitional housing designed to meet their unique needs and to overcome some of their most common barriers. If their challenges and barriers prevented them from qualifying for such transitional housing designed for them, imagine the difficulties they would encounter attempting to qualify for most traditional forms of "permanent" housing. To successfully move the 955 unsheltered homeless, or the 2,390 individuals experiencing homelessness (from the 2023 PIT Count), into a form of stable housing that they can both qualify for and then maintain, we need more housing options, and more wrap-around service providers, not more political rhetoric.

Additional Housing Successes

By the time Camp Hope closed, 216 residents (not including 3 who passed away waiting for their housing) had been moved into some form of housing or treatment that was appropriate to their needs or situations. In the absence of action by local governments to provide additional housing or treatment options, local service providers were forced to create an ad hoc network of alternative housing to meet the unique housing needs of many Camp Hope residents for whom traditional options or shelters simply would not work to address their needs. These included the Catalyst, Revive Transitional Housing, clean and sober Green Houses (JHH), Compassionate Addiction Treatment Transitional Housing, Miryam's House, Veterans Transitional Housing, Permanent Supportive Housing, and more. The lack of adequate alternative housing options for the chronically unsheltered homeless population of Camp Hope serves to highlight the challenges faced by any plan to meaningfully address unsheltered homelessness. Having such alternatives as a managed tiny house or pallet house village - had local jurisdictions leaned in to enable their creation - could have resulted in helping many more of the unsheltered homeless find meaningful transitional or permanent housing.

Epilogue

Measuring the "success" of work among the unsheltered homeless requires a different metric than anything you and I might be accustomed to, starting with the terms we use to frame that work. For example, what exactly is "permanent" housing? Is it a traditional single-family house? Is it an apartment, a duplex, or a condo? What about a clean-and-sober living house? What about a pallet house or tiny house in a village-type community arrangement? Wouldn't "stable" housing be a better and more inclusive term to describe a wider variety of housing options, especially for people coming out of the instability of unsheltered homelessness? And even a room in a transitional living facility like The Catalyst, while it may not be "permanent," is certainly "stable" for however long they are there before moving on to their next "stable" housing.

A similar problem arises when describing how we employ the "unemployable." We all want success stories like Sam's (and another former Camp resident - "New York" - who went to The Catalyst, graduated from the PEPP program and is waiting to start his new job). But not all of the 159 Camp residents employed at one time or another by JHH during the life of the Camp were successful. Some were hired one day, but didn't show up for work the next day. Some couldn't maintain the basic employment rules (show up for work on time, contact your supervisor if you can't be at work, pass your UA every couple of weeks, and a few others). Some had old offences that re-visited them, or new ones that side-tracked their journey. All 159 were hired and given the opportunity to work, but not all could maintain. And providing them with the opportunity to work - along with giving them grace that takes into account their challenges - is all we could do. You and I can't force people to be successful, regardless of how much we may want them to succeed. To succeed, they have to want it for themselves at least as much as we want if for them.

A Place to Exist

When I was filming my second documentary, *The Hidden Homeless: Families Experiencing Homelessness*, I interviewed Ryan Oelrich, the Executive Director of Priority Spokane. I served with Ryan on the leadership team of the Spokane Homeless Coalition which is how I came to know about his work among homeless school students in

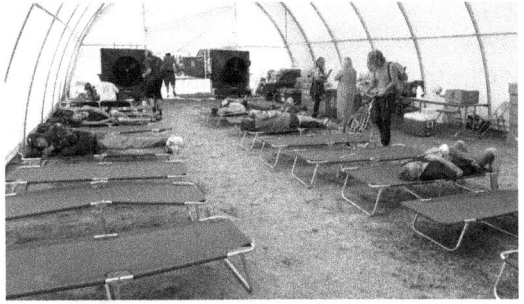
The Resource/Access Tent at Camp Hope

greater Spokane. Priority Spokane identified student and family homelessness as a major issue for Spokane County. In a multi-year pilot project they partnered with a local university that researched best practices and looked at what else had worked around the country. Ultimately, they came up with a plan to place community health workers directly into some of Spokane's highest need elementary schools to work directly with families to help them find housing. "We ultimately were able to house 70 or 80% of the students in those schools who are facing homelessness," Ryan told me. "So, of the families that we were able to house and stabilize after three years," Ryan continued, "95% of those families remained housed and stable and no longer in need of our services or help. So that was really exciting for us."[126] The success of Priority Spokane's pilot program for homeless school students and their families offers several practical take-aways. But one in particular stands out as relevant to what we discovered at Camp Hope: Offering help and services in as close proximity as possible to those who need them is very effective. But doing so requires that we be willing to change how we do things.

A well worn cliche, or better yet, a well known truism, says, *"If you continue to do what you've always done, you'll continue to get what you've always got."* A deep truth lies at the root of this truism: The price for effectiveness - regardless of the endeavor - is the willingness to change and to do things differently. But change involves risk, and the more established an organization becomes in a particular way of doing things, the more risk-averse it becomes, and the harder it becomes to change.

The Seven Last Words of Ineffectiveness

It was a Friday morning and I was at Huckleberry's at 10th & Monroe on Spokane's lower south hill to meet with Lisa Brown, Director of the Washington State Department of Commerce when the Right of Way Initiative began funding solutions for the residents of Camp Hope. We were discussing some of the challenges she faced getting State agencies to change the way they delivered services and to work "outside the box" in addressing some of the issues presented by the Camp. I mentioned that, having been an administrative pastor, we used to say that the last seven great words of a struggling church were, *"We've never done it that way before!*" We both laughed at the human reality that some things don't change, regardless of the bureaucracy. Welcome to the seven last words of ineffectiveness. We resist change, as if resisting change is part of our DNA.

The Cooling Tent That Became Much More

Earlier, in Chapter 5, I talked about the cooling tent that was set up on WSDOT property across the street from the Camp itself. During the Summer of 2022, it served as a cooling tent, giving Camp residents a place to escape the withering summer heat without having to walk over a mile to the nearest public library that the City promoted as a cooling center. This was the first instance of bringing much needed services to those who needed them at the Camp. But as

The Cooling tent became a Resource/Access tent and an all-purpose warming center (during the winter) as well as a hub for Camp Hope residents.

the month progressed, the tent morphed from a cooling tent to a resource tent where Camp residents could access additional services. The Resource Access Tent at Camp Hope came to embody a new post-pandemic reality. To truly be effective, homeless services needed to be offered as close as possible to where those experiencing homelessness live. And that included homeless camps. The Woodward Administration resisted this new reality (resisting change being part of their DNA), unsuccessfully attempting to forcibly close the Camp with no place to send the residents where they might find needed services, and attempting to force the Camp residents into the City's newly opened TRAC shelter (which never offered all of the services the City promised and promoted).

A Tent That Removed Barriers

As the months progressed from Summer to Fall and Winter, the Resource Access Tent at Camp Hope became a services hub for Camp residents where they could find food resources, meet with caseworkers and peer support staff, receive housing assessments, meet with *Identification Connection* staff to work on restoring lost IDs, be seen and treated by CHAS Street Medical teams, sign up for job training classes, talk with someone about substance abuse treatment, and much more. Community members at large used the Resource Access Tent as a drop-off location for food, water, clothes, and other supplies for Camp residents. In the process, the Tent illustrated an important principle. Successfully and effectively offering services to the unsheltered homeless (or to anyone experiencing homelessness) involves overcoming barriers. And historically, one of the most frequent and practical barriers to accessing services in the homeless community is transportation.

Consider Just One Practical Barrier

Consider this reality. There are roughly 253 million cars and trucks on the road in America, scattered among 115 million households. That's roughly two cars or trucks per household. How many do you and your family have now? Imagine not having any. Not one. How would you get around? How would you go to the grocery store, to church, to school? How would you get your kids to school? What about getting to that important doctor appointment, or to work, or to look for work? In a society built around the personal automobile, your life changes profoundly when you don't have a vehicle to drive yourself where you need to go.

Welcome to just one of the practical barriers faced by those experiencing homelessness in our community today. People experiencing homelessness, especially the unsheltered homeless, have additional unseen barriers, including the loss of a basic life-skill that you and I take for granted: a linear sense of time. You and I plan our days, our weeks, maybe even our months on a linear time-line: be at work by nine, child's athletic event next Wednesday, a doctor's appointment next Thursday at 2, a car service appointment in 2 weeks, an out of town business trip next month. But in the unsheltered homeless community (and even among the sheltered to a surprising extent), a linear sense of time is replaced by a survival sense of time: *Now*. Where will I find a meal today? Where will I find a restroom to use? Where will I sleep tonight? Their survival *Now* sense of time causes them to focus on their immediate needs and to miss even important appointments, ranging from service providers, to housing navigators, to doctors, and even court dates (partially explaining the large number of warrants for "Failure To Appear" in the unsheltered homeless community). The urgency of the *Now* replaces the importance of *later*. Add in lost cell phones, constantly being forced to move, and the general trauma of daily survival, and the lack of transportation to access services is one more barrier to overcome.

Epilogue

On-site services, like those provided at Camp Hope at the Resource Access Tent, as opposed to in-office services that require transportation and a linear sense of time, remove practical barriers and places much needed services within arms reach of those who need them most.

Historically, homeless policymakers have tended to create homeless policies and "solutions" for people experiencing homelessness without ever actually spending time with them, talking with them, and asking them what they need. Not to put too fine a point on this, but no one from the City of Spokane's Community Housing and Human Services (CHHS) department, responsible

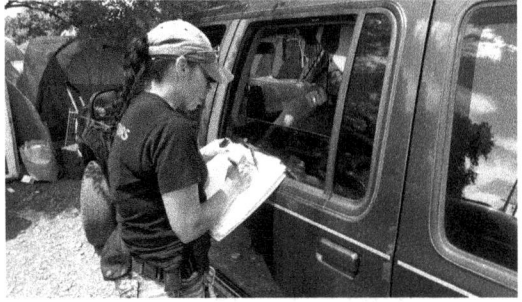

Assessments underway at Camp Hope in July of 2022

for making and implementing homeless policy for the City of Spokane, ever spent any time at Camp Hope, meeting with the residents and discovering what they needed or wanted. How can you know what people experiencing homelessness need, and what policies might be effective (or ineffective) if you never talk to the people affected by those policies?

In July of 2022, Jewels Helping Hands and a team of volunteers spent two days conducting 601 individual personal assessments of the residents of Camp Hope. Here's what the assessments revealed. Note that the percentages cited below represent percentages of the 601 total assessments. Of the 601 Camp residents who completed an assessment:

❑ 601 (100%) of residents assessed said they would accept a pallet shelter or tiny house, if available.
❑ 598 (99.5%) said they needed their identification (i.e., State IDs, Social Security Cards, birth certificates) restored. Valid ID is the gateway to all other services, placing the restoration of lost or stolen ID (very common in the homeless community) at the top of any homeless services needs list (More about this below, and in Chapter 9).
❑ 514 (86%) of residents said they needed help with laundry. As Julie Garcia noted earlier, this population lives in the weather with no ability to do laundry or take a shower or practice basic hygiene that you and I take for granted. Clothes are quickly ruined and need to be replaced. Again, ask yourself what you would look and smell like if you couldn't shower or do laundry for weeks at a time. You'd probably resemble a Camp Hope resident, too.
❑ 285 (47%) of those assessed indicated they had a phone, an essential (but frequently lost) communication tool for staying in touch with caseworkers, Parole Officers, Public Defenders, employers, doctors, DSHS, etc. This survey also means that 53% of Camp residents did not have a phone. Stop and ask yourself how long you would last without a phone?
❑ 51 (8.5%) of the Camp residents who participated said they would go to a shelter, depending on the operator. This also suggests that 91.5% of Camp

residents did not want to go to a shelter, begging the question, "Why?" This question, and its answers, would be addressed later through on-going individual housing assessments conducted by housing navigators.

Homeless journeys have many different causes, origins, and explanations. They're personal, not formulaic. When asked why they were homeless, 601 Camp residents revealed some of their personal journeys and reasons:

- [ ] 463 (77%) people cited a family conflict, including foster care, as the cause of their homelessness
- [ ] 286 (48%) people cited a loss of income as the cause of their homelessness,
- [ ] 232 (39%) people cited their criminal history. A criminal history often creates barriers to such basic things as employment and housing.
- [ ] 75 (12%) people cited an eviction as the cause of their homelessness,

The more than 600 assessments of Camp residents also helped to clarify what those experiencing homelessness in the Camp were thinking about housing, and how the homeless services system had let them down.

- [ ] 543 (90%) of those assessed said they had been previously assessed. In other words, at some point nine out of ten Camp residents had been through a needs assessment conducted by an agency or caseworker. This stunning reality begged a question: If they had been previously assessed, what happened and why were they still homeless and living in a homeless camp?
- [ ] 301 (50%) Camp residents said that their goal was to find transitional housing. Moving forward, this became particularly important in evaluating whether or not someone was actually ready mentally and emotionally to be placed into permanent supportive housing. Many were not and needed the intermediary step of transitional housing.
- [ ] 279 (46%) residents - nearly half - said that their goal was to find permanent housing.
- [ ] 43 (7%) of those assessed said they had a caseworker. This low number came as a surprise, but appeared to be related to the fact that they had been previously assessed, but were never followed up by whoever did the assessment.

What The Assessments Taught Us

Assessments alone don't solve problems. They simply provide a snapshot in time of where a particular person is on their journey through homelessness. Assessments are useless if, as activists, advocates, and service providers, we don't learn what they are trying to teach us about the homeless population we're trying to serve. These two days of assessments and the results they produced offered a handful of critical lessons that the Camp management team worked to digest and understand with an eye toward how best to move forward in providing services for the Camp residents. I want to suggest four critical lessons that should top the list of actionable take-aways.

Asking Is Better Than Assuming - When properly done, assessments don't just yield "data." Again, they simply provide a snapshot in time of where a particular person is at on their journey through homelessness. The questions we ask and the answers we get in response engage us with people experiencing homelessness, their journeys, their fears, their hopes, and their needs moving forward. The City of Spokane wanted to come into the Camp and do its own "assessments" with the goal of entering the people and their "data" into the Community Management Information System (or CMIS, also known as the Homeless Management Information System, or HMIS), a database used by various agencies to track the progress of (or at least the contacts with) those experiencing homelessness. More about this later. But there's a difference between treating those experiencing homelessness as a "data point" to be followed, and treating them as persons who need someone to walk along side them on their journey through and out of homelessness. When it comes to assessments, why you're asking (as a friend trying to help) is as important as what you're asking. Data is useful, but when it comes to successfully walking people out of homelessness, friends are more helpful. Friends ask, *"What do you need to get out of here?"*

ID Restoration Should Be A First Priority - Nearly every person residing at Camp Hope indicated that they needed some form of ID restoration in order to move forward. Some needed to replace a lost birth certificate. Others knew their Social Security number but had lost their card and needed a replacement. Still others needed to replace a State ID card (or license) that had been lost or stolen. The needs were varied, but widespread. ID restoration can cost as little as $5 or as much as $65 (or more, especially if starting from scratch with ordering a birth certificate and other state fees). Helping to cover those costs is a project that regional governments, policymakers, and foundations could easily fund, one that would make an immediate, practical, and meaningful difference. More about this later.

Appropriate Shelter Or Housing - In the months leading up to Camp Hope, there was a lot of chatter about the unsheltered homeless being "shelter resistant" or that they really didn't want housing because it was too "easy" and "comfortable" for them to be homeless. What the July assessments revealed was that the residents of Camp Hope were not shelter or housing resistant. Rather, what the assessments revealed was that Camp residents were "inappropriate shelter/housing resistant." Between 8 and 9 percent of respondents said they would go to a shelter, depending who operated it and how it was operated (such things as having trained staff that understand and practice trauma-informed care). Roughly half of Camp residents said they had a goal of either permanent housing (50%) or transitional housing (46%), and fully 100% of Camp residents said they would accept a pallet or tiny house if offered. These are not the statistics of shelter resistance. Rather, these are statistics that highlight a need for more and better shelter and housing options. These assessment results confirmed that, as a larger community - as well as a community of homeless services providers, we need to think outside of our traditional boxes, especially our shelter boxes, and offer more, better, and creative alternatives, including such things as pallet house or tiny house villages, and managed safe parking lots.

What Happened To Those Previous Assessments? Another eye-opening result from the July Camp assessments was the discovery that 90% of Camp Hope residents had undergone at least one previous assessment (some, more than one). This suggested that many of them were already in the Community Management Information System (CMIS) homeless tracking database, having been entered by a previous caseworker. So, what happened? A common response we received was, *"No one ever followed up with me?"* Whether rightly or wrongly, from their perspective, they feel as though they have been abandoned and have fallen through the cracks of a system that treats them as little more than a number and a data point. I understand there are many various reasons why our homeless population might not get the follow-up they need: they're forced to move by law enforcement; caseworkers lose contact because clients are very transient; they lose their phones and can't call or be called; caseworkers are overloaded and feel they have done all they can for this person without resolving their case. I understand. But that can't be where things end.

The City Administration wanted to do their own new and independent assessment of Camp Hope residents, with the goal of collecting personal data and updating the CMIS system.[127] But here's a novel thought. Why not work collaboratively with homeless service providers to go through the current CMIS data and follow up with what's already there? What does the existing CMIS data tell us about our overall success rate in exiting people from homelessness? Where are those people today? Who has gotten the help and wrap-around services they needed (and were promised) to successfully exit homelessness? Who hasn't been helped with no positive outcome. Discover why. Learn where the holes are in the reporting and tracking system, rather than filling a broken system with more data that won't get followed up on. Discover why people are not being followed up on. In other words, clean up your present CMIS house before you start adding more people who run the risk of disappearing into a data black hole, never to be followed up on. Why? Because that's what they fear will happen . . . again. Chances are good you might find many of the 543 previously assessed Camp residents who could still use the help someone once promised them in an earlier assessment. But at this point, they simply don't trust the system.

Final Thoughts. The 601 assessments done in July of 2022 were not the last assessments of Camp residents. However successful and revealing a single assessment might be, one snapshot in time is not a sufficient basis for identifying and meeting all needs. In the months that followed, throughout late 2022 and into early 2032, housing navigators, substance abuse counselors, identification specialists, peer support workers and others would do additional more specific assessments on specific issues to identify how best to remove obstacles to their progress and to move each person forward. It was slow, hard work, but it paid off as residents slowly moved on to better options.

Epilogue

We can't leave this discussion of assessments without re-emphasizing that of all the questions asked by these 601 assessments, only three questions received near-unanimous "Yes" responses:

1. Do you need your ID restored [99.5%],
2. Would you accept a pallet shelter or tiny house if offered [100%], and
3. Have you been previously assessed [90%].

Such near unanimity should move addressing these questions with meaningful solutions to the top of any homeless policy or services agenda. Otherwise, why collect data if we're unwilling to pursue the solutions that the data suggests?

A final important take-away from the assessment process and the needs it revealed should be obvious, but often isn't. We need more working hands at the table and more available options to serve more needs. Just as we've underestimated the size of homelessness in our community for many years, so too we've underestimated the number of caseworkers, case managers, staff, Peer Navigators, volunteers, and others that are needed to successfully move people forward, to identify and address their needs, and to provide on-going wrap-around services. If we don't come to terms with this reality, we'll break trust with the homeless community again by promising services we honestly are not capable of providing. And few things destroy trust faster among a population that already feels let down and left behind than over promising and under delivering . . . again.

14 - Peer Navigators - "I've Been There. Let Me Help"
by Sharyl Brown

Take a moment and imagine being 50 years old . . . living in a homeless camp . . . in a tent . . . in a wheel chair . . . and with no legs below your knees. In your imagination you just met my friend Top Hat (his street name). He had been homeless for twelve years when he came to live at Camp Hope, which is where I met him.

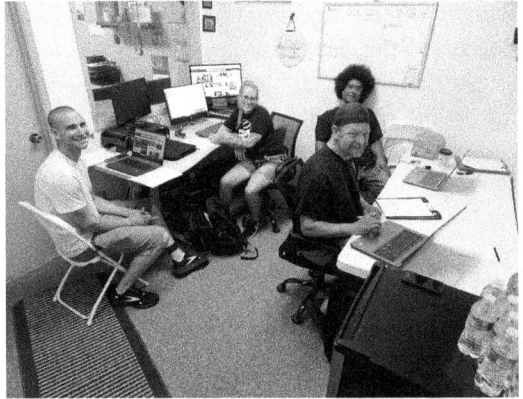

Sharyl Brown with Peer Navigators (Dann Babcox, Anwar Peace, and Chris Senn) from Jewels Helping Hands

I'm Sharyl Brown. I worked as the Lead Peer Navigator at Camp Hope, and Top Hat was one of my clients. A Peer Navigator is someone with lived experience with homelessness or one of the many contributing or "co-occurring" factors related to homelessness. That includes things like substance abuse, involvement with the criminal justice system (charges, courts, jails, prison, etc.), struggles to find medical care, housing, employment, and more. Peer Navigators are people who have walked some of the same paths as the people we're working to help, and we managed to find a way out to a better life. We can look our clients in the eye and honestly say, "I understand. I've been there. Let me help because if I could do this, you can do this." And I suppose that deserves an explanation.

My Journey Into Hopelessness

My downhill journey started when I was 24 years old with a 5-year old son and I was kicked out of where I was living. At that time, I was very anti-drugs. I didn't want anything to do with it. My whole family was in addiction, and I was like, "I don't ever want to grow up like that." I was a single mom with a 5-year old son and working as a waitress when somebody I knew approached me asking me if I would help them hide drugs and guns. I agreed, and it quickly escalated to me driving them around to sell guns for drugs. I still wasn't doing drugs. Things continued to escalate to where we were making a regular drop at a strip club. Having been sexually abused all of my life (another part of my personal trauma), I concluded that I might as well make some money off it. So, I started working at the strip club, which escalated my drug sales because I was selling to all of the people in the industry and to all of the top drug dealers that would visit the club. Things just escalated, escalated, escalated. Finally, I reached a point where the trauma I was re-traumatizing myself with by working in the strip club (I was literally putting myself through the same trauma I grew up with and trying to convince myself that it was okay, because I was "coming out on top") started catching up with me. I started using the drugs. Then my son started acting out because I changed as a human being, not just because I doing drugs, but because my life now revolved around gang life. I was not a healthy mother, so my son started acting up.

At one point I made a decision. I told myself, "I don't want anything to do with any of this anymore." I convinced one of the men who took care of me to buy me a condo. So, my son and I moved into a condo in Bellingham, far away from Seattle where all this chaos was going on. I stopped doing drugs, I stopped selling drugs. I tried really hard. I got two jobs. I was still not surviving and my son was still acting up. That's when I said, "I need you to go live with your dad." He was 13 and I was 32. The next day, after he moved in with his dad, I tried to kill myself. The day after that, I tried meth for the first time. After that, I was a full-blown addict.

In 2014, I moved to Spokane. I was homeless, couch surfing, addicted to methamphetamine, on probation, consistently having warrants, going to jail, and experiencing psychosis from the methamphetamine. Not the way most people want to start their day. From the outside looking in, most people would probably offer the most straightforward solution: stop doing drugs. But it isn't quite that easy. If drugs are the "tail that wags the dog", then the wagging tail of drugs was shaking my life apart and burying me with a deep-rooted layer of guilt and shame toward the life I was living. Quitting methamphetamine would mean confronting all that guilt and shame; addressing the guilt and shame of not being there for my son all of those years. Emotionally, that alone felt like a mountain I just couldn't climb. There was more, like significant childhood emotional, physical, and sexual trauma that I had experienced but had never addressed. I allowed that trauma to shape me as an adult, thinking that I was my trauma. I came to think that my only worth was my appearance, which years of drug use had slowly taken away. I had lost trust in myself, and in other people. So, reaching out and trusting anyone to help me out of my downward spiral did not feel like a real option. I felt like a passenger on the "train-wreck of life" and didn't know how or where to get off.

Prison And A Life-Changing Encounter

The day came when my addiction and all of the crimes I had been involved with caught up with me. In 2017 I was arrested in Idaho with a minimal amount of drugs. Idaho officials weren't in the mood to show me grace because I had some 35 previous charges. And for Idaho to show you grace, you have to show them that you can comply with probation. But I had never, ever complied with Washington probation in the five years I was on it. So Idaho said, "No, you're going to prison." I was disappointed, but in all honesty, it was when I was in Idaho that I had an overwhelming and life-changing encounter with God in which I experienced the unmistakable Presence of God. In that encounter, I truly, in my core and in my gut, knew that I needed a better way of life. I turned 40 years old in prison, and I knew something had to change. I understood that there was no way I could continue like that, not being able to talk to my son, and my son not wanting to talk to me. I just couldn't do it anymore. I knew something had to change and I "one-million-percent" experienced God's Presence while I was in prison, telling me that I could do it and I would do it.

When I got to prison, I didn't feel like I had any self-worth. And I think that's why I identify so well with the people I'm working with as a Peer Navigator. I just felt so low, like people wouldn't even look at me. When I got to prison, I had an idea that I could do better, but I didn't know how or what to do. While I was in prison there were people who believed in me and helped me believe in myself. I had no idea I was smart. I had no idea that I was capable of anything. I've never been a leader in my life. I've always been a follower. But between Narcotics Anonymous (NA) and God, I've become a whole different person that I don't recognize half the time. And sometimes thoughts creep in like, "*What do you think you're doing? You don't know what you're doing? You're not a leader.*" But God is good and He tells me, "*You are who I made you to be. And that's who you are right now.*"

A New Beginning

I got out of prison in January of 2018. When I got out I went to a few celebrate recoveries, but I felt kind of judged. So I ended up going to NA meetings, and that's where I met Ken (*Editor: Ken Crary, Director of Operations for Jewels Helping Hands*). Me and Ken have been like family friends for about five and a half years. I met Ken right after my mom died. We both were at an event, helping set up the meeting hall for the event and doing service work. Through Ken I met Julie Garcia. I was a SUDEP (Substance Use Disorder Professional) trainee at a treatment center when Ken asked me if I knew anybody who wanted to do peer support. I told him, "No, but I'll look around." At the time, I was in a good place in my job. I had a really good supervisor. I was the lead counselor. I was doing great. And I never thought I would leave. But God told me to pray on it. He told me the credential doesn't matter. It's how you treat human beings and it's what I'm doing in the world that matters. I knew He was telling me to take the next step. Today, I know this is God's will for me, and I know it without a doubt. And I remind myself of that on all the hard days. I remind myself every time I don't want to do it. There's no doubt in my heart that this is exactly where God wants me to be.

In September of 2022 Julie hired me to do Peer Support work at Camp Hope. At one point she said, "*I don't care who's working with what agency, they're all your caseload. I want you to make sure their needs are getting met.*" Wow. At the time Julie hired me there was over 600 people there, and my job was to remember everybody's name and try to help everybody that need it. I would show up at camp every day thinking, "*God, this is all you, because I can't do this.*" And I would look at that camp almost every day and think, "*I'm only human. This is a 'God job'*"

I started by just showing up, even when I was overwhelmed and not sure what to do. After all, I wasn't a trained or experienced homeless caseworker. But I wanted to make sure their needs were met, even if it was as simple as a smile, telling them that I loved them, telling them I'm here to support them. At the beginning I had a checklist. Working with so many people was challenging, but every time I'd meet somebody, I would write down if they needed Social Security, or their ID restored, or food stamps, a phone, everything down to a tee that would help them get to that next step. And that was all while we were waiting for housing options to come (the Catalyst Project didn't come until mid-December). We were basically preparing them for that housing option whenever it would come . We would take veterans to SSVF appointments (Supportive Services for Veterans & Families), we would take people to Goodwill for the HEN (Housing and Essential Needs)program, to doctor's appointments, to Social Security appointments to get their cards or benefits, to DOL for their IDs, to DSHS for their EBT cards, and more. We would utilize whatever resources were available, which were kind of minimal at the time. But we would do the best we could, including taking them to local shelters or wherever they needed to go to get to a better situation.

Understanding Their Trauma

At the end of the day, for our homeless friends at Camp Hope, their situations - like my own journey - all circle back to the trauma they have experienced. Like them, I am literally still facing and dealing with my own trauma. Someone may say to me "Well, I'm different," or "Maybe yours isn't as bad as mine." I can say, "First, you didn't see me six years ago. Second, I'm not saying your trauma isn't real, but you have to work to grow from it. Third, we can't just accept our trauma, if you want to get to a better place." So I'm still in counseling, I still have nightmares, and I'm still hypersensitive to people. Walking around camp, there were times that I would jump if anybody touched me. Because of my own journey through trauma - abuse, homelessness, drugs, prison, etc. - I can relate to the trauma of the people I'm serving. I understand it. I get it. Not everybody's trauma response is as minimal as mine, and a lot of people haven't started addressing their trauma yet. So, I understand. And I explain to them that I'm still not healed from my trauma. But I can tell them that this is what I did, and this is what you could do. I don't expect you to do it. But this is what I did, and I'm letting you know. By sharing my trauma and my journey, I've planted a seed in their lives, and maybe one day it'll flourish and grow.

And trauma brings me back to where I started this article - to my friend and client, Top Hat. He's doing well, even thriving, at the Catalyst Project. He is slowly working through his own trauma, which includes over a decade of street homelessness and repeated winters of frostbite that took his legs below the knees and left him in a wheelchair. I see him and talk with him regularly, which is what Peer Support Navigators do, and we're working to restore his lost ID and to help him build a meaningful pathway forward.

Lessons

As a Peer Navigator who came into this work without any professional training (I didn't even know what a "Peer Navigator" was), I've learned some important lessons along the way. Here are a few that stand out to me.

Don't Pre-Judge Outcomes. Maybe the first lesson should be to not pre-judge people's outcomes. I should have known this walking in, and it's embarrassing to even admit that I didn't. But you cannot look at somebody and know whether or not they will be successful. I feel bad even admitting it, but even as a team I've heard a people say about someone we're working with, "*Oh, they won't do well once they get inside,*" or "*They're not made for indoors*" and they go indoors and they're thriving. And then you're working with someone else and you're telling people, "*I'm so impressed that they're doing this, this, and this. They're going to be doing wonderful in housing.*" But then something happens once they get indoors and - surprise - they're not thriving! You simply can't judge their eventual outcome based on their current situation. People can surprise you, even shock you.

Get To Know Your Clients. Successful case management is all about getting to know the people you're serving. And getting to know your client takes time and thought. When we first started working with people at Camp Hope, we really didn't have everything planned. The plan emerged from the process. While we were at camp, it was go, go, go, house, house, house, act, act, act. There was so much to be done (with over 600 people) that there just wasn't a lot of time to decompress, reflect, and welcome new thoughts and energy into what we were doing. It was frenetic activity and constant action. We had a job to do and we were getting it done.

Now that the Camp has closed and I've had time to breathe, I've formulated a case management plan that will provide a format for me and the Peers I oversee to meet with our clients as we do outreach and ask, "*What are your goals? What are we going to do to move you forward?*" Yes, I know, this is traditional case management, and we should have been doing it from the beginning, and it's embarrassing that we didn't, but we didn't have time for that. During the height of the Camp, working with over 600 people, we simply didn't have the time or opportunity to do a lot of traditional stuff because we were living in constant, non-stop triage and emergency management mode.

We Can't Choose for Them. One of the big things I learned about case management is that we can't choose their options for them. We can't pick their housing situation. I can't tell them what to do. All I can do is be there, hold their hand, and give them options and let them know that I'm there for them if they need me. I tried it many times to pick for them, and it doesn't work, because at the end of the day, I can't live their life. So, why should I try to control their choice when I'm not the one who has to live with it. And if they think a different choice is a better option, I may look at it go, "Oh, well, that's not what I would have chosen," but I don't have to live with it. I get to go home. I don't have to experience the consequences of that choice. They do. They have to make their own choice. Then, if something blows up, I can come back to say, *"Well, that didn't work, so let's find something else."* I do that with recovery. I'll say to someone, *"Okay, you want to quit on your own? That's amazing. I'm so proud of you. I'll see you in a couple of weeks. How did it go? What are we going to try now?"*

The Importance of Teamwork. During my 10 months working as the Peer Support Lead at Camp Hope I co-ordinated a network of roughly 30 Peer Navigators (counting all of the come-and-go turnover) from several agencies. We became a very effective team that worked well together. And we all helped each other out. When you look just at the Jewels Helping Hands Peer caseload, you can identify whose clients are whose. But at the end of the day, they're all ours. For example, Joe, Bill, and Bob may be my clients. But if Joe, Bill and Bob need something and I'm not available to help, I know I have a team that will go and help them, and vice versa. That's the best dynamic I could ever come up with for our team, or for any team. And I love how it works because we're all here to support each other. We're all in it together. We can't do this alone.

Sharyl Brown was the Lead Peer Navigator for Jewels Helping Hands at Camp Hope. Following the closing of the Camp, she continued as the Lead Peer Navigator responsible for outreach and connecting with former Camp Residents who still need services.

15 - My Reflections On Camp Hope
by Julie Garcia

A Desperate Protest

I don't think most people in our community really understand what those homeless folks were doing at City Hall in December of 2021. Everybody calls it whatever they want to - a protest, a gathering, angry people upset with the City. But the truth is that these were desperate people who had nowhere to go. And the only thing that the protest provided them was a safe place to exist for a few days.

People still in the throes of experiencing homelessness don't know what the shelter count is at any of our shelters. They don't have a clue. They don't check it. They don't know. They don't see it. That's not their reality. Their reality is, "Where am I going to sleep tonight? Am I going to be safe? And what am I going to eat?". That's it. So, when we started this protest with a few folks who had really had enough with not having a place to go, people experiencing homelessness came, not because they cared to protest City Hall, but because they had nowhere else to go. Jewels Helping Hands just provided a safe place for them to sleep for the night. We had people who volunteered every single night to be there, to keep the peace, to make sure that they could zip up their sleeping bag and be safe. And that's how this all started, with desperation and with people who had nowhere to go.

A Disconnected City

The City's response to the desperation of these folk was to come in after three days and say, "Now, we're going to have to sweep this and get rid of these people." I remember what happened and it really underscored the disconnect of the City and its own employees. I was sitting in a meeting of the leadership team of the Spokane Homeless Coalition with Eric Finch, who at the time was the Interim Director of the City's CHHS (Community Housing and Human Services) Department. He and I were trying to talk through what Camp Hope was and how the City could fix it and what we could do to collaborate on a solution. And in the middle of that meeting, I got a call from my staff saying that Spokane Code Enforcement was there and issuing 48 hour notices to vacate. Some people may say Finch knew, and that was his reason for having me at this meeting offsite. But I saw his face. He did not know. He was as surprised as I was that there was going to be a sweep. And Eric was the guy who should have made any decision regarding a sweep. But, he didn't know. He had no clue. So, that shows me that the disconnect between the City and people experiencing homelessness is not just a disconnect between the City and those experiencing homelessness. It's also a complete disconnect between the City, the Administration, City staff, and those experiencing homelessness.

Leadership Matters

Because of this profound disconnect, there's no leadership involved in the decision making process to say, "This is the way we do this, and here are the steps we follow to get it done." It's not there. One of the things I've learned in running

Camp Hope and all of its related projects, all the way up until the day we closed Camp Hope, is that leadership matters. What you say, and how you say it matters, because everyone is looking to leadership to set the tone and give direction. Whether it's the leader of our City, or the leader of homeless services, or the leader of a Camp Hope, leadership matters. And if you can't work and function in that leadership role and take advice and expertise from folks, we'll never move the needle on homelessness.

I believe people experiencing homelessness should have their own voice. But people experiencing homelessness have trauma. They're in survival mode. Leadership is not at the top of their list of things they even care about, let alone do. It takes somebody exiting that situation who understands it or can empathize with the same feelings because that's how you build a relationship - through empathy. We know that what solves homelessness is housing. But what gets people into housing is relationships.

How Camp Hope Changed Us

Managing and closing Camp Hope had a profound impact on all of us. We began to understand unsheltered homelessness from a whole different level. When you're literally in a Camp with them, part of their everyday existence, every situation that they go through all day long, you begin to get a very different understanding of homelessness. You get the perspective of the affected person instead of the people who are causing the trauma or creating the policy. You get to see people experiencing homelessness in one spot, trying to maintain. Most people saw Camp Hope and they saw over 600 people on one city block. They saw what looked like a wreck, because sometimes it was a wreck. It really was. Let's be honest. People experiencing homelessness have issues. And to see that many of them all at one time in one place is really hard. If you're not okay with understanding what they're doing, it looks like a disaster. But when I looked at Camp Hope, I saw 689 people giving what they could, what they were capable of giving, to make it work. Is it wrong or right? Was it good or bad, right or wrong? I don't know the answer. But I've made a decision to always err on the side of humanity.

I remember one day getting to the Camp in mid-July when there was somewhere over 600 people in the Camp. I get to the Camp and I see tents on top of RVs. I walk in and I'm like, "Oh, God, what are you doing?" And they said, "Well, there's no more room on the ground, so we're building up." And my first thought was, "I'm going to prison for sure. There's no way that the city is going to allow this or see this and think it's okay." But then I sat back and I thought about it and I'm going, "Wow, that's pretty smart of them." Yeah, it was a dumb idea, and Code Enforcement would never allow it. But they were coming up with solutions, and that was their solution. It wasn't a good one, but they were literally working towards a solution for the overcrowding situation in the Camp. And that's where you have to start, with people who are at least willing to participate in something. And Camp

Hope showed that they were willing to participate in finding solutions.

The Fight Over An Access Tent

The city did everything in its power to shut Camp Hope down. From the day it opened until the last day that it closed, the Camp was a non-stop political issue, even a target. In August of 2021, the fight to close the Camp focused on what started as a Cooling Tent during a brutal heat wave, and later became our all-weather Access or Resource Tent. The Access Tent was literally a tent on the other lot across the street from the Camp. It was nothing special. It cost no money. We owned it. It was just a big, gigantic tent where people could go and access the things they needed, get supplies, talk to caseworkers. A lot of important activity took place there, including resident badging and the Identification Connection. Hot meals were often served there.

The Spokane Fire Department came in the same week we set it up, looked at everything, asked for structural information (which we provided) and said, "Okay, this looks permittable." They took our $250 for the permit and left. They came back a few days later and said, "We can't permit this." When we asked, "Why?" they told us the Mayor didn't want it permitted. So, they couldn't permit it.

Fighting over the Access Tent was a ridiculous battle that never needed to happen, and it continued through the entire existence of Camp Hope. From a common sense point of view, it made zero sense that you would not want everything to be under one roof and have a place for service providers to meet with their clients, a place to provide a safety net when it got too cold where we could put people so they didn't freeze to death, or in the summer when it got too hot with nowhere else to go.

But everything about Camp Hope was about the optic of it. If you were a citizen of Spokane driving to work on I-90, Camp Hope was something you saw every single day. And that's the problem the City had with Camp Hope. Once you've seen over 600 people struggling on one lot, you can't un-see it. And the Access Tent was a big part of that optic. It represented services being provided to more than 600 people. And it suggested "permanency." I think that was their biggest concern. It looked more permanent. The City's narrative, that they were in the process of getting rid of Camp Hope, wasn't supported by the Access Tent. The Access Tent publicly declared, "We're here. We're getting stuff done. This is where we need to do it."

I absolutely refused to take it down. Jewels Helping Hands racked up $5,000 worth of fines. They fined me every single day that I kept that building up. Eventually, as part of the settlement of our Federal lawsuit against the City, they dropped all of those fines. But there was one point where Jewel's Helping Hands owed $5,000 to the city of Spokane for every single day that the tent was open at Camp Hope. We didn't know how we were going to pay them. We just figured we'd raise the money somewhere and figure it out after we were done. The goal was always to close Camp Hope. It never was to keep it open forever. But I think that the Access Tent just became a visible representation of what was actually happening.

It All Started At The Convention Center

The growth and size of Camp Hope surprised a lot of people, including people at City Hall. But what eventually became over 600 people at Camp Hope really started at the Convention Center. Shortly after the City swept Camp Hope off the sidewalk in front of City Hall in December of 2021, the City opened a warming center at the Spokane Convention Center, thinking about 100 people would come. The day that the Convention Center shelter was about to open, I spoke with a representative from the service provider who was running the shelter. He told me, "Jewels, you'll never fill this place." And I said, "Watch me." So, that's what I did. I went and gathered all the homeless folks we could find and we made them go there. It was dangerously cold out, and they were going to die if they didn't go. We had a coalition of folks that went out every single night finding people in bad situations and dropping them off at the Convention Center. We convinced all the folks that we could find. "Please go there," we told them. "It's not safe this week to be out here. Just go to the Convention Center." The City had horrendously underestimated the number that would come. I was there on the day when they did a head count at 390. People can say whatever they want to believe. But I heard it from the Executive Director of the organization that ran the Convention Center shelter, that there were over 400 people in that building. When the Convention Center Warming Shelter closed after two weeks, that's when Camp Hope started to grow. It was the start of an enormous number of people going to Camp Hope. The Convention Center episode was one example of the City's underestimation of the number of people experiencing homelessness.

Jewels Helping Hands did two separate methodical head-counts of Camp Hope residents that Summer, one in June and another in July, in addition to conducting 601 physical written assessments of Camp residents. 689 residents was our last physical count in late July, but I believe there was more people than 689 who came into the Camp before the fences went up in late September and badging took place in late October. Personally, I believe upwards of 800 people called the Camp home at one time or another. That would be my estimation as someone who was there every single day for 18 months.

We Needed Structure And Police Help

Fencing the Camp and badging the residents in the Fall of 2022 is where we began to really structure the Camp. Before then it was volunteers who agreed to police each other. Jewels Helping Hands didn't have any money to pay people or pay staff. We were all just volunteers helping out and the residents were policing each other. That probably wasn't the best model, but up until late September it was the only model that was available. Up until that time, we begged the City for months, could we have a fence installed? It would help us create safety and security and some kind of structure. And every time the city told us, "No. No, we can't put up a fence. No, we're not going to pay for a fence. No, we're not going to do that." So, yes, we begged the City Council, "Please pay for a fence. We need to get control of this Camp. There's too many people coming and going. And we can't keep track of who's there and who's not there, because every day it changes."

We were very aware that criminals were hiding in the Camp as well. But we couldn't enforce anything because we had no power to do that. We could ask people to leave, but they weren't going to leave voluntarily. So, it got to a point where the residents (the Camp internal security) who were policing the Camp were literally beating people up and throwing them out of the Camp because it was the only way to get them off the lot. Drug dealers and traffickers and all of those criminal types hide among the homeless population because it's an unseen and un-cared for population. So, it's very easy to prey upon them while you're inside with them.

The lack of police involvement was a whole different nightmare of its own. The police refused to answer calls from us. Literally. They sat outside of the Camp for 18 months, usually with two police cruisers on adjacent property, would not help us in any way. They would literally roll up their window if we came and asked them for help, and we only asked for their help with crime related issues. They didn't want anything to do with us. But you have to remember, the police department is directed at the pleasure of the Mayor. So, when the Mayor said, "No, we're not helping them," the police department also said, "No, we're not helping them." The City wasted so much money and police overtime because they didn't actually do anything. They just sat there. Jewels Helping Hands has sent in enough records to the City to show that the police knew that we needed help, but didn't respond. They were literally a hindrance to everything that we did. We could have gotten the Camp under control, gotten rid of the criminal element that was in there, and perhaps made it a bit more productive had they helped.

Let's Talk Money

It's important to take a few minutes and talk about how financial resources did or didn't flow to the Camp. Here's the bottom line: all of the money that Jewels received for Camp operations came on an expense reimbursement basis. This type of financial procedure has been the standard for years. Every City contract, every government contract, every federal contract is on a reimbursement basis. It means that we first pay for things and then we send in receipts. The City (or whoever the payee might be) then decides if they're going to pay for it, that is, reimburse us for it. Every dime for the Camp went through layers and layers of oversight. The Department of Commerce contracted with the Empire Health Foundation and the Empire Health Foundation then contracted with Spokane Low Income Housing Consortium, Revive Counseling Service, Compassionate Addiction Treatment, and Jewel's Helping Hands to provide services at the Camp.

Jewels Helping Hands paid for things that we got approval for through Empire Health. We paid for it and then we sent our receipts to Empire Health who went through our invoices every single month, looked at the receipts, made sure they matched and were approved, and then sent everything on to the Department of Commerce Accounting folks. That's how the local funding and money-flow worked. And, for the record, Lisa Brown was never involved in that local funding process. None of the $144 million allocated by the Legislature in the Right of Way Initiative was ever supposed to come to Spokane, just as a matter of history. It was going to King County and the Seattle side of the mountains until Lisa Brown fought for the fact that there were more than 600 people on this WSDOT land in Spokane. If she hadn't fought for that, we never would have received $24 million into Spokane County.

Along Came A Lawsuit

What became a Federal lawsuit started when the Spokane County Sheriff, for whatever reason, who had never been part of homeless services, decided to jump on board with the narrative that the City Administration had put forward regarding Camp Hope. Soon there were videos being made along with press conferences being held announcing how they were going to come in and close down the Camp, knowing good and well that they couldn't. First, because *Martin v Boise* wouldn't allow for that, and second, because the Department of Transportation (which owned the property) said "We comply with federal law which is *Martin v Boise*. We can't move them and we're not going to until you have substantial and appropriate housing for them." Up to that point, the Sheriff had just talked about how he was going to close the Camp while making wild accusations - we were all just taking federal money and not providing any services, the Camp was a wreck, there was rampant crime and drug use.

The Sheriff's Office conducted helicopter flights with infrared lights flying over the top of the Camp, so close to the Camp that residents could feel the downdraft of the rotors, repeatedly terrifying the people who lived there, and using County resources to do this. It was absolute insanity. The Sheriff was trying to get a count of the number of people in the Camp. If he had just called us, we could have taken him in and he could have counted them individually if he wanted to. Or we could have given him the "by names" list from the assessments that we had done. But he didn't want to do that. He wanted the optics of the City and County doing everything they could to force the Camp to close. None of it was necessary, but he continued to keep doing it and it kept escalating. Soon he was talking about Antifa, and Jewels Helping Hands occupying the land. He went on Fox News to spout the same nonsense, as if his mental state was escalating into a really bad place. We knew we needed to put an end to it just to keep the folks on that lot safe.

About 200 Camp Hope residents left during that time. Why? Because they were just scared. And unfortunately for them, that was what led to only 467 residents being badged. It was detrimental to the people experiencing homelessness because the Department of Commerce only funded services for the folks who were badged. So, even though 467 were badged, there many more who went through the Camp at one point or another and left, people who could have received help and resources.

Finally, in December of 2022, law enforcement - SPD and Sheriff deputies - came into the Camp in force. They started posting ridiculous fliers with inaccurate information about what services to reach out to, and declaring in bold letters how the Camp was closing and everyone needed to move. They didn't come in offering resources and bringing resource officers. It was literally a show of force. So, I called an attorney and the next day, when they came back, our attorney was there with us and he was able to document everything that happened. He went into Federal Court and filed for a Temporary Restraining Order against the city of Spokane, the County of Spokane, Sheriff Knezovich individually (not the sheriff's department), and Chief Meidl (not the Spokane Police Department) in his capacity as Chief. We won the day and the Judge granted us a Temporary Restraining Order for the protection of the Camp.

Things That Closed Camp Hope

We closed Camp Hope on time (actually, three weeks early) and on budget. Successfully closing the Camp and moving people forward required a hybrid of all the successful models that we've seen used elsewhere. Best practices were utilized, trauma informed care was utilized, people-centered approaches were utilized. But badging, providing abundant resources, and using people with lived experience as mentors is what closed the Camp.

Peer Navigators. Peers with lived experience walk others through the process of homelessness from beginning to end because they've already dug themselves out and they know the way. That's what really closed the Camp. It was creating and building relationships with the residents, taking them and helping them get to their appointments.

The Identification Connection. The Identification Connection was a gigantic part of closing Camp Hope. It was a partnership between the Department of Licensing, the Department of Health, Jewel's Helping Hands, and the Department of Commerce. What happened with the ID Connection was all the parties came into the Camp where we were at. They didn't expect people to come to the DMV. They came into the Camp. They were able to identify residents, get them an immediate temporary ID, help them apply for a birth certificate, and basically get all their core documentation all at one spot. And that's what made it easier for us to navigate people into housing, because you can't complete a housing or job application without ID.

Scattered Site Shelters. The Spokane Low Income Housing Consortium (SLIHC) really supported the on-the-ground service providers by freeing up Rapid Rehousing dollars that allowed us to open up *scattered site shelters*. We call them transitional housing but, in reality, they're scattered shelters, houses in the middle of communities and neighborhoods. They house anywhere from 4 to 8 people, with onsite staff 24 hours a day, and they teach people what's needed to maintain housing. They break down barriers that would otherwise keep them from being housed. And it's all done indoors in transitional housing.

The reason scattered site shelters work is because we already know, according to any kind of scientific data, that when you're out in the elements and your basic needs are not met, you are not utilizing all of the skills you have in your brain to be able to, one, acknowledge the problem and to work towards getting out. Your focus is on survival mode and you're only focused on "Where am I going to sleep? What am I going to eat? And am I going to be safe tonight?" Once you get those things under control and we move people into these houses where they have a bed to sleep in and they have consistent food, and they know they're not getting kicked out tomorrow, they begin to be able to address all their other issues. Once they go inside, they're able to work towards advancing their own lives and breaking down their barriers, including addiction.

To address the addiction barrier, we collaborated to create a sobering center. Compassionate Addiction Treatment received funding from the Department of Commerce to provide Peer led sobering services, something we lacked in our community. The Camp Hope folks were able to utilize the sobering center to break down some of the barriers of their addiction, which then made the transitional houses more functional while they waited for permanent housing to open up.

Recognizing Mental Illness. We had to accept the painful reality that there's a group of chronically homeless folks that are never going to be able to maintain housing on their own due to their own mental illness. We don't lock up people with mental illness anymore, like we used to do back in the fifties and sixties. If you were mentally ill, you went to a psychiatric hospital, and that's where you spent the rest of your life. There were lots of problems with that. So the fact that we stopped doing that probably isn't a bad thing. But we never created an alternative for those folk. Even if they are a danger to themselves or to others, they just live homeless on our streets. There's no place for those folks to go.

That's when permanent supportive housing became a thing. So, we had to create spaces for people who were never going to be able to maintain their housing on their own. We created spaces where they could go and live together, where there was a staff member present, where they could live long-term and not be sleeping downtown on the streets. They have a safe place where the requirements are a lot less than if they had to pay their own bills and get their own food.

A Handful of Lessons We Learned From Camp Home.

I think the number one lesson I learned was that 689 people on one lot have a gigantic impact on the community. It's a big lesson that I'm still processing.

The second lesson I see is that the narrative we're allowing to be told isn't the truth. People experiencing homelessness are not shelter resistant. They don't want to live in tents on the side of the road. They want to participate. They just don't know how or they've participated before and have been let down. And that's a lot of the reason. You don't live chronically homeless in our city, or any other city in the United States, and not access resources. You've just been let down by resources. You've been told, "Yeah, we're going to get you housing" and then it doesn't happen, or "Yep, we're going to come visit you tomorrow and bring you something." And they don't. There's no trust whatsoever.

And you can correlate that with poverty. It's the same thing if you're in a home and you're in poverty. The programs that are set up to help you are only set up to keep you in poverty. They're not set up to advance you getting out of your situation. We've turned people's poverty or homelessness into a moral and character issue. If we help them, then we must be making a moral judgment and saying, "Oh, they morally deserve to be housed, and it wasn't their own bad choices that got them to that situation." I don't know whether it's because of people's bad choices or if it's because of their particular set of circumstances. But what difference does it make? They're living on the streets in our city and dying every day. They deserve a place to go inside. They deserve to be treated humanely.

I've made more mistakes in my entire life than most people have made. But our pasts shouldn't determine our future. We have to be able to accept that people make mistakes, even if their mistake got them to that lot on 2nd and Ray. Some people's bad choices got them there, and some people were there because of the circumstances they were given. But they still deserve to be inside somewhere. I don't know that we will ever solve homelessness - people are always going to become homeless for a variety of reasons - but it should be rare and brief. If we can get to that place where we stop judging people on their situation and seeing poverty as a character flaw, we could actually get out of this situation that every city in America is in.

Community And Collaboration. Camp Hope showed community. It showed participation. And most of all it showed collaboration. Collaboration is hard because we have to admit that our particular way of doing things isn't the only right way, that there are many different ways to get to the same point. And we have to support each one of those ways. I can't come to you and say that the collaboration behind the scenes was amazing and everything was good. No, there were a lot of fights, a lot of crying, a lot of tears, a lot of yelling. But we were committed to making it work. We may not have agreed on how to get there, but we sat at that table until we had compromised enough to get it done.

Moving forward, I don't know how we move the needle in homeless services without collaboration. It's hard and it's brutal to do, but it has to be worth a shot because Camp Hope showed all of us what 689 people suffering from unsheltered homelessness looks like. It showed us where we're failing so many of our citizens.

And it showed us that if we collaborate, we can get people out of that situation and into something better.

The Story of "Firestarter Robert"

Another lesson Camp Hope taught us is that everyone can get housing. I want to share a true story from the Camp that illustrates this truth.

We called him *Firestarter Robert*. He came to Camp Hope on the day it opened because he'd pretty much been banned from everywhere else in Spokane. We called him Firestarter Robert for a reason. He loved fire. He was a pyro and an arsonist. He was also severely mentally ill due to a traumatic brain injury. Once the Camp started getting organized, the Campers literally booted him from the island with nowhere to go. Because of his brain injury, Robert can't remember what he did yesterday. But no matter where we took him, he always remembered his way back to that Camp. The next day he was there. We dropped him off at the shelter, and he walked back. We dropped him off downtown. He walked back. We finally realized that he wasn't going anywhere. He was just going to keep coming back. So we talked to the Department of Transportation and told them, "This guy is dangerous. He can't be in the Camp because he keeps trying to light people's propane tanks on fire. He can't be in the Camp with the Campers, but he keeps coming back and we have to give him something." So they allowed him to stay on the lot next to the Access tent, which probably wasn't the best place for him, but it was the only place that he could exist and where we could keep an eye on him. And we spent a lot of time just watching and monitoring and making sure he wasn't lighting fires in the neighborhood.

I honestly believed that we would never, ever find a place that would take Robert. I thought he would be homeless forever. But today, he is living in his own place. He is completely sober. He is court ordered to take his meds. He's also court ordered to never enter the property at 2nd and Ray again. But he is maintaining in society like we want all of these folks to do. Throughout his entire time of being homeless, which I'm sure was most of his lifetime, no one ever had an answer for him. And somehow, through relationships and building trust, we were able to get him the help he needed, to get him to his Court dates, to get the judge to understand the situation, and to get him into housing. And he's thriving. And that's a success.

If Firestarter Robert's situation is the only thing that went well at Camp Hope, that alone was worth it. And there are 289 other former Camp residents with similar stories that are maintaining housing right now because of Jewels Helping Hands saying, "Nope, we're not going to move today. Nope, we're going to continue to provide services." I understand they're going to come after us. I understand it's going to cost us a lot. It has already cost me a lot. It has cost me my reputation. Half of the city loves me and half of the city hates me. Half of the city thinks I'm embezzling money and half of the city thinks I'm an angel sent from heaven. But the only One that matters is the One I answer to when God asks me to do something. And I completed the task that He asked me to do. As for the folks that are still out there on the street, we're still working to get them in housing. It's my goal and my moral obligation, from here on out, to make sure each one of those folks has an opportunity to get housing.

Closing Reflections

It's scary when you're standing in court and the City of Spokane and the County of Spokane and the Sheriff and the Police Chief are literally threatening you. It was scary, but we stood our ground anyway and we proved it could be done. And we shut Camp Hope down before the deadline that they wanted. We shut it down compassionately with kindness and love. We didn't just tell people to get out and leave. We found them appropriate housing and we used appropriate interventions to get them there and that lot went back to exactly the way it was before the Camp.

I remember standing with Governor Inslee when he came to visit a couple of weeks after we closed the Camp. And I remember how, after he left, I was so happy because he told us what a good job we had done. And whether you like the Governor or you don't, he's the Governor. And our progress went all the way to him. So, that's good. But I also remember standing in front of that empty lot, and for the first time in 18 months I cried and cried and was able to really breathe because it was done, and I felt like, "Oh, we accomplished something."

Whether or not anybody ever sees or notices what happened at Camp Hope, we spoke truth to power and we completed the tasks given to us. And at the end of the day, all I can do from here on out and on every other day, is to continue to speak truth to power. That's what Jesus would have done. He flipped over the tables of the money-changers, because they were unjust and wrong. Injustice is still wrong. And we can't not fight injustice, because I hope for you what I hope for myself and for my kids. I hope for myself that I'm safe, that there's peacefulness, that I have a home to come home to, that I have food to eat tonight. I hope that for my kids, I hope that for John who lives on the side of the freeway. Or I hope that for the guy who smells really bad, who yells at me every time I bring him a sandwich. That's what is important, that we want those things for our community members. We want those things for others. And I'll continue to do that, whether or not there's another Camp Hope, which I hope there's not (and I might have made promises to the Washington Department of Transportation that I would never start a Camp on their lot again). But I'll follow homeless folks wherever they go, and I'll try to continue building relationships and providing services, wherever they happen to be.

Julie Garcia is the Founder and Executive Director of Jewels Helping Hands, a non-profit homeless services provider, and the overseer of Camp Hope from the day it started at Spokane City Hall in December of 2021 until the day it closed in June of 2021.

16 - Here Come The RVs!

In addition to being a Day Manager for the largest homeless encampment in the State of Washington, I also found myself a Manager of what was probably the State's largest "safe parking lot."

There's a lot of conversation today among homeless service providers and advocates about the need for "safe parking lots" where people experiencing homelessness and living in their vehicle can safely park without fear of harassment. I want to be clear that I understand

The owner of this Bounder RV eventually left the Camp for better housing.

the need for - and the importance of - safe parking lots.

In the Summer of 2021, I filmed a law enforcement sweep of homeless camps along the Spokane River across from Mission Park. During that sweep, on the hottest day of the year, Spokane law enforcement impounded the camper of Schell and his wife, Tanya, for expired tabs, making them effectively homeless. Their home was impounded and Schell was told he could go to a downtown city warming center. It was absolutely heart-wrenching to witness and film his despair and brokenness as he said, *"I simply want to die."* [128] Trust me, I understand the need. A personal tragedy could have been avoided if a safe parking lot had been available for Schell and Tanya.

Based on my experience as a Day Manager at Camp Hope, I want to offer some observations about the idea of safe parking lots. Here's my up-front caveat: *Homeless Camps - and by extension, safe parking areas - are easier to get into than they are to get out of.* That doesn't make them good, bad, or wrong. It simply means we should be very thoughtful about them.

At the peak of Camp Hope, we had no less than 34 RVs and camper/trailers in the Camp (I have pictures of 34, but I know we had a few more before I started recording them. I would place our peak at about 40). We could have had even more, but once we began receiving funding from the Department of Commerce, the Camp was closed to new residents and we had to turn away several additional vehicles. Of those 34 vehicles, roughly 1-in-5 (~20%) was able to run or move on their own without assistance from Camp Managers. In other words, they had been able to get to the Camp (although a couple actually had to be towed in) but could not get out under their own power. Why? The reasons varied: dead batteries, flat tires, engine problems, other mechanical issues, no registration, missing titles, and even broken steering columns One RV we removed from the Camp had no steering wheel or ignition. I towed it out while Ken Crary (Jewels Director of Operations) "steered" it with a pair of vice-grip pliers locked onto the steering hub. Ken and I agreed. We'd never seen that done before!

I could tell more stories, like the trailer I pulled out before we realized that it had no wheels on the left side! Long story. Sigh. I like to say that I earned my official "Camp Hope RV Towing Merit Badge." But my point is this. Our experience with nearly 40 RVs and trailers in what was essentially a "safe parking lot" revealed that many of those needing safe parking areas have vehicles that will never leave without either having to be towed out or someone spending considerable funds to make them driveable.

One of our Camp staff preparing to remove an RV from the Camp as the owner prepares to go to his new apartment.

In addition, you quickly discover that people still want to use the "facilities" in the RV, but without any ability to empty the waste tanks. I've seen broken (i.e., missing) steering columns, 10-year old registrations (an RV or trailer that had not been registered in 10 years), RVs with no registration or Title to prove ownership, RVs with engines completely torn apart, and more. I had one RV owner who was crest-fallen when I informed him that we didn't have the resources to pay for an engine and transmission re-build for his RV! He eventually resigned himself to the reality that we would have to tow it out of the Camp when he left for housing and place it in the neighboring Camp parking lot. From there, he would have to figure out his next step. And, unfortunately, on many occasions WSDOT had to arrange with a local towing company to tow, hold, and eventually dispose of numerous RVs and camper-trailers. We've bought batteries, fixed flat/damaged tires, and helped with other minor repairs and expenses, but the needs and the expenses can mount quickly, as any vehicle owner knows.

I have no desire to discourage anyone from offering a safe parking lot for people experiencing homelessness and living in their RVs or camper-trailers. After all, I spent close to a year helping manage what - at its peak - was the largest homeless Camp and safe parking lot in the State of Washington. But I would encourage *any* potential operator to go into such a project with their eyes open and with a plan for how the lot is going to be managed. As I said at the beginning of this chapter, homeless camps - and by extension, safe parking areas - are often much easier to get into than they are to get out of. Here are my general suggestions for operating such a safe parking lot:

1. Understand and clearly define what you're getting involved with before you find yourself involved and overwhelmed.

2. Have a clear plan for what you can realistically do to help those utilizing the lot to eventually leave the lot. Do they have a plan for what they are going to do moving forward, and the ability to implement that plan?
3. Have clear rules, in the form of a contractual agreement to be signed BEFORE they are allowed in. The violation of those rules then becomes the basis for asking them to leave.
4. All vehicles (RVs, camper-trailers, and the vehicles pulling them) must be in good running order. No vehicle can be towed in.
5. All vehicles in the safe parking lot must have current, valid registration (and/or a Title proving ownership), and current proof of insurance (such as minimal state-required liability insurance).
6. There should be no buying, selling, or trading of vehicles while in the parking lot (unless you want to get entangled in someone else's legal mess, because you're the lot manager).
7. No use of sanitation facilities in the vehicle without a prior arrangement for when, how, and where to regularly empty tanks at an approved facility. You don't want that problem on your property, unless you enjoy enforcement visits from the local health department declaring your property to be a public health hazard. Not good.

Epilogue

Again, the goal here is not to discourage anyone from considering sponsoring a safe parking lot. They are certainly needed. But there is also a need for potential sponsors/operators to think through some of the real-world challenges they are going to face and to make realistic plans. Be compassionate, but be smart, too.

A Place to Exist

17 - The Right of Way Initiative
By Lisa Brown

Background

My name is Lisa Brown, and I had the privilege of serving as Director of the Washington State Department of Commerce from February of 2019 until March of 2023. Commerce's mission is to strengthen communities. One of the five divisions of the agency is the Housing Division, which funds a variety of programs for affordable housing and homelessness. Since 1986 the Housing Trust Fund has invested more than $1 billion in capital funding and helped build or preserve more than 50,000 affordable housing units statewide. [129]

Washington State Director of Commerce Lisa Brown visiting Camp Hope in late September of 2022

As housing affordability and housing supply emerged as a major challenge all over the state over the last decade, the Governor and the legislature significantly expanded funding into the Housing Trust Fund and other housing, homelessness, and home ownership initiatives. State funding usually comes as a competitive award of capital dollars that co-invests with housing developers and local governments to create housing units that are required to remain affordable for decades. A new program, the Rapid Capital Acquisition program, was launched during the pandemic with hundreds of millions of dollars of new funding. It was frustrating for me to see that the City of Spokane and Spokane County were not as involved as other local governments in the state in partnering with non-profits and applying for these resources which could be used to convert existing buildings into permanent affordable housing. Instead the city administration spent millions of dollars on a large leased warehouse.

When I started at Commerce, as someone who came from eastern Washington, I challenged my leadership team to look at regional equity in all our programs. We also led a statewide study analyzing racial disparities in home ownership. [130] We embraced a directive from the legislature to bring more capital resources for assets like affordable housing and childcare facilities to historically marginalized communities and to build capacity in organizations led by people from those communities, who work to become trusted messengers and serve those communities. This was the context in which the Commerce team began the Right of Way work on homelessness in Spokane.

A Personal Discovery

Perhaps the biggest discovery for me personally regarding homelessness in our state is how the annual point -in-time count counts only the visibly homeless. In reality there are so many more people who are housing insecure, rent burdened, or spending too much of their income on housing, whether they're renting or owning. That phenomenon is significant all over our state, but particularly in Spokane. So, it's one thing to figure out programs and services and methods for working with people who are chronically homeless. And we have had success with that, especially with homeless youth in our state. However, the faucet is still on and the sink is filling up. There are still more and more people falling into homelessness all the time. So, we need to do two things at once. We need to address the people who are visibly homeless or chronically homeless on the streets, but at the same time, we've got to be thinking about how we can address the upstream issues before people become homeless in the first place. And that's big and it's tough, but we need to meet the needs of people at risk of homelessness, or we will end up doing a lot of remediation after people have lost community and have lost resources that could have been utilized to keep them housed in the first place.

Collaboration and Individual Assessment

In the 2022 legislative session, Governor Inslee proposed specific funding to address those camping on State Rights of Way. He could see the growing number of camps on the I-5 corridor from Olympia to Everett. On I-90, in Spokane, Camp Hope had formed after a shelter in the city was closed and a protest camp at City hall was dispersed. The Governor and legislature realized that camps on state property posed a unique challenge. The camps were on Department of Transportation land, an agency that doesn't have housing or homelessness funds. The State Patrol's authority to enforce no trespassing laws was limited by legal rulings that prohibited sweeping campers if there was not housing or shelter available. The Department of Commerce administered housing and homelessness funds, but did not directly build housing or provide homeless services. Commerce had contractual relationships with most local governments and many non-profit housing and service providers but no authority to direct local governments or providers to address camps on state property. To address the gap, the budget appropriation for the ROW Initiative directed the Department of Commerce and Department of Transportation and the State Patrol to work together and with local governments and providers to close camps by individually assessing people, offering appropriate behavioral health, addiction treatment and employment services and referring them to a housing solution better than the camp. The idea was for state funds to incentivize cooperation to close camps by transitioning people to housing, not merely dispersing them into local communities. The Commerce team saw the challenge as housing people, not just moving them.

Build Affordable Housing Inventory In Communities

Legislators were concerned that the funding for the Right of Way initiative not be taken out of planned investments already slated for the Housing Trust Fund and the Rapid Capital Program, so the ROW funding had to identify new housing solutions in a community before a camp could be closed. The budget proviso also specified that significant funding go to long term affordable housing, not just shelters. The time frame for bringing on new units was the primary challenge in every community, especially at Camp Hope, which had grown to the largest Camp in the state by the time the funding was appropriated.

Deciding How To Allocate Resources

The inter-agency ROW team, which met at least weekly, was led by Deputy Directors. That team oversaw the work to identify and prioritize camps for closure in Snohomish, King, Pierce, Thurston and Spokane counties. Commerce's role was to convene participation of local governments and providers of housing and services and solicit proposals in each county. Tedd Kelleher, Senior Managing Director for Housing Assistance at Commerce, developed a formula for the five counties, starting with a base amount for each county. Then, he added to that base amount a variable percentage amount that was linked to the Point In Time Count numbers in each County, understanding that those are not perfect numbers, but that we had to have some kind of starting basis. So, that's essentially what resulted in Spokane receiving $24 million from the ROW Initiative.

That didn't mean that Commerce would simply write a check to the city. Commerce had to insure that the funding followed the directions of the legislature, and it was the same in the other four counties. We worked both with local governments and with service providers, creating the plans and then executing the contracts, sometimes with local governments and sometimes with service providers.

The Catalyst Controversy

What I've described so far is the basic process that we utilized in all five Counties, with local variations from community to community. Spokane County did not send in a plan. They said the timeline was too short. The City of Spokane sent in a list of projects recommended to be funded, with a letter signed by the Mayor and the City Council President. Near the top of the list was the Catalyst project, which was a hotel on Sunset Highway proposed to be renovated and operated by Catholic Charities of Eastern Washington. The project would be a secure facility providing nearly 100 units of housing and was designed for people ready to enter treatment or counseling, which they would receive in the facility, as a plan was created for their long-term housing. At some point in the future the facility could be converted into affordable apartments adding to the inventory of permanent supportive housing in the community for decades. Knowing that it would likely take several months to open the facility and that winter would be treacherous for the camp, the Commerce team quickly executed the contract. When some people in the neighborhood objected, the Mayor attended a public meeting and said that

Commerce was responsible for the decision and mentioned my name specifically, even though she had requested in a signed letter that the project be funded. Soon I had protesters at my house. Neither the Mayor nor the City Council took responsibility for siting new facilities and this delayed the closure of Camp Hope.

The Trent Shelter Controversy

Another conflict emerged between the ROW agencies and the City of Spokane regarding the Trent warehouse leased by the City and converted into a large congregate shelter known as the Trent Resource Assistance Center (TRAC). The city administration repeatedly asked that most of the Spokane County ROW funding to go to TRAC. Commerce agreed to fund operational expenses for people who moved to TRAC from Camp Hope, but did not agree to funding capital improvements in the leased facility. The first operator apparently misused funds, which delayed the execution of the contract between Commerce and the City. The facility was expensive to maintain as millions of dollars went into basic water and waste water services as the warehouse did not have bathrooms, showers or laundry facilities. The Mayor and former Sheriff repeatedly asserted that the state could just close Camp Hope and force everyone there to TRAC, but from the state team perspective this was not practical, legal or humane. There were many other homeless people in the county who were filling up TRAC and it was not a suitable referral for many of the people at the Camp.

Setting Closing Dates

Because camps in other parts of the State were much smaller, the process of working with the people in the camp, assessing them, figuring out the right housing referral and services, happened faster. The State team could set a tentative date by which everyone would have received referrals to services and housing. Then they could say, "We're going to close the camp on a specific date." But, of course, Camp Hope was completely different than that because of its size. When Commerce first became involved, we didn't know how many people were there, possibly 500 to 600 people and dozens of vehicles and tents. Camp Hope required a whole different approach. That different approach started with a decision that there had to be some structure brought into the camp to identify a specific population. And that's when the work began with fencing the Camp and badging the residents. Most of the on-the-ground services to keep people alive (water, sanitation, cooling, heating) and manage the site were provided by the Department of Transportation, while Commerce contracted with the Empire Health Foundation to coordinate service providers in the Camp. Non-profits, churches and volunteers were providing food, clothing and basic necessities. Hundreds of people in the community helped sustain people in the camp while housing options were being developed.

Collaboration - the Good News

Services for people who are homeless, especially the chronically homeless, are fragmented and uncoordinated. One of the lessons learned at Camp Hope is that bringing the services to one location is effective. At the request of the three agency team, the Department of Health and the Department of Licensing came to the camp to help people get birth certificates and ID's. The Department of Social and Health Services brought a mobile unit to the camp which helped connect people to public assistance. A project of the Department of Transportation, labor organizations and philanthropy utilized a program known as the Pre-Employment Preparation Program that resulted in some campers becoming certified to enter employment or paid apprenticeship programs. Some people went directly from the camp into drug or alcohol treatment or recovery programs and some people were reconnected with family or community without needing a housing referral. After the fencing and badging took place, the relative stability of the camp combined with service providers and navigators with lived experience of addiction, mental health challenges and homelessness to build relationships of trust with camp residents, allowing for individuals to build paths out of homelessness.

Collaboration - the Bad News

The ROW team and local governments had tensions and disagreements in other counties, but the relationship was clearly most dysfunctional in Spokane County. The City administration held that the state was responsible for the camp and at the same time criticized and obstructed the approach the state was taking to closing the camp. The Spokane Police Department deployed officers on over-time outside the camp, but would not come in to remove people who were reported by providers as not badged or breaking camp rules. The Department of Transportation ended up hiring private security and significant financial resources and agency time went into legal disputes that could have gone into closing the camp more quickly.

There was a period of time when the downtown organization *Hello for Good* tried to independently convene meetings of what you might call the "principals." They invited agency directors or secretaries, the Mayor, the City Council President, County Commissioners, the Sheriff, the Police Chief, and select representatives of downtown business interests. At those meetings, we would discuss the ROW Initiative and how we were proceeding. Zeke Smith of the Empire Health Foundation usually reported on behalf of the providers in the camp. Transportation reported on the logistics of the camp, things like garbage and RVs being moved, and Commerce reported on housing solutions being developed. The business representatives wanted a date certain for Camp closure, which the state could not give due to legal reasons and uncertainties around when housing options would open.

I would have to say that despite what were good intentions, the meetings called by *Hello for Good* didn't tend to result in much progress. They became particularly problematic, in my opinion, because of Sheriff Knezovich's participation. He wanted to take things in a completely different direction, saying that he was going to personally sweep the camp and demanding that everyone report to him in an emergency communications framework. He went on a national conservative television programs making allegations against the state and non-profit providers. Ultimately his threats resulted in a lawsuit against the County and an injunction that prevented a sweep.

At the same time, the Commerce and Transportation staff were meeting regularly with both City staff and with providers. And while collaboration at the basic staff level was fairly good, it tended to be inconsistent. The (former) City Administrator would abruptly cancel meetings and would bring different staff and elected officials to each meeting. Sometimes the Sheriff was brought to the meetings, which was completely unproductive. Ultimately, as it turned out, there was a mutual agreement to not have elected officials at those meetings. Further complicating things, there were still a lot of COVID protocols in place. As a result, a lot was being done by phone calls and through virtual meetings. The ROW Initiative was ongoing in all five counties. Ultimately, small commerce and transportation teams were doing the same work in five different counties at the same time and I commend the work they accomplished under very trying circumstances.

Lessons We Learned Along The Way

Collaboration. One of the most fruitful products of the ROW Initiative was the amount of state agency collaboration that took place. For example, being able to pull in both the Department of Licensing and the Department of Health to provide identification restoration and birth certificate services in the camp was really a very positive part of the experience at Camp Hope. In addition, the Department of Social and Health Services (DSHS) brought their mobile unit to the Camp, and that allowed people to be validated for certain things they were qualified for, such as food stamps and other services. Another important collaboration was between the Department of Transportation and State Patrol in terms how to prevent the re-opening of camps once there were closed.

On-site Services. While it wasn't a full navigation center model, many aspects of a navigation center model occurred at Camp Hope, and there were important lessons learned about how you could do things more effectively, and save time and save money, by having the services on-site in one location versus homeless individuals having to navigate from this agency to that agency in this location to that location.

Peer Support And Lived Experience. The utilization of people with lived experience to really create relationship with people in the various camps became a very important part of successfully moving people out of the camps and into better situations. One of the questions I hear from people all the time is, "Why would anyone in Spokane prefer to stay in a tent to a shelter?" It just doesn't make sense to most people because you think that a shelter is going to be warmer or safer. As people were interviewed, we learned lessons about understanding that some people's reluctance to stay in the shelter was very real based on past experiences. They had either witnessed violent events, or had their possessions stolen, or found it difficult to maintain their sobriety, or whatever the case may be. Just understanding the significance of individual people's different experiences relative to why they would be in a camp - maybe with a partner or a support animal versus a shelter - and then also understanding the role of peer navigators with lived experience with homelessness or trauma or addiction who could have that relationship, build trust, and have more success in the creation of the plan for where that person would go from the camp - that was a hugely important lesson.

Identification of people by name. We already do this in our youth homelessness system, but I believe it's a very important piece of the equation. Our homeless system already has what's called the CMIS (or Community Management Information System) on-line system. But I've heard from providers they don't find it very useful in actually coordinating people, service providers, services offered. I believe there's a lesson here about how to really create accountability for the system when an individual is being assessed and offered services, etc. Tracking people by name is important, both for the person being served as well as for the system itself.

Some Closing Takeaways

In every county, the process of resolving camps happened slower than people wanted it to happen and had controversy. The biggest obstacle to that faster resolution was siting and constructing or procuring housing units that would accept those individuals. You might have thought this was unique to Spokane and Camp Hope. But, in reality, the same thing was happening in all five counties, though it was easier to see the progress in the other counties as small camps were closed one by one. In Thurston County, the City of Olympia had given the ROW Initiative a piece of land on which to construct a tiny home village. While that village was being constructed, camps were not being rapidly closed, which frustrated the Governor and local legislators. Using hotels as emergency housing was controversial in other counties, not just in Spokane.

In Spokane, lack of proactivity by local governments in creating shelter or housing options and lack of cooperation and agreement on how to proceed, initially between the City of Spokane and the Department of Transportation, then between the City, County and State agencies, was unfortunate and unproductive and resulted in the chaos of hundreds of people living outside at Camp Hope and delay in its closure. Focus on Camp Hope deflected attention from the hundreds of other unhoused people in the County. In my opinion, people in the camp, along with people and businesses in the surrounding neighborhood, were victimized by too much political posturing and blaming by elected officials and too little good faith negotiation and cooperation.

Even without the political distractions, having people with lived experience working to build relationships and taking the time to really create a path out of homelessness for chronically homeless people took longer and was more expensive than people wanted it to be. But it's cheaper and more effective than the alternative. The alternative would have meant a lot of resources going into moving people who are visibly homeless without addressing the fundamental issues that have led them there. Moving the homeless around by playing homeless wack-a-mole is not good for them, it's not good for the public, and it's not a good use of taxpayer dollars or of law enforcement resources. The lesson I've taken away from this is that we need a coordinated homeless navigation center system with cooperation between local and state governments, not lawsuits and threats of lawsuits.

Final Thoughts On A Regional Homeless Authority

A regional homeless authority to coordinate homeless policy and resources is a promising concept. Elected leaders from local governments can create agreements or a separate entity to integrate federal, state, local and private funding streams into a system in which providers can be more effective in sustainably transitioning people from homelessness into appropriate services and housing. With feedback from providers and people with lived experience, I believe we are capable of creating a better homelessness response in our region.

However, the structural issues of lack of affordable housing and lack of sufficient behavioral health and addiction resources are bigger than any regional homeless authority can solve. We need state and federal action as well as local to take on the big picture challenge of housing insecurity in our country and state.

Lisa Brown is the former Director of the Department of Commerce and former state legislator and senate majority leader representing Spokane's 3rd legislative district from 1993-2013.

18 - Respite and Legal Protection
By Jeffry Finer

Chris Senn, age 51, in a new-ish suit, clean shaven with an unaccustomed haircut, left the federal courtroom less anxious than when he had entered minutes before. But just as disbelieving. It was early Winter 2022, and the court just signed its Order granting Camp Hope protection from law enforcement efforts to sweep the camp and permanently close it. (Chapter 20 on how law enforcement operates sweeps.)

For Mr. Senn, Courts were not places to find help. "I didn't think unhoused folks left a courtroom by the front door."

It wasn't any courtroom. The ceilings were 40 feet tall and the case was not against Chris, or anyone living at Camp Hope: it was about stopping local law enforcement from sweeping the Camp. [131]

It only took a few minutes. Federal Judge Bastian courteously thanked Chris, his two co-plaintiffs along with his employer Julie Garcia, plaintiff's lawyers, defense lawyers, the media, and everyone else present. The judge was gratified with the parties' decision to settle the first stage of a federal lawsuit between Chris and his co-plaintiffs against the City of Spokane, the City's Chief of Police, the County of Spokane, and its Sheriff. The settlement meant the City and County, along with its top law enforcement officers, would not raid Camp Hope as planned. It meant that Chris and hundreds of others sheltering in their own tents and RVs could remain without fear of Spokane's promise to "sweep" the hundreds of campers off the WSDOT property. Although the hearing lasted minutes, the preparation took weeks. The relief was instant and, to Chris and everyone at Camp Hope, miraculous.

A Sword or a Shield?

For anyone experiencing homelessness, in particular chronic homelessness, the legal system is a grinding trudge through impatient security officers, crowded hallways, overworked public attorneys, unapproachable prosecutors, and weary antagonized judges. Court hearings generally end in grief, expense, aggravation and a pointless spin through the system. Or just as often more delay.

For folks without a place to live, the law is the sword used by cops, landlords, neighbors, and the public to threaten people with little-to-nothing left to lose. For folks without a place to live, often their best outcome is to scrape by and ignore whatever just happened.

Relocating the Problem: Bus Tickets and Sweeps

The threat to sweep the Camp clean was law enforcement's toughest move yet. It began when the State's Department of Transportation, which operated the property on which Camp Hope was located, refused to ask for trespassing citations. DOT decided to allow campers to remain in place. The City decided to make things as hard as possible for anyone to stay. The City's building department began ticketing Jewels Helping Hands for operating an uncertified 1800/ft^2 Quonset-style hut... and did so thirteen times. The City ruled it would not provide water to the Camp, nor electricity, not even waste removal. Instead, law enforcement stationed permanent overtime surveillance to simply sit back and watch from a block away. The stationed officer was unresponsive to pleas from Camp organizers to help with law breakers inside or outside the Camp's boundaries.

Not content with making living in the Camp intolerable, the County stepped up the attack: "Leave or be arrested." The plan was simple: if the State's Department of Transportation would not agree to trespass the campers the County would deem the population to be an ongoing "nuisance" needing to be disbanded. The Sheriff offered bus tickets to anyone at Camp Hope wanting to go anywhere but made it clear if anyone tried to stay they would be arrested.

Deadline after deadline went by, however, with no sweeps. No one knew what was holding back the Sheriff. It was known that the county's jail could not hold hundreds of new arrestees, especially if they were charged with a mere nuisance camping offense. Spokane's jail was at capacity and was in another "catch and release" phase. There was hardly enough room for felony offenders. There was no real jailing option available.

Despite the impracticality of sweeping hundreds of campers, messaging from local businesses (impacted by increased crime) blamed the Camp and its guests and demanded action in ads displayed in the local paper. By early October 2022, print and broadcast media coverage turned harsh.

Campers and staff sweated out each announcement, knowing that Spokane's super-hot summer and fall was only weeks away from a predicted tough Spokane winter. In mid-October 2022, the Sheriff demanded the camp be closed, pointing to a vocal community organization demanding he empty the Camp by any plausible means. Portions of Spokane's business community would be happy to see it done

Camp Hope needed legal protection. Federal court and recent civil rights caselaw was the key.

Success lay in the numbers. Camp Hope organizers had argued in emails to elected officials that Spokane simply had no where near the capacity to house the 400+ adults living at Camp Hope. If swept, campers having no place to go would have to take to living on the streets, unhoused and unsheltered. These arguments went unheard. No one in command was listening, and those who did listen had no authority to stop a law enforcement raid.

Financial Relief Leads to Internal Organization

At the same time State-based relief money had begun to flow from Washington's transportation and commerce agencies (chiefly through the efforts of Commerce Director Lisa Brown) into hiring housing teams, counseling providers, sobriety programs, and funds for direct operations.

On-site the funds were used to pay for two tiers of security, fencing, screening, and a vastly improved utilities and waste management program. Funds brought onto the site medical care, ID recovery programs, job training, sobriety programs. Campers were issued numbered badges that were necessary for entry; a curfew was imposed.

Every Camper signed the Camp's good neighbor agreement and understood that multiple infractions of the basic rules could lead to loss of the entry badge and termination of benefits. The Camp's paid internal security team comprised of peer campers living on site kept watch for fire risks, fence jumping, and health crises. A separate professional security team staffed the front gate and liaised with the internal peer team. The Camp learned how to protect itself.

All for naught if the Sheriff had his way and swept the Camp. Everyone knew the sword was coming. Despite the obvious improvements from the State funding program, trust was lacking on every side.

And with that, Camp Hope decided its community needed a legal team to stop the sweep. Legally. Using the federal law.

The Nature of Litigation: Having a Winning Theory of the Case

Clients tell me they want to sue, or are being sued. They want help, they need relief, or they don't even know what to ask for.

The lawyers job is to step into the client's world and figure out a solution. There are so many factors but they always begin with the *facts* of the case and the *law* that governs the dispute. Other things matter: the resources of the parties (to win or lose), the judge who may be deciding critical questions, the population of jurors that could be summoned, the skill of opposing counsel, and a slew of imponderables on top.

And with all those factors in mind, a lawyer constructs a "theory of the case." How does a "theory" win a case? The theory is where the lawyer analyzes the facts and the law (and considers the other factors) and looks for the route to a successful case. There may be many possible types of suit one can bring, or many possible defenses to a suit, but a good lawyer will sift and select the type of suit or defense that makes legal and common sense, that's aligned with the available resources, and that meets the client's needs.

Camp Hope was already on its back foot, being sued by the City in State Court for violating a city nuisance ordinance. There were limited resources, just enough to hire experienced counsel at a reduced rate. The Camp faced a tough battle in the media, in the affected neighborhoods, and needed something strong for the legal battle.

How to turn this around? What would a win in court look like? Given the resources available, what is Camp Hope's attainable goal? [132]

Theory of the Case: the Facts and the Law

First, a lawyer considers the bad facts: the initial months of Camp Hope's existence were chaotic: no one was in control, there was little to no order, no resources, not even drinkable water except what one neighbor agreed to send over via a 700 foot hose.

A vocal and hostile set of commercial and private neighbors were determined to write up declarations for the court to read describing Camp Hope in the bleakest possible terms. The local media were aligned with the beleaguered community, based on the stack of complaints. There was a single operations hut (cooling campers in the summer, warming in the winter) where campers could get such services as were offered by volunteers and the few paid providers hired by Empire Health Foundation - but the City was hitting Jewels Helping Hands with weekly tickets signed by the fire-marshal tickets, running up fines, for operating an unlicensed structure.

On the other hand, Camp Hope had some good facts.

Money was coming from Olympia and that meant several things: security (two teams, one internal staffed by campers with some background in the work and the other a professional team hired by Empire Health Foundation); medical care; restoration of identity documents; sobriety programs; a security fence around the perimeter (often cut and repaired nightly but giving the Camp some security from outside predators); badging of each camper with a personal identifier so the Camp could determine with precision who was on site and keep out any who were not authorized; and the beginning of an peer-to-peer organization.

Jewels Helping Hands was actively working on accountability: a first step was its Good Neighbor Agreement aimed at getting campers to pledge better behavior inside and around the Camp and in the local neighborhood. Plus Jewels developed a written "due process" promise so that campers who violated the rules knew there would be consequences, including having their badge taken and future access denied.

And finally the Camp had one really good fact on its side: there was nowhere for all its campers to go.

In contrast to the mix of good and bad facts, Camp Hope had *great* law on its side. The City's lawsuit was totally based on a local ordinance meant to close local nuisance properties. The City's suit was filed in the county courthouse where, for good or bad, the judges are elected and sensitive to local feelings. The Camp filed its suit in federal court, based on two powerful federal circuit cases (just one level below the United States Supreme Court). From the looks of things, these two federal cases could overcome anything the City and County planned.

And the law relied on by Camp Hope was the perfect tool to buy some stability for the Camp to use its funding to draw down the population humanely, safely, and legally.

Caselaw: "Boise" and "Grants Pass"
The two powerful cases focused on a simple rule: if a city does not have the capacity

to shelter its unhoused population, then it cannot criminalize or enforce nuisance ordinances against folks experiencing homelessness. The two cases are *Martin v. Boise* and *Johnson v. Grants Pass.*[133] Here's how it read in the Camp's opening Complaint filed October 29, 2022. (Found at ECF 1, in case number 22-254-SAB, Eastern District of Washington).

"In *Martin*, the Ninth Circuit held that "so long as there is a greater number of homeless individuals in [a city] than the number of available beds [in shelters]," a city cannot punish homeless individuals for "involuntarily sitting, lying, and sleeping in public." [920 F.3d 584] at 617. That is, as long as there are insufficient emergency shelter beds available to homeless individuals, "the government cannot criminalize indigent, homeless people for sleeping outdoors, on public property, on the false premise they had a choice in the matter."

The rule applied to *criminal* citations only. As of September 2022, the *Boise* rule was extended in *Grants Pass* to cover civil infractions as well. In other words, if Spokane did not have sufficient beds it could not sweep Camp Hope using city nuisance ordinances and could not arrest residents for trespass.

And how did Spokane's municipalities react? They argued that the Camp was filled with lawless drug users and besides, there were plenty of beds.

As lawyers like to note, the issue for the judge was set. The question turned to who had the actual facts about local government's capacity to house its homeless? By that, the Camp meant the current facts on the City's capacity to shelter its homeless population, substantiated by hard evidence.

A Different Kind of Lawsuit

Most often we think of lawyers filing suits to fix something that has already happened. "You drove your car through the stop sign and hit me; my lawyer is suing you for tort damages" (medical expenses, lost wages, repairs to the car, etc). "My boss fired me because he thinks I'm too old to do the job; my lawyer is suing for job discrimination." "My supplier failed to deliver as promised; my lawyer is suing for breach of contract." These cases look back in time to something that has already happened and looks for money to make the outcome fair.

This type of suit was not what Camp Hope needed. It needed an "injunction," a court order forbidding *future* acts. In fact it needed an emergency temporary injunction to keep things frozen until it could get a permanent injunction.

Enjoining two municipalities (the City and the County) and both their top law enforcement officers (the Chief of Police and the Sheriff) could be a tough sell. Camp Hope would have to show that there was an immediate threat to its legal rights, requiring immediate court intervention to keep the status quo, assuming once the case went to trial there was a strong likelihood that Camp Hope would be the winner. That meant, in the space of a few days - maybe a week or so - Camp Hope would have to go to court and prove its campers were genuinely threatened with an unlawful law enforcement action (the sweep) and that the harm from such action would be too severe to remedy (money could not fix the threatened harm).

We needed an immediate "temporary" injunction order freezing the current situation. These can be had when there is urgency and a strong likelihood of winning. Then, having bought a bit of time, we needed to win a permanent order once everyone had time to put together the full lawsuit. We filed on October 28, 2022, a few days ahead of the rumored "November sweep" and gave the County and City copies of our suit. Our suit demanded the following relief:

(a) Enter a declaratory judgment that Defendants' announced plans to remove all people and property from Camp Hope violate Plaintiffs' rights under the United States Constitution and the Americans with Disabilities Act;

(b) Enter a declaratory judgment that Plaintiffs and other current residents of Camp Hope are legally entitled to reside at this location so long as they have the consent and permission of the property owner, WSDOT;

(c) Issue a permanent injunction restraining Defendants from arresting and removing residents of Camp Hope from their current location without specific and individualized probable cause to arrest a person for a criminal offense unrelated to an order given by Defendants to disband, move, or otherwise leave Camp Hope;

(d) Award to Plaintiffs their expenses, costs, fees, and other disbursements associated with the filing and maintenance of this action, including reasonable attorneys' fees under 42 U.S.C. § 1988 or other applicable law; ...

Each paragraph had significance, either in its tactics (such as paragraph c, which made it clear we were not asking that there be no laws at Camp Hope, just no arrests based on an order to disband, move or leave), or as a strategy (such as paragraph d, which put a financial risk on the City and County to compensate for the costs of the suit and the fees owed to Plaintiffs' lawyers).

A Winning Theory of the Case

Camp Hope had the facts to make its theory of the case win. Even in the face of the many dozens of sworn complaints by local business and a few neighbors, the fact of the matter was Spokane did not have adequate shelter space - nowhere near it. Without adequate shelter space, the City and County could not criminalize being homeless. The City and County could not proclaim an encampment to be a legal nuisance.

The City and County were unprepared to shelter its homeless population and therefore it could not arrest the campers (who were not given trespass notices by the Department of Transportation - the actual land owner). Lacking shelter capacity, the City and County could not declare the Camp to be a nuisance and use the ordinance to sweep everyone.

Worse, for the City and County, Camp Hope's residents included dozens of folks with severe physical limitations. There were campers needing to be in hospice, campers who had bi-lateral amputations, campers who were so impaired they could not perform the national standards for "activities of daily living" (clothing, cleaning, feeding). This disabled population was among the critical factors that the federal judge had to take into account. Even the City had to acknowledge that its offered shelter facilities (far too small in number for even the able-bodied) were utterly unavailable to anyone with severe physical or mental disabilities.

For these reasons, the parties arrived at court knowing that the facts and law would tip to Jewels Helping Hands and Camp Hope. And with the reality of the situation revealed, the City and County agreed to a courthouse steps solution: a temporary order to not sweep the Camp as threatened, followed several months later with agreement to a permanent agreement to allow a full state-court state law procedure to determine the Camp's continued operation.

And this pair of rulings got Jewels Helping Hands and Camp Hope what it needed: peaceable security and time to humanely and legally close. The record of successes and benefits is found in other chapters. The legal work was just a simple act to protect the voiceless - for a brief while - so that peer-to-peer and professional collaborations could bring a genuine solution to the many hundreds who constituted Camp Hope.

Jeffry Finer, Attorney-At-Law, is a long-time civil rights attorney in Spokane and was the lead counsel for Jewels Helping Hands and the other Plaintiffs in the Federal lawsuit against the City and County of Spokane regarding the disposition of Camp Hope.

A Place to Exist

19 - Law Enforcement As A Tool Of Homeless Policy
By Anwar Peace

The solution to our homeless crisis won't be found in the continuation of "criminalizing homeless individuals." It won't be found in any kind of "Sit & Lie" or "No Camping" ordinances that target those same folks. In fact, these kinds of policies are ultimately counter-productive and harm our Community's goal of ending this crisis. City governments that choose the path of criminalizing the homeless, whether they know it or not, are

Anwar Peace, Chair of the City of Spokane's Human Rights Commission and a Peer Navigator with Jewels Helping Hands.

compounding the crisis by alienating and re-traumatizing this vulnerable population. In defending their strategy of criminalization, some City Leaders have said that "we make it too easy to be homeless in our society," and so a tougher approach and tougher tactics must be utilized in order to declare victory on the homeless crisis. From my perspective, this strategy seems like a classic "the Carrot or the Stick" approach, just minus the Carrot and very heavy on the Stick.

Tactics That Break Trust
The primary mechanism City Governments use to criminalize the homeless is law enforcement - their Police Departments. Now made a tool of homeless policy, the Police-Force goes forward with enforcing the policies that those Cities enact. But, because Police Departments aren't designed or setup to compassionately interact with the vulnerable population of the Homeless Community, the result of that policy is the homeless feel alienated and re-traumatized by the very same Police-Force that's supposed to keep them safe as well. Studies have shown that the Homeless Population is one of the most victimized populations in our communities, but at the same time crimes against the Homeless go significantly under-reported due to lack of trust with the Police.

Let's take a moment and key-in on that "lack of trust" issue and examine the root of the problem. Now, everybody has some kind of trust issue that they're working on in their life, and typically those trust issues are rooted in a historical-pattern of trust being broken in their life. Once trust is broken it is hard to earn that trust back. But it can be done starting by 1st admitting trust was broken and ending that historical-pattern that led to the harm. For the Homeless, the very real trauma of broken trust plays out for them daily when interacting with Police, due to the ongoing historical pattern of Police tactics that further erode the "Community-Police Relationship". Those Police-Tactics that erode the

"Community-Police Relationship" within the Homeless-Population typically consists of the following: 1) "Street-Sweeps" of Homeless encampments, 2) "Emphasis-Patrols on Pedestrian-Interference or Jaywalking" where the Homeless congregate, and 3) "Patrol-Car-Mugshot-Books & Databases" of Homeless folks that Officers have deemed "problematic."

Each one of these Police-Tactics is specifically designed by the Police Department, often in collaboration with local business leaders (more about that in a moment). Whether they know it or not, Police officers who utilize these tactics are compounding the crisis by alienating and re-traumatizing this vulnerable population with their flawed tactics. Plus, all parties acknowledge that these are flawed tactics, mainly because the only thing the tactics really do is to push those folks into a different neighborhood for the time being. Those kinds of tactics will never address the root of the Homeless crisis. Also, these flawed tactics by Police Departments typically have been crafted & designed without the collaboration/partnership of the community's social service entities. Lacking that collaboration/partnership from service providers, the Police miss out on learning from those providers about national- best-practices on how to engage with our Homeless community. What those national-best-practices show is that engaging with folks using a "Person-Centered & Trauma-Informed" approach produces far more positive results, as well as creating space to build rapport and trust between the parties. It's been found that this "Person-Centered" approach helps reduce trauma in a person. For those experiencing Homelessness, just the process of becoming Homeless can be very traumatic. So, the goal of any Police-Tactics should be to do the least amount of harm while providing professional Police-Services, with Officers using empathy and compassion toward our Homeless neighbors.

Tactics And Consequences In Real Time

It's important for us to see and understand how these Police-Tactics are playing-out in real time on our streets. Looking at the Police-Tactic of conducting "Street-Sweeps" of encampments, you will be able to see for yourself how this tactic can erode the trust with Police in the Homeless-Population. A Homeless encampment can take many forms; an encampment could be a bunch of cardboard boxes put together or some pallets covered in tarps, and most commonly camping-tents are utilized at these encampments. These encampments typically take a lot of time and energy to setup, and the folks that build them take pride in creating a home-like environment which is their safe-zone from the dangers of the streets. So, think back for a moment about the last time you went camping in the woods. How long did it take you to setup your campsite? Did you take pride in picking the perfect tent spot? When taking down your campsite, how much time and energy did you use packing your things away the right way and getting them into those right bags. Well, that's just a little taste of what it is like setting up a Homeless encampment without the stress of Law Enforcement being involved.

Law Enforcement As A Tool Of Homeless Policy

Law Enforcement involvement in "Street-Sweeps" of Homeless encampments here in Spokane involves amassing large numbers of Police and large amounts of City resources, none of which are geared towards providing services to those being relocated. During a Spokane Police "Street-Sweep," it is very commonplace for there to be anywhere between 5 to 8 Squad Cars present, sometimes more. Also present at these Spokane "Street-Sweeps" are many vehicles from the City's Code Enforcement Department along with several City dump trucks. Once all those City resources gather, Spokane Police & Code-Enforcement issue what's called a "Notice to Disperse" with a time limit. At that point Officers & City Officials wait around until the end of the allotted time limit. They then proceed to go about physically dismantling that encampment. Typically, these time limits from Police aren't enough time for folks to pack & haul their belongings away. Sadly, quite often their personal items get thrown like trash into the dump trucks and then hauled to the dump. Sometimes these personal items that are thrown into the dump trucks by City Officials are items like Personal IDs, Social Security cards, food stamp (EBT) cards, medications - all of which are vitally important to the daily survival of a Homeless individual. During these Spokane Police "Street-Sweeps", folks who attempt to gather their personal items *after* the time limits are arrested by Police and charged with "Obstructing a Law Enforcement Officer" (RCW 9A.76.020). Anyone who attempts to stay and not disperse from the encampment are arrested and charged with either "Unauthorized Camping on Public Property" (SMC 12.02.1010), "Interference with Pedestrian or Vehicular Traffic" (SMC 10.10.025), and/or "Obstructing a Law Enforcement Officer" (RCW 9A.76.020). For those folks who are lucky enough to be able to walk away from the encampment with some of their things, the whole merry-go-round starts again - the very familiar circular-pattern of scouting out another safe spot for them and their belongings (that often takes a lot of time and energy to do), setting up their new living-space, and then trying to quickly grab some rest and sleep before the next Police-Action is taken against them. It should be clear to all of us that these Police-Actions clearly do produce trauma & harm to our Homeless neighbors - unwanted trauma & harm simply for the crime of trying to find a safe place to sleep.

Complaints About Police Tactics

Throughout the years, several City of Spokane Human Rights Commissioners have received many complaints about the Spokane Police "Street-Sweeps" and the heavy-handed tactics used toward the Homeless. These complaints range from community members/organizations to even complaints from those directly affected by the "Street-Sweeps". Those complaints to the Commission commonly center around the inhumane treatment by Officers at these "Street-Sweeps", as well as concerns over use-of-force issues. What these complaints also reveal is the troubling pattern of Officer behavior while interacting with our Homeless neighbors. Multiple reports of Officers intentionally being very sarcastic, rude, profane, intimidating, harassing, mean, and in some cases downright "cruel with evil intent." The Spokane Police Ombudsman classifies these kinds of behaviors from Officers as "Demeanor-Complaints", and sadly, over the last 5-years, the rate of "Demeanor-Complaints" has remained consistently high citywide. Perhaps most disturbingly, what these complaints to the Human Rights Commission have very clearly shown is that there hasn't been just 1 or 2 "Bad-Apple-Officers." Rather, there has historically been a large number of Officers who act in an unprofessional manner towards the Homeless, by either talking down to them, demeaning them, insulting them, or just treating them as less-than-human.

An Unconstitutional Policy?

Many in the Spokane community - including both service providers and legal experts - believe that these "Street-Sweeps" are, in fact, unconstitutional and illegal. Back in 2018, the 9th-Circuit Court of Appeals ruled on the Boise, Idaho case of *Martin v. Boise*, finding that criminalizing resting or camping on public property is a violation of the 8th-amendment when unhoused

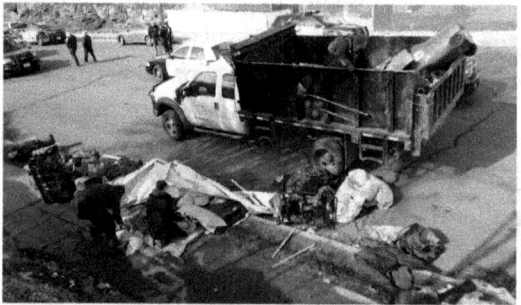

A Law Enforcement sweep of a group of homeless campers in downtown Spokane.

people don't have access to adequate shelter. A year later, the United States Supreme Court upheld that ruling (by choosing not to review it, but allowing it to stand). Spokane does not now have, nor ever had, access to adequate shelter for our unhoused. If that is the case (and it is), then by this Federal ruling (or "Case Law") Spokane Police have violated prevailing Federal Case Law by conducting "Street-Sweeps". And the numbers don't lie about shelter space in Spokane. As of the mid-2023 there was a total of 1,015 beds in the citywide emergency shelter system, while this year's "Point-in-Time" count of the Homeless population found our community has at least 2,390 folks who are unhoused. So, as you can see, even a Federal District Court and the United States Supreme Court have acknowledged that these "Street-Sweeps" clearly do produce trauma and harm to our Homeless neighbors. At this point then, a question must be asked as to why Spokane Police continue with these flawed & unconstitutional Police-Tactics, simply for the crime of trying to find a safe place to sleep.

A Troubling Collaboration

Another troubling Police-Tactic in Spokane that erodes the "Community-Police-Relationship" within the Homeless-Population are its "Emphasis-Patrols on Pedestrian-Interference or Jaywalking" in places downtown where the Homeless congregate. Again, you will see that these "Emphasis-Patrols" are flawed tactics, mainly because the Police Department's tactics typically have been crafted & designed without the collaboration/partnership of the community's social service entities. What is even more interesting as we dig deeper is who the Department does choose to collaborate and partner with for these "Emphasis-Patrols." Instead of partnering with the community's social service entities, they collaborate closely with the Downtown Business Association. Through Public Records Requests, private citizens found out in the spring of 2023 that, over a 2-year period, thousands of emails had been sent between the head of the Downtown Business Association and Spokane Police Chief Craig Meidl about these "Emphasis-Patrols". These emails clearly showed that the Downtown Business Association was directing the Police Chief to do these "Emphasis-Patrols." They were also collaborating together to brainstorm other ways of harming the Homeless. Together, the Police Chief & the Downtown Business Association devised and executed a plan to install fencing under downtown overpasses to keep our homeless friends from seeking shelter from the frigid Spokane weather. Plus, these two entities also created a database of homeless folks who Officers and the Police Department have deemed "problematic." Thousands of emails revealed to the Spokane Community the special treatment that Spokane Police Chief Craig Meidl showed to the Business Association regarding our unhoused friends by utilizing cruelty and callousness to accomplish their goals with these flawed tactics. This is why, once these emails became public, over 20 state and local diverse Community Organizations called for the resignation of Spokane Police Chief Craig Meidl.

Again, what is interesting about all of this is that all involved parties acknowledge these are flawed tactics on the part of the Police regarding how they deal with our City's Homeless-Crisis. The only thing these tactics really do is to push those folks into a different neighborhood for the time being, and that kind of tactic will never address the root of the Homeless crisis. Once more, through Public Records Requests, community activists were able to map-out arrests of the Homeless using arrest reports for "Pedestrian-Interference or Jaywalking" in a 5-year period. What the Spokane arrest-map revealed to the public is that for 5-years the only arrests for "Pedestrian- Interference or Jaywalking" happened in known locations where the Homeless congregate, mainly in the downtown core. Few arrests took place in middle-class-neighborhoods and no arrests happened in affluent-neighborhoods like Spokane's South Hill. Apparently, rich people never cross the street to see their neighbor without using a crosswalk. A rational person could reasonably conclude that the enforcement of "Pedestrian- Interference or Jaywalking-Laws" is not equally applied by Police and the application of the law is only used as a tool of homeless policy towards those folks who are financially disadvantaged. Whether we're examining "Emphasis-Patrols on Pedestrian-Interference or Jaywalking" or "Street-Sweeps of Homeless encampments," the reasonable conclusion is the same: These are failed Police-Tactics that do nothing but create a "War on being poor and homeless." One side of this war consists of human beings carrying tents and sleeping-bags and just trying to figure out where their next meal will come from. The other side of this war consists of state-actors wearing matching uniforms with bullet-prove vests, guns & weapons with arrest authority - which, in my opinion, seems like a terribly lop-sided war.

Let's Conclude With A Real-Life Story

I have a real-life story that reflects the real-world impacts of these failed Police-Tactics used towards our Homeless neighbors. For 4 months I worked at Spokane's newest Homeless shelter on Trent Avenue, where I was employed by a mental health/housing agency providing wraparound services at the shelter. One day at the shelter, after my co-workers and I had built a lot of rapport with a guest, she then opened up to us about a traumatic situation that she recently went through and desperately wanted help and assistance on coping with. This shelter-guest then disclosed to us that a few nights earlier she had been sexually assaulted at the shelter and that she never told shelter staff nor called the Police. At that point we supported and worked with this victim. She then felt comfortable enough to allow us to contact the authorities about this crime. The victim was very eager to get justice for what had happened to her and to make sure no other victims had to go through what she did. Before Police arrived, she expressed that she was very willing to fill out a victim-statement with the Police. But when those 2 Patrol-Officers, not SVU Detectives, walked through our door the victim's whole demeanor changed. My co-workers and I later found out that those 2 Patrol-Officers were part of the "Street-Sweep" that broke up the encampment where she had been living, which then forced her to be at the shelter where she was then victimized. These Officers had treated her and the others very inhumanely during the "Street-Sweep." It should be no surprise that, at the shelter she became uncooperative and eventually ran out of the shelter to avoid dealing with those Officers. Sadly, a few weeks later the victim returned to the shelter. We tried to help again but with two different Officers. Unfortunately, again the victim ran away from those Officers because of the same "Street-Sweep" that had evicted her from the camp and eventually produced her victimization at the shelter. As a result of that terribly unfortunate episode, the victim's attacker is still at large and roaming free in our community, the consequence of failed Police-Tactics that are truly harming public safety - for you, for me, and for our unhoused neighbors.

Anwar Peace is the Chair of the City of Spokane's Human Rights Commission, a member of the Washington Coalition on Police Accountability, a Fellow at JustLead Washington, and a police accountability expert & activist with 23 years of experience.

20 - Homelessness Is A Housing Problem
By Ben Stuckart

Spokane entered a housing crisis in 2017, and I use housing crisis really as too broad of a term. When we talk about housing, we need to talk about three different types of housing. And we have a housing crisis in all three levels. The *first* crisis involves a lack of low-income or subsidized housing, which means government money helps to build that housing so you can hold rents low. *Second,* we have an ownership crisis which means that prices of housing are now too high and have risen too high for

Ben Stuckart (left) at Camp Hope, along with Julie Garcia, Lisa Brown, Barry Barfield, and Lerria Schuh, on the day before closing

somebody to buy a home. Home ownership is important because that's how people build generational wealth. *Third,* we have a crisis in market rate rentals. Somebody builds an apartment building and rents it at market rates. Both home ownership and market rate rentals have increased over 60% in the last three years, which basically makes housing unattainable.

Homelessness Is A Housing Problem

This three-part housing crisis is important because there is a direct relationship between housing and homelessness. In March of 2022, a book came out from the University of Washington Press, written by an Assistant Professor at the University of Washington and a data analysis from the Tacoma Tribune. The title and premise of that book is that *Homelessness is a Housing Problem.*[134] What they did was they looked at more than 30 metro areas across the United States. Then they tried to do correlations. They looked at poverty rates in those communities. They looked at whether they were mainly urban or suburban metro areas. They looked at age populations that lived in those areas. And the only correlation they found was that high rental rates equaled an increase in the number of people experiencing homelessness.

Now, you and I might make an assumption that it's really high poverty rates that are driving homelessness. But the authors discovered that in areas like Detroit, Michigan, where you have high poverty rates, housing prices and rentals are low. And you don't see the high rates of homelessness. So, the housing problem - that housing crisis I mentioned earlier - is really the reason why we see an increase in homelessness, especially in Spokane and other West Coast cities

A Place to Exist

Housing Density

In keeping with the Post-World War 2 housing boom in America, we've often idealized the large suburban yard with single family homes. What we haven't done is build up density. But if you go to cities like Prague or Budapest, or even if you're standing on the Eiffel Tower in Paris and you look out, you find human sized cities where there aren't big skyscrapers. All of the buildings are 3 to 5 stories high. There are multiple people - individuals and families - living in every building and you have much denser environments than on the West Coast of the United States. We've heard about the homeless problems in Portland and San Francisco, San Diego and Seattle. That's because those cities are younger and haven't figured out density yet in order to drive prices down. In Spokane, when we saw rental prices increase by 60% over three years, what we were seeing was a lack of supply (and housing density) in the city of Spokane. When I say lack of supply, I'm also including the issue of vacancy rates. Think of it this way: out of 100 apartments, our vacancy rates were below 2% for three years in a row. That means for every one hundred apartments that exist, there were less than two available. That's a seriously constricted supply, and when the supply of available rentals is constricted, a landlord in a market economy raises rents because the market will bear those raised rents, because there are so few available.

A Stalled System

A healthy vacancy rate where you can stabilize rent is about 5%. After the housing crash in 2008, housing prices stabilized because over 5% of the homes in Spokane were available. Then the vacancy rates for those homes plummeted as the economy and the real estate market recovered. When people go out looking to buy a home, and there's less than one and a half percent vacancy rate, the price for those homes rises. The lack of supply and rising prices stalls the whole housing system and makes low-income housing even harder to find. To get into low-income housing, we currently have a three year wait-list. So, even if you've done everything right and filled out all the paperwork, you have to wait an average of three years. Some people do get in quicker, but for some people it takes a lot longer.

Currently, what we have is a system that's completely stalled. Even if I build 100 low-income housing units and I house 100 people off the streets into those subsidized units, there's only so much subsidy money available from the government. Then, once they've stabilized in low-income housing, if those people can't move on to market rate housing, their unit can't be freed up for the next low-income tenant until a new unit is built somewhere else.

Now, some cities have been successful at this. The best example we have of a city that's been successful in decreasing their homeless numbers over the last ten years is Houston, Texas. Houston decreased their homeless numbers by over 65%. And they did that in a combination of ways. They built a whole bunch of low-income housing, but they also used rapid rehousing dollars, rent subsidies, and vouchers to move people on from those low-income, permanent supportive housing because they provided services as part of that housing.

You can never simply put somebody in a house if they have a mental illness, or if they have substance abuse problems, or other co-occurring disorders, and expect them to stabilize. But if you do housing with services, they can stabilize and eventually move out. So, what you see in Houston is within 3 to 5 years, 80% of the people who had come off the streets and into low income housing had moved on, using other subsidies - rapid rehousing or rental assistance or vouchers - to move into market rate apartments.

What we've got in Spokane, with the 600 plus permanent supportive housing units that we've built since 2014, is a complete flip of the Houston numbers. In Spokane, only 20% of low-income tenants are moving out within 3 to 5 years into market-rate stabilized housing. 80% are still in the same low-income housing they originally moved into. They aren't moving out and making room for the next tenant who needs that low-income supportive housing. The system is stalled.

A Broken Continuum

Spokane needs a system that functions as a continuum - transitional housing, low-income supportive housing, market-rate housing. Oftentimes, what we have in Spokane is a process where somebody will move off the streets directly into permanent supportive housing. But there's a lack of transitional housing, intermediate places that are set up with really robust services that enable someone to stabilize before moving into permanent supportive housing. We have no tiny home villages that offer housing, services and a sense of community. And one of the things we know from Camp Hope is that people form relationships and a sense of community. When they move from a tent in a camp, they still want that sense of community. And if they're just moving into an apartment by themselves, they're very isolated and not likely to succeed. There needs to be housing options in between living on the streets or in a camp and living in an apartment building. I believe we've completely failed on that transition part of our homeless system and our housing system, what many people refer to as our continuum of care. Our continuum is broken because we have nowhere for people exiting homelessness to immediately go where they can have that sense of community and can receive those intensive services. Then, once they go into permanent supportive housing, they lose that sense of community or they don't have *enough* services they need to stabilize. And even if they had the community and the services they needed, there's not a light at the end of the tunnel to move forward into market rate housing. We've got a stalled system at every level, and a stalled system and a broken continuum set people up to fail.

Changing How We Advocate

Let's look at how we advocate for things in our community. I work for the

Spokane Low Income Housing Consortium. But if we want housing to be affordable, I can't spend all of my time advocating for just subsidized housing. If we want a successful continuum, we're going to have to take ourselves out of our comfort zones where we want to be as individuals and are more comfortable and can get really settled in, and where I could spend all my time advocating for money for low income housing. But if the continuum is broken, we all need to be advocating together for the entire continuum. People who are left leaning often want to demonize developers. And I see this weekly in meetings. I truly believe their heart is in the right place, and they believe that all low-income housing should be subsidized and we should all have a right to housing. But we're nowhere close to getting there as a society. We're actually moving away and cutting funds for low-income housing. So, how do you make market rate housing affordable? By building more. And that's really uncomfortable for some people because they want to demonize all developers. But if we do not build more market rate apartments and more market rate housing, we will not stabilize those prices, and we're going to continue to see homelessness rise in Spokane.

If you look in Spokane at the Real Estate Association, who in the last ten years has become the major player in politics in Spokane, they will tell you that they're advocating for home ownership and that's it. And they'll fight apartment complexes tooth and nail, not understanding that you need people in a continuum and advocating for all levels of the housing continuum in order for it to be successful so that people can afford to buy a home later. If we just had homes and no apartments, our system would be irrevocably broken. It's just as important that we have apartments and low-income housing as it is that we have an ownership option for people to increase generational wealth. They're all equally important. I believe everybody has a right to housing, but I understand where I'm at in this world - we need market rate apartments and market rate housing.

Right now, when it comes to subsidized housing in Spokane, we have 6,000 units and we know we need 6,000 more, right now. We know we also need 19,000 market rate units in the City of Spokane, right now. So we need 25,000 units in Spokane to completely stabilize the market and maybe reduce rents and reduce home prices some. But it's going to take a combination of market rate housing and it's going to take a combination of low-income housing, and then it's going to take innovation on how do we build tiny home villages to get people off the streets.

The Kevin Bacon Housing Study

There's a great study that the University in California put out in 2018, and it's called the Kevin Bacon Housing Study, based on the notion of six degrees of separation and that everybody is separated from Kevin Bacon by six degrees. The study really busted some mythology and showed that even if you build a $1,000,000 home in a community, you free up homes at six levels below that (hence, six degrees of separation). They showed this by looking at like 60,000 different home sales, over seven different communities,

Let me illustrate this by starting with a housing shortage. So, there's a shortage of $1,000,000 homes just as much as there's a shortage of $200,000 starter homes. And if I build a $1,000,000 home in a community, somebody with a $750,000 home can move up, which allows the person in a $500,000 home to move up into the $750,000 home, and someone in a $250,000 home can now move into that $500,000 home and so on for a total of six levels down.

I hear people complain and ask, "Why are we building high end homes?" Whenever I send that study to somebody asking that question, they get really mad at me at first and they're like, "This is junk!" But then they read the study and they read the articles about the study and I never hear from them again. And it's because it's really hard to demonize developers if you understand that whatever they're building somewhere, it's helping all of us in our housing system. And that's why it's important sometimes to question yourself and the assumptions you make about who people are or what they're doing. I could lament the fact that somebody on the far south end of town builds a $1,000,000 home. But if somebody built that and it frees up other housing, then we're all benefitting. And that study has never been refuted. Nobody has ever done a study that says that's not true. All the articles that have studied that have said, "Yes, that's valid. The data is right." So I think it's really up to us to stop demonizing others in our community and find those people who want to work with our housing system.

The Zoning Challenge

This raises the issue of zoning. We know that Spokane has a zoning problem. I think the most interesting fact that describes Spokane's zoning problem is that over 70% of the land inside the City of Spokane is zoned single family. And there are areas of Spokane zoned single family that should not be. They should be zoned multi-family. We passed a comprehensive plan in the early 2000s, and that comprehensive plan basically said, Okay, based on the Washington State Growth Management Act, we're no longer going to sprawl out. We as a community are going to densify. And our strategy in Spokane was we're going to have these what's called centers and corridors. There are 28 centers and corridors. And if you want to think about it, when I say centers and corridors the examples would be the Perry Street Business District, or the Garland Business District, or the area of North Monroe that we've just renovated and spent millions of dollars on the streetscape from Northwest Boulevard to North Hill right below Garland.

These are all small business districts that are really the lifeblood of small businesses, and where we should be seeing density. But 80% of our centers and corridors are surrounded by single family homes instead of apartments. Zoning for greater housing density for two or three blocks around each of those business centers would make a massive amount of difference. And it's not just that it would provide dense housing, because you need the land to build apartments on. It would also take the pressure off the outskirts of our city. If we had land inside the city and in our core and around business centers, where transit lines are, it would take pressure off of our transportation network at the outskirts of our city, which is inevitably where it goes if you don't have it zoned correctly inside the city.

In addition, we often talk about public safety and we talk about that in a vacuum. But the thing that is more effective than 100 police officers on the street is eyes on the street - each of us out walking in our neighborhoods. So, if we had density in our small business centers, we would have a safer environment because more people would be out walking and watching.

You often hear of conflict around our small business centers where people don't like all the cars in their neighborhood. You go to the Perry Street neighborhood during the farmer's market on a Friday night and parking becomes a problem. That's because those areas don't have enough density to support their business district with just the people that live nearby. In order to survive, they have to have people driving to those business districts. But if you had enough housing density around the business district itself, you would have enough local people for those small businesses to survive, even if nobody drove there. It's the people who live there that should be supporting these small business districts. But without the density and the apartments surrounding those, we totally miss out on that. Today what we see is a place like Perry Street, which was the fastest growing area in our town from 2007 through about 2017. But new businesses are no longer opening there. They're only replacing ones. And there are several vacant buildings that have been vacant for over five years, and that's in what was the most successful small business district for ten years in our city. To see a vacancy there means something's wrong. And what's wrong is there aren't enough people that live nearby in order to support it through walking. So, by changing zoning code and creating density around our small business districts, you get better land use, you get a safer environment, you get healthier small businesses, and you solve the housing crisis by creating a space for all of those apartments to be built.

Tiny Houses

I think in multifamily areas where we already allow apartment buildings, tiny home cottages, tiny homes, pallet homes should just be outright allowed. And that needs to be a change in the code that as we move forward and densify our city, it should just be outright allowed. You shouldn't have to get special permits in order to build tiny homes. If it's okay to build 40 apartments on a space, then it should be okay to have 40 tiny homes on the same space. There's no reason why not. They're building tiny homes now that pass fire inspection, they're built out of cross laminated timber and they're just as inexpensive as the ones that you see on the west side of the state. And so the technology exists to build a tiny home that is just as safe as your big, large one two bedroom house. So there's no reason it shouldn't just be outright allowed.

A Handful of Takeaways

I want to close with a handful of takeaways.

First, I believe we're missing that transitional step between being on the street or living in a tent and then moving directly into a 40 unit apartment building or permanent supportive housing. I think there needs to be more transitional housing, and we really need to get our act together as a community about tiny homes at one of those transitional options.

Second, we need to embrace the reality that if any one level of our housing system fails, the system fails in a way that affects all the other levels. We could have all the low-income housing in the world that we can possibly build, and the system could be as efficient as possible, and we could be putting millions more dollars into it, but if market rate apartments and market rate ownership are broken, whatever we do isn't going to be enough. It has to all work and the system has to work in concert.

Third, when we really look at the data, it shows us that homelessness is a housing problem. High rents and lack of availability are what are driving people onto the streets. I know the talking points are that it's a mental health issue, and, yes, there are people who have mental illness. But there are also people who are mentally ill that are stably housed. But the rising rents are what's pushing them out of housing and onto the streets as well. There are a lot of people with addiction issues that have housing, but when somebody with addiction issues sees their rent double, they're also pushed out onto the streets.

Fourth, by saying that homelessness is a housing problem, we can't ignore those other problems. We need a better community mental health system. Community mental health is not working correctly for those people in our community in need, and we need more treatment services.

Finally, increasing homelessness and addiction and the increasing mental health crisis that we're seeing are not going to be solved just by building housing. They are a sign of deeper problems. There's a reason why people use drugs, including a sense of hopelessness, a sense of a lack of community. There's a reason we're seeing more outward mental illness. Maybe it manifests itself when things are broken. I think we have really high poverty rates and a lot of problems that are bigger than just us looking at this one issue - homelessness. It's part of a larger problem. Why are we so broken as a species? Why is everything solved by violence? Why are we so hopeless that we need to numb ourselves constantly, looking for that next best high? Why is mental illness manifesting itself in what appears to be much higher rates than we saw 40 years ago? Until we have some honest conversations about things like wealth inequality, the loss of community, our loss of trust in each other and institutions, I see us just trying to Band-Aid problems. Until then, we can't even entertain the thought that housing or health care is a right in our country. Until then, we're not ready to entertain a conversation about taking care of each other as a community. I think we need to have some bigger conversations about how we how we interact with each other and how we treat each other and what it means to be part of a community.

Ben Stuckart is the Executive Director of the Spokane Low-Income Housing Consortium (since March of 2020). He has been working on housing issues in the City of Spokane since 2017 while serving as the City of Spokane City Council President from 2012 to 2019.

"Progress, far from consisting in change, depends on retentiveness. When change is absolute there remains no being to improve and no direction is set for possible improvement: and when experience is not retained, as among savages, infancy is perpetual. Those who cannot remember the past are condemned to repeat it."
~ George Santayana, Philosopher

"The past cannot predict the future, but it can show the dangerous consequences of certain ways of thinking and behaving." ~ Edward J. Watts[135]

By the time this book is in print and you read this closing chapter, Camp Hope will be gone. If those of us who worked with the residents of the Camp did our jobs carefully and thoughtfully, most of the residents will have moved on to better options and, hopefully, fresh chances at a better life. In the 18 months of its existence, Camp Hope impacted not only the unsheltered homeless who lived

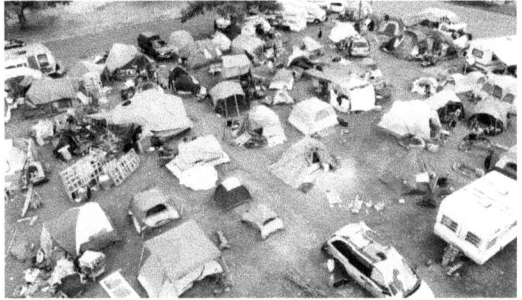

One of the four quadrants of Camp Hope in the early Summer of 2022

there, but the individuals and agencies that serve the unsheltered homeless. It changed the face of homeless services and how those services should be delivered (on-site rather than in-office) It also challenged the City of Spokane's understanding of homelessness, forcing the opening of new shelters and housing options, revealing the barriers that prevent those experiencing homelessness from exiting the cycle of homelessness that has held them prisoner, and forcing our community to confront its own failures that have held back meaningful solutions in the past.

For those willing to listen and learn, Camp Hope taught important lessons for any future plans to meaningfully address homelessness. A very real danger exists that we might ignore or forget the lessons that Camp Hope taught us. For that reason alone, we need to identify and explore those lessons, making certain that they don't fade away along with the Camp. We paid a high price in "treasure, time, and toil" for those lessons. Forgetting to learn and failing to pass those lessons on would result in our community paying an even higher price - the price of forgetfulness . . . and repetition. The Spanish-American Philosopher George Santayana famously observed, "Those who cannot remember the past are condemned to repeat it." Historian Edward J. Watts agrees when he observes, "The past cannot predict the future, but it can show the dangerous consequences of certain ways of thinking and behaving." Repeating the mistakes that led to Camp Hope and forgetting the lessons we learned from the experience of moving the unsheltered homeless of Camp Hope forward to better lives would·be a price too high to pay . . . again, and too painful to risk.

Philosopher A.N. Whitehead, the godfather of Process Philosophy (which I studied in graduate school but could never completely wrap my head around), famously observed that the history of European philosophy could be summarized as a series of footnotes on Plato.[136] As we review the lessons that Camp Hope taught us, you may feel like you're reading a series of repetitious footnotes on things we've already discussed, and at length. Well, you would be right. You and I learn with difficulty and struggle to remember what we've learned. Repetition is an important memory key. We remember what we struggle with, what we emphasize, and what we repeat, until the struggle, the emphasis, and the repetition become part of our DNA. Or, to abuse the words of another famous philosopher, Yogi Berra, until it becomes "like déjà vu all over again." The lessons explored in this chapter range from the philosophical to the spiritual to the political to the historical and, yes, to the practical. Each represents an indispensable part of a greater whole, the whole story of Camp Hope, and, hopefully, the beginning of a new story of what comes after.

1. A Journey From Chaos To Cosmos To Shalom

In her wonderful book, *Walking On Water: Reflections On Faith And Art*, author Madeleine L'Engle describes the work of the artist as bringing *cosmos* (order) out of *chaos* (disorder).[137] Welcome to working among the chronic unsheltered homeless. Meaningfully addressing homelessness is an ongoing exercise in bringing *cosmos* out of *chaos*. We walk with the unsheltered homeless, assisting them to take the necessary steps on their journey from their current *chaos* and survival mode of existence to a place of personal *cosmos*, stability, and Shalom (peace, wholeness, and well-being). Our role is not to impose our view of stability on them, but to help them discover the form of stability that works for them. At the end of the day, it's their life. They must live it out for themselves. We can only coach and encourage them along the way.

For the residents of Camp Hope, this movement from the *chaos* of unsheltered homelessness to the *cosmos* of an appropriate form of stable housing was different for each unique individual. But, in spite of the differences, all of those individual journeys involved a handful of commonalities that I've labeled "steps." For the service providers who worked with Camp residents, taking the steps from *chaos* to *cosmos* meant doing the hard work of assessing needs and offering appropriate options, rather than imposing cookie-cutter solutions that were part of someone's pre-conceived homeless plan. Let's take a few moments and briefly reflect on the "steps" that are common, in varying degrees, to each Camp resident's journey out of homelessness.

Step 1 - Unsheltered Homelessness. This is the beginning step where we connect with the unsheltered homeless in the midst of the *chaos* of their journey through unsheltered homelessness. It is often a place of personal *chaos* and hopelessness where many of the unsheltered homeless have given up any realistic hope of something better. Reconnecting with them on their terms where they are offers the hope that someone still cares.

Step 2 - A Low-Barrier Shelter. A certain percentage of the unsheltered homeless are, in fact, ready and able (emotionally, mentally, physically) to go to a low-barrier shelter, if approached and encouraged in the right way (and a law enforcement sweep is not the right way). The assessments we conducted in July of 2022 revealed that 51 Camp residents (or 8%) were willing to go to a shelter, depending on who was operating it. In the months that followed, we estimated that roughly 42 Camp residents actually went to the TRAC shelter (see our earlier comments in the Epilogue of Chapter 10). There is a lesson here. To be effective, a shelter must be appropriate to the needs and challenges of the people who stay there. Otherwise, they will not be able to "maintain" there, assuming they're even willing to come.

Step 3 - Assessments. We dealt with this earlier in Chapter 13, but individual assessments became an important (even invaluable) component of the journey out of *chaos* and into *cosmos* because they helped camp managers and caseworkers better understand the unique needs of each person in the Camp, why they were there, and what it was going to take to move them forward toward a better future.

Step 4 - On-Site Services. As we discussed earlier in Chapter 12 ("On Site Services Remove Barriers"), at Camp Hope personal needs assessments were combined with on-site services, including an on-site resource fair. Prior to COVID-19, most homeless service providers connected with those experiencing homelessness by asking those seeking help to come to their agency office. Direct outreach was minimal, while office visits were normal and expected. COVID-19 changed everything, as direct outreach was suspended and service provider office hours and availability were curtailed. Many offices were simply closed. As COVID-19 restrictions were slowly lifted, the unsheltered homeless did not begin showing up at offices in significant numbers. To complicate matters, the 2022 Point-In-Time Count, the first full post-COVID homeless census, showed a dramatic 56% increase in the number of unsheltered homeless from the last pre-COVID Count in 2020. Not only were the unsheltered homeless not showing up at agency offices, their numbers had increased, with many experiencing homelessness for the first time. The old service model of "come to my office" simply wasn't adequate to meet the new need. What Camp Hope demonstrated was that engaging in direct outreach while offering on-site services works.

Step 5 - Identification Restoration. The next critical step toward personal *cosmos* and stability for camp residents, and the first major application of assessments and on-site services, came in the form of a newly created program called *The Identification Connection.* The assessments conducted in July on 601 camp residents revealed that 598 of those residents needed some form of ID restoration (lost birth certificates, Social Security Cards, and/or State-issued IDs). The journey out of *chaos* requires the *cosmos* of ID Restoration, because having current valid ID is the gateway to most of the services the unsheltered homeless want and need.

Step 6 - Peer Support. While working on this book, I had a conversation with the Director of a large homeless services agency about our work at Camp Hope and the challenges we faced in getting people into housing. I began describing the current shortage of, and glaring need for, more wrap-around service providers when this person nearly finished my sentence. It's common knowledge in the homeless services community that we do not have the number of trained people needed to provide the wrap-around supportive services needed to help the newly-housed homeless successfully maintain in their new environment. In a very real sense, policymakers who continue to talk about the importance and availability of wrap-around supportive services are over-promising and under-delivering. One of the note-worthy successes of Camp Hope was our ability to hire and deploy a motivated team of Peer Support workers who worked and walked tirelessly alongside Camp residents as they built their personal exit ramps out of homelessness and into some form of appropriate housing. Because of their background of lived-experiences (substance abuse and recovery, criminal records, prison, homelessness, and more), they were able to say to those they worked with, *"If I could do this, you can do this,"* as they worked with them on paperwork, appointments, referrals to treatment, court appearances, housing, and much more.

Step 7 - Substance Abuse Treatment. In data collected during the 2023 Point In Time Count, the top three causes people cited for their homelessness were 1) lack of affordable housing, 2) lack of family/support network, and 3) substance use. For some people, substance abuse caused their homelessness. For many others, the substance abuse came later and simply complicated their effort to build an exit ramp out of homelessness. As a result, for many in the sheltered and unsheltered homeless community, substance abuse has become "the tail that wags the dog." They are no longer in control of their lives. The drugs are in control. Regardless of how the substance abuse started, unresolved substance abuse is a barrier. It jeopardizes employment, and a lack of employment means a lack of income, which jeopardizes any housing achieved.

Step 8 - Physical & Mental Health Assessment. As I mentioned earlier, I once heard the Director of a major homeless services agency say that the chronically homeless they were placing into housing had been homeless for an average of 11 years, and that the majority of them would die within three years of getting housed due to untreated medical conditions left over from their years of homelessness. Unsheltered homelessness impacts the long-term health of those experiencing it. Since 2020, Street Medical Teams have significantly improved the medical care provided to our street homeless, but a thorough assessment of their medical needs and potential medical barriers is an important step toward their overall well-being.

Step 9 - Re-Building Life Skills. Chronic unsheltered homelessness rewires the brain for survival mode. The casualty in this process is many of the life skills you and I take for granted and practice every day, things like communication skills (helpful in conflict resolution), personal hygiene, household skills like cleaning up and taking out the trash, time management (helpful if you want to keep a job), money management, and more. Moving someone experiencing unsheltered homelessness from *chaos* (the loss of life skills) to *cosmos* requires some degree of intentionality on our part as service providers to set them up for success when the day comes when we are no longer part of their journey. By teaching and modeling life skills, we work to set people up for success after we're gone. To do otherwise is to set them up to fail.

Step 10 - Resolving Legal/Court Issues. For those who have been homeless on the streets of Spokane for any length of time, the probability is high for having an encounter with local law enforcement. Such encounters frequently result in legal citations being issued for such things as Trespassing or 3rd Degree Possession of Stolen Property (usually, a shopping cart). These citations and court appearances (or failures to appear, resulting in warrants being issued) create additional barriers for those experiencing homelessness.

Step 11 - Employment. Employment means income, and income means stability and the ability to pay bills, maintain housing, and build a life moving forward. But many of the unsheltered homeless have barriers that make finding employment difficult, as we discussed earlier under "Employing the Unemployable" in Chapter 11.

Step 12 - Housing. When all of the previous steps have been completed, those experiencing unsheltered homelessness are ready for the goal they (and their support team) have worked so hard to achieve: appropriate, stable housing. They have now moved from *chaos* to *cosmos*, and to the beginning of building their personal Shalom. Welcome home.

CHAOS/SURVIVAL
UnSheltered Homelessness
A Low Barrier Shelter
Assessments
On-Site Services
Identification Restoration
Peer Support/Community Building
Substance Abuse Treatment
Physical & Mental Health Assistance
Re-Building Life Skills
Resolving Legal/Court Issues
Employment
Housing (appropriate & affordable)
COSMOS/STABILITY/SHALOM

2. Optic, Narrative, and Tone Matter

In early 2019, as I was beginning my documentary work on homelessness in Spokane, I was part of the Leadership Team of the Spokane Homeless Coalition when we met with the President of the Downtown Spokane Partnership, an organization representing the interests of the downtown business community. "If we're going to meaningfully address homelessness in our community," I said, "we need to do three things. *First*, we need to change the optic of what people see when it comes to those experiencing homelessness. *Second*, we need to change the narrative - the story - that people hear about those experiencing homelessness. And *third*, we need to change the tone of our community conversation about those experiencing homelessness."

We live in a generation that listens with its eyes and thinks with its feelings. What they see is what they hear, and how it makes them feel becomes their truth. And that includes what they see, hear, and feel about those experiencing homelessness. A community experiencing a constant media bombardment consisting of

> We live in a generation that listens with its eyes and thinks with its feelings. What they see is what they hear, and how it makes them feel becomes their truth. ~ The Author

pictures depicting homeless individuals sleeping on sidewalks or under bridges or in homeless camps, combined with a narrative of *they're all criminals, drug addicts, and nuisances*, will come to perceive homelessness in those terms. A negative optic combined with a negative narrative creates a negative community tone of an "us-against-them" war, not against homelessness, but against those experiencing it. Whatever the endeavor we engage in, from politics to homeless policy, to homeless services, leaders impact our community through the optic we show, the narrative we tell, and the tone that we set. It's true on a national level, and it's true in your home town . . . and in mine.

Unfortunately, three years later, at the advent of Camp Hope, Spokane business and government leaders continued to promote and practice an "us-against-them" optic, narrative and tone regarding people experiencing homelessness, facilitated by a local media acting as a megaphone for this narrative.

These things (optic, narrative, and tone) matter, and the role of leadership at every level is to set a better tone, tell a better community story, and to promote a better optic when it comes to homelessness and those experiencing it. Front page newspaper ads declaring "Camp Hope Must Close," without offering any tangible or practical solutions, don't meaningfully address homelessness, but serve only to polarize the community into camps of "us-against-them." Political leaders declaring that we make homelessness too easy and comfortable, or declaring those experiencing homelessness are nothing more than nuisances, criminals, and drug addicts, betray their out-right ignorance of homelessness and of those experiencing it while setting a tone of waging war against "those people." Such narratives and tone are dangerous and dehumanizing because *how we see people is the beginning of how we treat people.* History warns us that dehumanizing any marginalized group is to the first step down a slippery slope that never ends well for anyone involved. Our community, including those experiencing homelessness, deserves better. In addition to dehumanizing those experiencing homelessness, the promotion of a negative optic, narrative, and tone has a long-term and widespread impact upon our community as a whole. It fosters and encourages a growing NIMBYism.

3. NIMBYism Limits Community Options

In the Summer of 2019, the City of Spokane wanted to site a new homeless shelter somewhere outside the downtown City core. Their plan coalesced around a recently vacated Grocery Outlet store on the boundary between the City of Spokane and the City of Spokane Valley, located at the corner of Sprague and Havana. Plans were made. The Spokane City Council approved a $50,000 earnest payment to purchase the property. A public meeting was announced where top City employees responsible for homeless services would lay out the formal proposal to the neighborhood.

I attended that meeting, and the kindest description I could offer would be that it was, well, a disaster. It was obvious from the moment the meeting started that the City had not done its ground work to educate and address the concerns of the neighborhood. The audience was surly, and the meeting quickly degenerated into angry chaos. For me as an observer, the death knell of the proposed shelter came when an audience member stood up and declared (to widespread applause), "I'll spend the rest of my life fighting you on this."

The planned new shelter died that night at the hands of NIMBYism writ large and loud.

NIMBY is a well-worn acronym that stands for "Not In My Back Yard," best summarized as, *I want to solve that problem as long as the*

What I learned from Camp Hope . . .

The surrounding community of housed individuals have passionate and polar opposite responses to the visible houseless. Some are moved to provide their time, meals, services and donations in response to human suffering. Others are moved to hate, derision, and even physical assault of human beings. I suspect that for some people, seeing the visible houseless triggers their fears of economic instability and potential houselessness.

Breean Beggs, Attorney
Spokane City Council President

solution doesn't involve me or my back yard.

NIMBYism is an aggressive cancer that eats away at the soul of a community. Unopposed NIMBYism limits the options available to policymakers and service providers when it comes to meaningfully addressing homelessness. Everyone wants to solve homelessness, but no one wants a homeless shelter in *their* neighborhood. When NIMBYism takes hold of a community, you could announce that you're moving Camp Hope (or any proposed homeless shelter) to the middle of no where, and the Middle of No Where Neighborhood Association would miraculously appear and announce their opposition to whatever you're trying to do, declaring, "Not in my back yard, you're not! Not even in the middle of no where!"

In any community, NIMBYism flows from the top down, from political, business, neighborhood, non-profit, and media leaders, which is why the optic, narrative, and tone promoted by all such community leaders is so important. Only by changing the optic, narrative, and tone that leaders promote and that our larger community sees and hears can we hope to eventually change the tone at the grassroots and effectively combat anti-homeless NIMBYism.

4. Law Enforcement Is Not A Solution To Homelessness

It was closing day at Camp Hope when Jonathan Choe arrived to cover the event. Jonathan is a video journalist with the Discovery Institute and is based out of Seattle. I first met Jonathan back in late August of 2022 when he came to Spokane to do a story on the Camp at its peak (before WSDOT got actively involved).[138] On closing day he was back to see how things had changed. In the course of our talk, Jonathan asked me what I thought were the top lessons we had learned. "That law enforcement shouldn't be a tool of homeless policy. It doesn't work," I said. "But can't law enforcement be there in a support role?" Jonathan asked. "I don't know," I responded, "we haven't really experienced that here."

I suppose that my answer embodied 18 months of frustration with law enforcement and its relationship with Camp Hope, along with my experience of filming multiple law enforcement interactions where the homeless were forced to move with nowhere to go, often experiencing the loss of their belongings. With respect to the Camp, we had experienced very little in the way of "supportive" help. We could count on our fingers the number of times our calls for assistance had been answered. But you would need an abacus to count the number of times our calls for assistance went unanswered (even after the City and WSDOT entered into an agreement that allowed SPD to enter the Camp in response to calls for assistance). The City assigned two SPD patrol cars to literally sit and watch the Camp - one on the property diagonally west of the Camp and the other on the property diagonally to the east of the Camp. But Jonathan Choe's question regarding the involvement of law enforcement in a supportive role is a valid one that makes a valid point.

In the Spokane Community, law enforcement provides valuable - even indispensable - services that we all count on: responding to our emergency calls for help, protecting and guaranteeing public safety, enforcing our laws, investigating crime, apprehending those (including those experiencing homelessness) who break our laws, and more. But when used as a tool of homeless policy, law enforcement is out of its element. Painful experience teaches us that, all too often, the interaction between law enforcement and those experiencing homelessness becomes an ongoing game of homeless wack-a-mole, forcing the homeless to move with no effective options while generating new and additional barriers that only complicate their journey out of homelessness. Handing out citations for trespassing, or 3rd degree possession of stolen property (i.e., a shopping cart), or obstructing a sidewalk may send you to Community Court, but the service providers at Community Court don't have any more services, resources, or housing options available than anyone else does. Using law enforcement as a tool of homeless policy simply isn't a meaningful solution to homelessness (as described earlier in Anwar Peace's excellent article).

Whether or not we as a Community can find effective ways for law enforcement to play a supportive role in homeless services is yet to be determined. Efforts have been made to partner law enforcement officers with mental health professionals, but so far those efforts have been short-lived, even when successful. Unfortunately, they have also been misused, as when "mental health outreach workers" accompanied law enforcement on their visit to Camp Hope in December of 2022 (as we described earlier in Chapter 6) in an event that had the net effect of traumatizing a large number of Camp residents and negatively impacting their mental health. For law enforcement to play a positive and supportive role in homeless policy, some things will need to change.

5. Shelters Aren't The Silver Bullet Solution To Solving Homelessness

Earlier we looked at the extent of homelessness in the Spokane community and compared the number of known-and-counted homeless (via the PIT Count) with the number of shelter beds in Spokane's city-wide shelter system. We saw that in mid-2023 the city-wide shelter system had total bed capacity for only 46% of the known-and-counted homeless in our Community (and that true homelessness could be larger by a factor of 10!). Our first response might well be, "We need more shelter beds!" and I would agree. But increasing shelter capacity will not solve homelessness. If the new beds are filled, the guests will be off the street (and that's a good thing), but they remain homeless (or "houseless"). The long term solution to meaningfully addressing homelessness is housing - more housing options, including tiny houses, more affordable and appropriate housing, and for those who need additional care, more wrap-around supportive services to help them maintain that housing.

Over a period of 18 years I've been directly involved in the operation of four (4) low-barrier shelters (and the State's largest homeless camp). Shelters are an important component in any homeless policy. But all shelters should be treated as transitional housing, a gateway to better housing (more about this under Lesson 12 below). Homeless shelters should be temporary places where people can received appropriate services while they wait until they can leave for their true destination: stable housing. Shelters, while needed, are not the silver bullet solution to meaningfully addressing homelessness. Housing is. Ultimately, homelessness is a housing problem, not a shelter problem.

6. Direct Outreach And On-Site Services Represent The Future Of Homeless Services

As we describe in Chapter 12 ("On Site Services Remove Barriers"), Camp Hope taught us both the importance and the effectiveness of providing on site services. Effectively serving those experiencing homelessness in general, but unsheltered homelessness in particular, can be divided into two phases: Phase one is outreach where service providers find and contact those experiencing homelessness where they are, whether under a bridge or in a homeless camp. Phase two is providing services on site where the homeless live, not waiting for them to come to an office or other location. At Camp Hope, our outreach phase was no problem because 84% of the known-and-counted unsheltered homeless were in the Camp. The Administration's "Homeless Plan 2.0" envisioned something described as "Compassionate Accountability" that involved using law enforcement to force those experiencing homelessness (such as the residents of Camp Hope) into shelters (particularly the City's TRAC shelter) where they could be held accountable for any services received.[139] While shelters should offer needed services, forcing people into shelters (that may be inappropriate to their needs) to receive services is not particularly effective. Direct outreach and on site services are effective, and Camp Hope demonstrated it. Taking this lesson forward, homeless services providers will need to factor in how to better engage in direct outreach and provide on site services. Direct outreach and on site services do NOT represent "enabling people to be homeless." Rather, they represent empowering people to survive until something better is available. What else are they supposed to do in the midst of an historic housing shortage when affordable housing options could be as much as three years away and there are no available shelters that are appropriate to their needs (mental health issues, substance abuse, physical challenges, etc.)?

7. Identification Restoration Is A Priority

When Jewels Helping Hands conducted 601 assessments of the residents at Camp Hope, the results were eye-opening. Out of 601 Camp Residents assessed 598 (or 99.5%) said they needed their identification restored. In other words, nearly every person residing in the largest homeless encampment in the State of Washington said they needed some form of ID restoration in order to move forward. Welcome to what is perhaps the most common barrier in the homeless community: lost or missing ID. As experienced homeless service providers know, valid and current ID is the gateway to all other services. Without it you can't access State social services (DSHS), or other government benefits, complete a housing application, complete a job application, and more. This reality places the restoration of lost ID at the top of any homeless services needs list. As we saw earlier, *"The Identification Connection"* program was able to coordinate on site ID restoration services resulting in the restoration of 106 birth certificates and 400 State IDs. When issued, new IDs were sent to a centralized location where they could be received and copied into a permanent file before being distributed to the client .

ID restoration can cost as little as $5 or as much as $65 (or more, especially if starting from scratch with ordering an out-of-state birth certificate and other state fees). Let's talk hypothetically for a moment. If ID restoration for 598 people averaged $20/person, that's a potential price tag roughly $12,000 (okay, $11,960). That's a project that a municipal government or a foundation could easily fund. It's also a project that would have a practical, immediate, and meaningful impact on eliminating a common and crucial barrier for those experiencing homelessness. In other words, it would be money well spent, even an investment in eliminating one of the most common barriers for people working to exit homelessness. It's time for our Community to prioritize - even centralize - identification restoration so that a stream-lined and more permanent process is in place to address this need whenever it arises (and it arises a lot).

8. Peer Navigation Works

As I described back in Chapter 8, our staff and our network of Peer Navigators with lived experience became the "secret weapon" in our work to move the unsheltered residents of Camp Hope forward, helping them solve practical problems and remove potential barriers to building their exit ramp out of homelessness. They worked hard to rebuild trust with people who had lost their trust in caseworkers and systems. And among the homeless, re-building trust - and a sense of community - is as important as finding housing.

But the amazing work of Peer Navigators at Camp Hope also exposed some cracks in the system that need to be addressed by the homeless services community as we move forward (we'll develop some of these further in Lesson 12 below).

First, it revealed that we simply don't have enough qualified people working as Peers in the homeless services community.

Second, the need for additional qualified Peers leads to the issue of preparation and training. We saw too many recently hired Peers who (for lack of a better description) were simply tossed into "the deep end of the pool" at the Camp and told to figure it out on their own without the preparation and training they needed, and should have received, to be successful. Many eventually became disillusioned and overwhelmed by their caseloads and issues, left the Camp (and their agency), and are no longer working in homeless services. We need better and consistent Peer training.

Third, I'm going to call this the issue of *"time, trauma, and triggers."* People with lived experience are often working through their own personal trauma left over from their journey. On a timeline, some may be only a few months out of addiction and into sobriety. If mental and emotional stability are a function of truth embodied over time (and they are), then many newly-hired Peers have not had the time they need to process their old traumas. Their old trauma can return like an unexpected wave - a tsunami from their past - triggered by working closely with people who are also deeply traumatized and haven't begun their own journey of healing. Working among the unsheltered homeless is very intensive and demanding work, and those we onboard into our agencies as Peer Navigators should be closely examined as to their *"time, trauma, and triggers."* Otherwise, like inadequate preparation and training, we may be setting them up for profound failure and their own personal set-backs.

9. Life Skills Must Be Re-built

We touched on this earlier under "Step 9" but its importance warrants repeating it here. As service providers, we need to re-think whether we are setting people up for success or failure in the process of helping them find stable housing. It's only stable if it can be maintained long-term. And the loss of many basic life skills among the unsheltered homeless (and even among many of the sheltered homeless) often jeopardizes the housing they've worked so hard to obtain. When I was on the board of a local men's shelter, we used to require the men staying there to sign up to do basic chores. Each chore was designed to take no more than 15 to 20 minutes, and taught a basic, practical life-skill. Chores included such things as wiping down tables after dinner, doing dishes and cleaning the kitchen after dinner, mopping the floor, cleaning the 2 bathrooms, cleaning the shower, emptying the trash cans, and a few others, all of which were activities that they would one day be doing in their own places (hopefully!). In other words, basic life skills. Trust me. As a Camp Manager (and chief garbage collector) at Camp Hope, I've witnessed up-close-and-personal what happens when people lose (or forget) such basic life skills. Helping them recover those lost life skills can be as important to their success as helping them find housing. It may prevent them from losing it.

Taking this lesson forward, classes on basic life skills should become an integral part - if not a required part - of any plan for wrap-around supportive services that we offer to those we work with for stable housing. For many of those we serve, keeping what they have gained is as much of a challenge as getting housing (which is why many of them have gained and lost housing more than once).

10. Employing the Unemployable

One of the requirements for maintaining stable housing is income. After all, sooner or later you have to pay the rent and utilities (and that little nuisance thing called "eating and living"). And, generally speaking, income means employment. For the unsheltered homeless (and for many of the sheltered homeless), finding employment can be a challenge, due to barriers that can make them "unemployable." After all, who wants to hire someone with a "criminal record" or a history of drug use, or who has no ID and can't complete a required Form I-9?

Camp Hope taught us the importance of offering employment opportunities to people considered "unemployable" due to their journey through homelessness and the accumulation of barriers that must be overcome in order to achieve their personal *Shalom* of stable housing. As a community of service providers, as well as a larger Community, we need to consider how we can sponsor, fund, and offer on-going pre-employment programs like the PEPP program offered by WSDOT (that we described in Chapter 9), or the "Roadmap to Success" job-readiness program offered by Pioneer Human Services, to those experiencing homelessness and needing to find meaningful employment. Even a website-based centralized information hub of groups or agencies offering pre-employment training would be a helpful start.

11. Safe Parking Areas Are Important

As we discussed at length in Chapter 14, during the 18 months of its existence, Camp Hope was the largest "safe parking lot" in eastern Washington, and maybe in the state. Camp Hope demonstrated that the need for safe parking lots is very real (we eventually had to turn people away who wanted to bring their RVs into the Camp. No room). This important need could be met in a couple of different ways. *First,* non-profits, such as Churches, could use surplus property or unused parking lot space to offer a safe parking lot (be sure to read Chapter 14 before you do!). *Second,* municipalities could lease or donate appropriate surplus property to an organization or agency that wanted to offer (and had a plan to manage) a safe parking lot. Safe parking lots represent one more option for people experiencing homelessness where they can legally and safely exist while they figure out their next step. And municipalities that don't want to sponsor safe parking lots could play a meaningful role by making them legal (perhaps via a zoning and permitting process) and eligible for municipal services.

12. We Need To Quantify The Holes In Homeless Services

Camp Hope exposed serious cracks - even glaring holes - in our system of social services that serves those experiencing homelessness. And a basic principle should inform us, namely that "You can't fix what you don't know." A brief list of some of the most important and glaring holes that need to be fixed should include the following.

"You can't fix what you don't know."

Insufficient Shelter/Transitional Housing Beds. As we detailed in Chapter 4, "Homelessness Is Larger Than You Think," Spokane has sufficient shelter beds for only 46% of its known and counted homeless population. This presents a problem for how we care for those experiencing homelessness while they wait for affordable housing options to become available, or while they work on eliminating the barriers that prevent them from accessing housing when it is available. As a Community, we need to figure out how to provide additional appropriate and "comprehensive" shelter space, if even on a temporary basis. I use the word "comprehensive" intentionally. For example, why would anyone open a large congregate shelter whose operating cost is unsustainable long-term, with no restrooms, no showers or hygiene facilities, no laundry, no storage, and no kitchen facility for preparing meals, and that you don't own and which could be sold out from under you whenever the owner chooses to do so, while the owner retains the value of any improvements you paid to make? A "comprehensive" shelter would be one that satisfies all of these requirements while serving the purpose of providing a transitional living arrangement for those waiting for stable housing to come available.

Let's take a moment and think of our City's shelters like the boarding gate areas of an airport. The purpose of any airport boarding gate area is to allow people to temporarily congregate while they wait for their flight to their ultimate destination. It isn't the purpose of an airport boarding area to simply accumulate people with nowhere to go and no plan for leaving. They may have food and restroom facilities available while they wait, but the goal isn't to stay there and enjoy the facilities. No one should live permanently at a boarding gate waiting for a promised plane that never arrives. The goal is for them to move on to the next leg of their journey and to do it as quickly and safely as possible. Our shelter system should be like that, *We're glad you're here, and happy to serve you while you wait. Now, let's figure out where you're going next and how to get you there as quickly and safely as possible.* That should be the role of such a "comprehensive" shelter, and it should be the topic of a meaningful Community discussion that rises above NIMBYism and political divisiveness.

Mental Health Services. As I write this, I'm sitting at a table next to the resources trailer at Camp Hope. Sitting behind me is a homeless individual who has hung out around the Camp off and on for several months. She's known to the staff and security as having serious mental health issues. This morning she has spent the past hour or more having a verbal conversation with the voices in her head. At a recent symposium, I listened to a mental health professional, who specializes in mental health issues among those experiencing homelessness, tell the audience that the largest supplier of mental health services in America is . . . wait for it . . . our nation's jail and prison system! Last week, we had to get law enforcement involved for a Camp resident whose mental health challenges caused her to act out and be disruptive. We called in a behavioral health team from a local agency. They determined that she was delusional, was a potential threat to herself and others, and was resisting any attempt to offer services. The agency made a call to law enforcement and requested a "DCR" or "Designated Crisis Responder." Law enforcement eventually came (when an officer was available and not on a higher priority call) and removed her from the Camp for a 72-hour mental health hold and evaluation.[140]

The woman behind me this morning is not disruptive, violent, or acting out, so a call to either the county-designated mental health professional or the police either wouldn't get a response, or wouldn't result in any action. Where is this person supposed to go to get help? In September of 2021, Spokane County - in partnership with Pioneer Health Service - opened a new Spokane Regional Stabilization Center with 47 in-patient mental health "stabilization" beds to be used by law enforcement for "pre-booked individuals, or those who have not been charged with a crime but were escorted to the center by police."[141] Another regional health care provider announced plans in May of 2023 to offer mental health services at a new behavioral health clinic in Hillyard.[142] What remains unknown is how would such facilities serve an individual like the person I described above, or the many others in the homeless community in need of mental health services? Will there be an outreach program to the 955 unsheltered homeless, and will potential patients be required to make an appointment and come to the office? And if it's found that they need professional help - even civil commitment - are these in-patient mental health facilities open to that portion of the homeless community struggling with untreated mental health issues? And why is involving law enforcement our only "treatment" option in the homeless community? We need a better plan and better options.

One of those better options could be Street Psychiatry. Just over a year ago, a local provider of health care services to the homeless community sent me an article from the *Community Mental Health Journal* titled "Implementing the Street Psychiatry Model in New Haven, CT: Community-Based Care for People Experiencing Unsheltered Homelessness."[143] Those of us involved in homeless services are very aware of how Street Medical outreach (based out of the downtown CHAS Denny-Murphy Clinic) is a proven and valuable - even indispensable - service among the unsheltered homeless in Spokane. Today, as detailed in the article, many communities around the country are discovering that Street Psychiatry is also proving to be a valuable and practical outside-the-box corollary to street medical outreach. Such a mental

Community Mental Health Journal (2021) 57:1427–1434
https://doi.org/10.1007/s10597-021-00846-1

FRESH FOCUS

Implementing the Street Psychiatry Model in New Haven, CT: Community-Based Care for People Experiencing Unsheltered Homelessness

Emma Lo[1] · Brooke Lifland[2] · Eliza C. Buelt[3] · Lilanthi Balasuriya[4] · Jeanne L. Steiner[1]

Received: 15 January 2021 / Accepted: 22 May 2021 / Published online: 31 May 2021
© The Author(s), under exclusive licence to Springer Science+Business Media, LLC, part of Springer Nature 2021

Abstract
"Street psychiatry" is an innovative model that serves people experiencing unsheltered homelessness, a vulnerable population with increased rates of mental illness and substance use disorders. Through community-based delivery of mental health and addiction treatment, street psychiatry helps the street-dwelling population overcome barriers to accessing care through traditional routes. Throughout the United States, street psychiatry programs have arisen in multiple cities, often in partnership with street medicine programs. We discuss the philosophy of street psychiatry, document operational highlights involved in the development of a street psychiatry program in New Haven, CT, suggest key ingredients to implementing a street psychiatry program, and explore challenges and future frontiers. Street psychiatry is an effective person-centered model of service delivery with the potential to be applied in a variety of urban settings to serve people experiencing street homelessness.

Keywords Street psychiatry · Street medicine · Homeless · Unsheltered homelessness · Serious mental illness · Implementation

Introduction

Mental illness and substance use disorders are disproportionately prevalent among people experiencing homelessness. Estimates suggest that between one-quarter and one-half suffer from a serious mental illness or substance use disorder (The, 2010 Annual Homeless Assessment Report to Congress, 2010). They exhibit significantly higher prevalence of psychotic and mood disorders (Fazel et al., 2008), in addition to high rates of childhood trauma, family instability, and poverty (Sullivan, 2000). People experiencing unsheltered

homelessness, also known as "street homeless" or "rough sleepers," bear a particularly heavy burden of mental illness and substance use disorders. They are 1.6 times more likely to suffer from a mental illness or substance use disorder than their sheltered counterparts (Levitt et al., 2009; Montgomery et al., 2016). Meanwhile, health care access for people experiencing homelessness and serious mental illness can be a challenge due to barriers like insurance, transportation, access to phones, mistrust and stigmatization, and prioritization of survival (Martins, 2008); these barriers are magnified for the unsheltered population. When accessing health care, people experiencing homelessness use emergency and hospital care over preventive or primary care; as a result, those who are unsheltered generate costs to the health care system that are more than three times those generated by the sheltered population (Folsom et al., 2005; K. A. Koh & Bencarati, 2019).Unmet mental health care needs are enormous for people experiencing homelessness—21% of respondents of one survey reported an unmet mental health care need (Baggett et al., 2010); though this may be an underestimate since many feel stigmatized if they admit to having a mental health problem. Despite best efforts to refer to mental health or substance use disorder treatment, follow-up does not always occur. While 37% of homeless individuals in one

✉ Emma Lo
Emma.lo@yale.edu

1 Department of Psychiatry, Yale University School of Medicine, Connecticut Mental Health Center, 34 Park St, New Haven, CT 06519, USA

2 Department of Psychiatry, Yale University School of Medicine, 300 George St, New Haven, CT 06511, USA

3 Massachusetts Mental Health Center, 20 Vining St, Boston, MA 02115, USA

4 Yale National Clinician Scholars Program, Yale University School of Medicine, 333 Cedar St, New Haven, CT 06510, USA

health outreach to the unsheltered homeless could prove to be a valuable - even indispensable - service to the Spokane homeless community as well.

Substance Abuse Treatment. Let's start with a question or two. How many in-patient substance abuse sobering and/or treat beds are there in Spokane? Where are they? And how long is the wait to get into one of those facilities? Next, let's pretend for a moment that you are homeless and drug addicted, but you woke up this morning and made the potentially life-changing - even life-saving - decision to break this gawd-awful habit and seek treatment at an in-patient or residential treatment facility. Good choice! Now, you want to know where to go, and how soon they can get you into treatment (yes, back to our original question). Here's your answer: Best case scenario, 2 weeks. But probably longer. Getting Camp Hope residents (who wanted to enter treatment) into detox and/or treatment was so difficult due to a chronic lack of treatment beds that the Department of Commerce funded a new 16-bed sobering unit at Compassionate Addiction Treatment as part of the Right of Way funding initiative. [144]

Welcome to the first set of barriers experienced by anyone in the homeless community looking to break free from substance abuse and needing a place to detox and recover. In the homeless community, a two week wait seems like an eternity, and might as well be never. Then, once they're released from detox or recovery, where can they go, other than back to the street (after all, they're still homeless), for an environment that will support and encourage their new-found sobriety?

Wrap-Around Supportive Service Providers. As I stated earlier in this chapter, it's common knowledge in the homeless services community that we do not have the number of trained, qualified, or experienced people required to provide the wrap-around supportive services needed to help those exiting homelessness to successfully maintain what they've achieved in their new environment. In private conversations I've asked experienced caseworkers how many clients they are working with on their current case load. The average response is around 25, with some carrying a caseload of as many as 40. Best practices calls for a caseload of between 12 and 15. Using the higher-end best practices caseload, the 633 person increase in total homelessness found by the 2023 Point In Time Count should require an *additional* 42 caseworkers. Where are they? Again, policymakers who continue to promise wrap-around supportive services are over-promising and under-delivering. Where are the wrap-around service providers who can provide the needed follow up for the formerly unsheltered homeless who have transitioned to housing, but still need assistance with the adjustment?

My friend Ken Fay is an award-winning documentary filmmaker who worked for NBC/Universal for many years. He has been a Consulting Producer on some of my documentary film work. Ken recently worked on a series of videos for the State of California Education system about McKinney-Vento students. The State is working with McKinney-Vento service providers to develop a web-based training curriculum and tool kit for Schools and law enforcement to help them work more effectively with families and students experiencing homelessness. They're planning to launch the program (called HOPE for Homeless Outreach Program for Education) statewide.[145]

I use my friend's video work on the HOPE program to frame our local issue. The need for many additional wrap-around service providers (caseworkers, outreach workers, peer support workers, etc.) inevitably raises a practical question: where's our training curriculum for the basic aspects of effective homeless services? Let's illustrate this with another hypothetical scenario. You've decided that you want to work in homeless services, but you have no experience and little knowledge of what it involves. Where can you go to learn the basics about such things as homeless outreach, conflict de-escalation, working with homeless families and school students, how to locate and access various housing options and programs that might be available, how to understand and work with the unsheltered homeless, how to work with those staying in homeless shelters, the basics of ID restoration. There's more, but you get the idea. We need consistent base-line training on critical topics that new homeless service workers could access to prepare themselves for working with those experiencing homelessness, or that existing staff could use as continuing education to improve their job skills.[146]

Medical Respite. Every shelter director who has been operating a shelter for any period of time has faced this dilemma. I lost count of the number of times it happened at the shelter where my wife and I served for many years. The phone rings. It's someone from the hospital. They're releasing a patient who is homeless. Can we take them in for the night? (This is a best case scenario. We experienced hospitals simply placing the patient in a taxi and sending them to us unannounced!!) How do you say "No" to someone in need? But how can you care for someone who isn't ambulatory (able to move around and care for themselves) or who needs to have their wound bandage changed daily, or their medications taken regularly (it's illegal for you to dispense them if you aren't a licensed medical professional)? Where are the Medical Respite beds for those experiencing homelessness who have been released from the hospital with no place to recover (there are roughly 20 beds in two or three shelters that have been designated as "respite beds" in Spokane)? There have been recent discussion within the City of Spokane about turning the former Cannon Street Shelter into a medical respite facility, but there is no money to operate it and no designated medically qualified operator to run it. We had to turn people away from Camp Hope simply because we were not equipped to help people with chronic medical conditions or recovering from medical procedures, and we had no appropriate places to send them.

A Handful Of Additional Lessons

We've touched on some of the major lessons, but there are more lessons, both large and small, that deserve mentioning. Here is another "handful" of those lessons.

Grandma Doesn't Belong In A Homeless Camp. During the 18 months of Camp Hope, we had numerous elderly homeless individuals pass through the Camp ("elderly" being defined as 55 or older). They were exceptionally vulnerable and simply did not belong in a homeless camp. We reached out to other agencies for help, such as Washington State's Aging And Long Term Care, but other agencies were as much at a loss for what to do as we were. People elderly and homeless embody a sub-group of overall homelessness that has fallen through the cracks of our homeless and social services support network. We owe it to them to let them know that they haven't been forgotten.

Meaningfully Addressing Homelessness Requires A Community. Homelessness is a Community issue, and meaningfully addressing it will require a broad-based community effort. One of our more encouraging experiences during the 18 months of Camp Hope was the positive response and engagement of so many community members - both individuals and organizations - who simply wanted to know how they could help. Churches came to the Camp and fed the residents. Individuals sponsored pizza-feeds, purchasing 50 large pizzas and dropping them off at the Resource/Access Tent. Others donated clean socks, bought replacement tents (we had to replace a lot of tents after a major wind storm), delivered cases (even pallets) of bottled water, and more. Needs posted on Facebook were quickly met by average community members who simply wanted to serve and make a difference. We experienced on a limited scale what Spokane needs to experience on a much larger scale - our Community rallying and stepping up to serve the homeless, hungry, and marginalized of our Community. What's too often missing is Community leaders with the vision, courage, and willingness to lead and bring the larger Spokane Community together to address our shared, common issue of homelessness and housing insecurity.

Agency Communication, Collaboration, And Cooperation Are Imperatives. Agencies addressing homelessness in Spokane have traditionally been guilty of living and working in their own silos. This tendency to silo off is understandable. Each agency serves a certain clientele, has its own constituency support network (i.e., fund raising, volunteers, etc.), and operates within its own cultural environment and way of doing things. No secrets there. And nearly every agency (I suppose there's an exception out there somewhere) experiences a sense of being overwhelmed by their particular workload. But the size and unchecked growth of homelessness in Spokane - up 36% from 2022 to 2023, and up 119% since 2017 - is going to require more inter-agency communication, collaboration, and cooperation than we have ever seen in the past. Moving forward, it isn't going to be enough to simply "be bigger and do more." We're going to need to communicate, collaborate, and cooperate better - communicating our plans and our target clientele, collaborating with individuals and agencies that do certain tasks better and with greater expertise than we do, and generally cooperating with others who labor in homeless services. That's what a healthy community does. A good example and foreshadowing of what that could look like can be seen regularly on the email list-serve (a GoogleGroup) of the Spokane Homeless Coalition where more than 1,800 Spokane individuals and agencies share information and post specific needs that the poster alone can't meet or solve. At Camp Hope, we worked with multiple agencies that "leaned in" to serve Camp residents, and we were glad to have the advantage of their unique knowledge, skill sets, and expertise. But we also had agencies that, for lack of a better description, "leaned out" and chose not to engage on-site with the Camp or its residents. To meaningfully address and even reduce homelessness in our Community, all of us involved in homeless services will need to become better at our communication, collaboration, and cooperation, because that's the future of homeless services.

We Need A Comprehensive Regional Response To Homelessness. Early 2023 saw the emergence of a group of community leaders with a vision for moving homeless policy out of the world of partisan politics and into an independent regional homeless authority that would oversee, coordinate, and fund a regional response to homelessness. In mid-July of 2023, as I was finalizing this book and preparing it for publication, I spent some time with one of the driving personalities and visionaries behind the proposed regional homeless authority that was being considered for adoption by local elected officials. [147] From my own perspective, I believe Spokane is at a tipping point when it comes to homelessness, homeless policy, and homeless services moving forward, and I believe a regional coordinated policy under a separate umbrella entity is the best pathway forward.

We talked about many things, but specifically about their discussed goal of cutting regional homelessness by 40% in two years. I countered by suggesting that the goal be re-focused on eliminating *unsheltered* homelessness in two years (not reducing, but eliminating), getting the 955 unsheltered homeless off of City streets, out of City parks, and into appropriate housing and services. Eliminating unsheltered homelessness in two years would effectively reduce overall homelessness by 40%. That would be my recommendation for a specific targeted goal. We also talked about their vision of a Navigation Center similar to "the Beacon" in Houston. Such Navigation Center would be a campus, as opposed to a warehouse, spanning 2 or 3 acres. It would be a place where those experiencing homelessness could do laundry, take a shower, get a real meal (prepared on-site in an actual kitchen), get a bed if they need one, and (very important) be assigned to a Peer Navigator who could help them work on a personal exit ramp out of homelessness.

The things we discussed about what a regional homeless authority could do are very achievable goals. But nothing will be achieved if we put the same people in charge of the new entity who got us into this mess in the first place. It's time to "do different," unless we want to be having these same conversations at a higher frustration level a year from now. That's the problem with tipping points - if they don't tip forward, the alternative all too often is to go backwards. And I don't want to go backwards. Do you? [148]

Epilogue

The lessons of Camp Hope are many and varied, some large, some small. Taken as a whole, and embraced by homeless policymakers and service providers - as well as by you and me - they could change our Community for the better. Taking this conversation about Camp Hope and homelessness full circle to where we started it in Chapter 1, we should think of these lessons as our Community stepping stones toward "the way things ought to be" - toward genuine *shalom*, peace, and well-being - not only for those experiencing homelessness, but for ourselves as well. We help them build their *shalom* because, in the process, we build our own *shalom*.

> "But seek the Shalom of the city . . . .
> and pray to the LORD on its behalf,
> for in its Shalom
> you will find your Shalom."
> ~ Jeremiah 29:7

Lessons Camp Hope Taught Us
Summary

1. A Journey From Chaos To Cosmos To Shalom

CHAOS/SURVIVAL
UnSheltered Homelessness
A Low Barrier Shelter
Assessments
On-Site Services
Identification Restoration
Peer Support/Community Building
Substance Abuse Treatment
Physical & Mental Health Assistance
Re-Building Life Skills
Resolving Legal/Court Issues
Employment
Housing (appropriate & affordable)
COSMOS/STABILITY/SHALOM

2. Optic, Narrative, and Tone Matter

3. NIMBYism Limits Community Options

4. Law Enforcement Is Not A Solution To Homelessness

5. Shelters Aren't The Silver Bullet Solution To Solving Homelessness

6. Direct Outreach And On-Site Services Represent The Future Of Homeless Services

7. Identification Restoration Is A Priority

8. Peer Navigation Works!

9. Life Skills Must Be Re-built

10. Employing the Unemployable

11. Safe Parking Areas Are Important

12. We Need To Quantify The Holes In Homeless Services

A Place to Exist

✓ Insufficient Shelter/Transitional Housing Beds.
✓ Mental Health Services.
✓ Substance Abuse Treatment.
✓ Wrap-Around Supportive Service Providers.
✓ Medical Respite.

A Handful Of Additional Lessons
✓ Grandma Doesn't Belong In A Homeless Camp
✓ Meaningfully Addressing Homelessness Requires A Community.
✓ Agency Communication, Collaboration, And Cooperation Are Imperatives
✓ We Need A Comprehensive Regional Response To Homelessness

Appendix: Framing A New Model Moving Forward

It's not an extreme exaggeration to say that much of what has passed for homeless services in America since World War 2, especially when it comes to homeless shelters, was originally built around a model of soup kitchens and shelters developed during the Great Depression of the 1930s. Until fairly recently, homeless services consisted primarily of warehousing and feeding those experiencing homelessness. In recent years - and 20 years is relatively recent - we have slowly added such things as housing counseling, diversion services (giving people assistance to keep their housing and "divert" them from becoming homeless), social services, EBT cards to replace the literal food stamp coupon books of prior generations, some employment training, minimal drug treatment opportunities, and a few other related services. But the model of a shelter and soup kitchen has remained the core of much (if not most) of how we have cared for those experiencing homelessness.

Can you say, "rut"? A quick internet search finds two basic definitions of the word "rut":

1. a long, deep track made by the repeated passage of the wheels of vehicles

2. a habit or pattern of behavior that has become dull and unproductive but is hard to change (e.g., "the administration was stuck in a rut and was losing its direction")

I'll let you - the insightful reader - guess which of these two definitions comes closest to describing the rut that homeless policy in Spokane was stuck in during the years leading up to Camp Hope.

Is comparing present day homeless services with the 1930s and the Great Depression an overstatement? Of course it is, but it's an overstatement with a purpose. If we are to meaningfully address homelessness in its many variations, we have to change the way we do things, the way we deliver homeless services, and the options we offer those experiencing homelessness who are stuck in the ruts we've created. For people emerging from unsheltered homelessness, *Housing First* may not mean a house or an apartment in traditional terms. Their needs may be better met by a pallet house or tiny house in a managed community, or a managed clean and sober house, or a room in a transitional project like the Catalyst project, or some other form of transitional housing that gives them time to make the adjustment from their old life to their new life (and if you don't think such an adjustment is needed, you haven't spend much time working with the unsheltered homeless).

Is There A Camp Hope Model?

Let's be clear and up-front. None of us who were involved in creating Camp Hope wanted or expected to create and manage the largest homeless camp in the State of Washington (and perhaps in the entire Pacific North West). Nope, didn't see that coming. And I'm pretty sure our team would be the first to caution others against it. But reality is a harsh mistress to all who ignore or try to cheat on her. And unsheltered homelessness and homeless camps are a part of reality for communities all across America, but particularly on the West Coast from Spokane to Seattle to

Portland to San Diego. Ignoring them won't make them go away, and using law enforcement to sweep them won't create the services and options they need to build their individual exit-ramps out of homelessness. So, at the risk of irritating pundits, politicians, business leaders, service providers, and a host of others, what follows is a suggested model (or at least suggestions for creating a model) for managing the homeless camp that may be forming in your community. Consider it the practical application of everything we've covered in this book. Not everything will apply to your particular situation, but at the very least it will help you think through your decision making process.

In many ways, what follows represents an ongoing lesson on how collaboration and cooperation between governments, non-profits and community partners is more effective and productive than confrontation, obstruction, and resistance. We are a better community and can meet more challenges when we work together.

Securing The Basics To Survive

There are times in managing a homeless camp when you find yourself multi-tasking many things, and many priorities, all at once (which, I suppose, is the definition of multi-tasking). But there are a handful of items that should be considered high priority, some of which Julie Garcia touched on in Chapter 6 and that we need to expand on here, including: Food, Water, Garbage, Sanitation & Porta Potties, Fire Safety, Winter Warmth/Summer Cooling ,and Health & Medical Support. We discovered that meeting many of these basic needs for the Camp eventually came down to funding, in-kind donations, and community participation.

Food - The residents of Camp Hope ate their way through mountains of peanut butter and jelly (PB&J) sandwiches, assembled and delivered by volunteers. Individuals and organizations purchased and donated hundreds of pizzas. Churches came down and did hamburger & hot dog BBQs for the residents. Food banks donated a variety of food supplies. Community partners delivered fresh food boxes. Local Cafes and pastry shops donated breakfast pastries. A local soda pop distributor donated pallets of soft drinks. Donors purchased pallets of bottled water (especially important during the summer months). And residents used their EBT cards to purchase personal groceries. And while we didn't have a budget to prepare regular meals, we always tried to have something to eat available for residents every day (yes, even if only PB&J!).

Make the food needs of the Camp you're managing known to the wider Community. You'll be surprised by who will respond. Set up a Facebook page. Establish a GoogleGroups email list-serve where management can post needs and interested people can respond. Many people in the Community want to help. They just need some practical guidance on what you need and what they can do.

Practical Takeaway - Create a food plan for the camp you manage.

Water - Even inexpensive bottled water can get expensive when you're using pallets of water at a time. But don't hesitate to let the Community know that they can donate cases - and even a pallet - of water. Everything helps. To meet peoples' need for drinking and washing water, we purchased three 300-gallon plastic water tanks from a local farm supply company and fitted them with spigots (plastic spigots are best because they won't freeze as easily in cold weather) so that residents could re-fill their personal containers whenever they needed to. During the cold winter months we inserted heaters to keep the tanks from freezing. Before WSDOT and Commerce funding came available, we filled the tanks using a garden hose that ran from a neighbor's house a block away, and across two streets (forcing yours truly to become an expert in broken hose repair). This work-around was necessary because the City of Spokane refused to authorize residential water service to the Camp (unfortunately demonstrating confrontation and obstruction, rather than collaboration and cooperation). After Commerce funding came available, we contracted with a private company to fill the tanks once a week.

Practical Takeaway - Create a water plan for the camp you manage.

Garbage - A homeless camp is like any small town or community. It produces garbage, but without any infrastructure for handling it. With 689 residents, Camp Hope at its peak was a small eastern Washington town on one city block, but without city services. To its credit, the City of Spokane provided 3 medium-sized dumpsters (eventually, they added a fourth) for Camp use. One of the early routines I established as Camp Manager for water, garbage, and sanitation was daily garbage collection. We kept an ample supply of 40-gallon trash bags and handed them out to Campers to use for their garbage. Each morning the first thing we would do was to go through the Camp collecting any garbage left outside tents, and picking up any stray garbage we could find (especially food that had been left out), and hauling all garbage out of the Camp to the dumpsters on the perimeter. I regarded this a health priority for the Camp. Garbage, especially open food, attracts mice and other vermin. Mice equals mouse droppings which equals a health hazard. On a practical level, I taught those who worked with me to always handle garbage with gloves, a snow shovel, and a rake. I made it a point to avoid handling garbage with my hands (even with gloves) as much as possible. Raking up garbage, collecting it with a snow shovel, and placing it in a trash can equipped with a trash bag liner made it much easier and safer to handle.

Practical Takeaway - Create a plan to regularly handle garbage in the camp you manage.

Sanitation & Porta Potties - Welcome to no one's favorite topic. While the City of Spokane was willing to provide trash dumpsters, they refused to provide porta potties (the only rationale I could find was that the City owned the dumpsters, but not the porta potties). Lack of adequate sanitation is a health issue, and providing adequate sanitation should be a top priority. Fortunately, at Camp Hope, a private party initially paid for four porta-potties. As the Camp grew, four porta potties quickly became twelve, which were emptied and cleaned once a week. Again, after Department of Commerce funding came available, the cleaning schedule became more frequent . . . to everyone's relief!

Practical Takeaway - Create a plan to handle sanitation in the camp you manage.

Fire Safety - We worked pro-actively with the local Fire officials on fire safety protocols such as the placement of approved fire extinguishers in key locations throughout the Camp as directed by the Fire Department (and, yes, they got used). The Fire Marshall would also pay us regular visits to check on our compliance with such things as unfettered egress from the Resource/Access Tent and the proper placement of sufficient fire extinguishers. When WSDOT assumed oversight of the Camp, we worked with WSDOT and the Fire Department to create a graveled fire lane through the center of the Camp, so that in the event of a fire, the Fire Department would have the ability to bring heavy equipment into the Camp to fight it. Thankfully, it was never needed, but a Fire Battalion Chief told me that, in his opinion, it was one of the wisest management decisions we could have made. "With the right tent fire and a strong wind," he once told me, "half this Camp would be ashes over the freeway before we could get here."

We worked with Fire officials to reconcile two conflicting realities. Most Camp residents had no way to cook or prepare food without some form of open burning, while the Fire Department had a reasonable safety concern that open fires around flammable tents could result in a fast moving and disastrous fire in the Camp. We compromised with rules that no open fire could be left unattended (I got yelled at by one resident when I used his coffee pot to douse the open fire he was using to heat it up while leaving it unattended), and that all open fires had to be in fire-proof containers (like a grill-basket) and preferably six feet from any tent.

During the Winter months, propane for personal "Buddy Heaters" became an issue, first supplying enough propane to make a difference for so many people, and second teaching people how to use it safely. We found it necessary to outlaw "hijackers," adapters that allow someone to transfer propane from larger tanks to smaller tanks, like campers use for their camp stoves, and we used for "Buddy Heaters." Transferring propane can be dangerous, as two campers discovered when transferring propane near an open flame resulted in a flash fire, an exploding propane tank, and a trip for one of them to Seattle's Harbor View Burn Unit. Thankfully, only one tent was destroyed, and both campers recovered from their experience, but the entire Camp learned a lesson in the dangers of mishandling propane. In the 18 months of the Camp, and among the 689 residents, we only experienced three serious fires - two RV fires (one caused by an electrical overload and one gas related) and one serious tent fire caused by mis-handled propane.

Practical Takeaway - Work with local Fire Officials to create a plan and protocols to handle fire issues and concerns.

Winter Warming/Summer Cooling Plan - Weather can be brutal on the unsheltered homeless, especially when no provision is made by homeless policymakers to provide 24/7 warming or cooling centers. At Camp Hope, the Resource/Access Tent (located directly across the street from the Camp) became both. It began as our cooling center during the summer heat of 2022. When Fall arrived with much cooler temperatures, it became our warming center for Camp residents. To cool the tent we rented two large industrial-sized swamp coolers. To heat the Tent, we rented a large industrial heater that burned diesel fuel and blew hot air into the Tent to keep the inside temperature tolerable. For additional winter warming, inside the Camp itself we set up two large 10X20 warming tents with propane heaters to keep them warm. Camp residents needing to warm up at night could visit these smaller warming tents. Our goal was simple: to prevent people from experiencing heat stroke in the summer, or freezing to death during the hard winter months (especially at night), or from experiencing hypothermia and frostbite.

Practical Takeaway - Start early to develop your summer cooling and winter warming plans.

Health & Medical Support. Camp Hope managers had two basic health and medical concerns. First, we knew we needed the involvement of the local County Department of Health (known as the Spokane Regional Health District). So, we decided to be pro-active and invite SRHD representatives to come to the camp and look for community health concerns that we should address. They agreed to come, to look for potential health issues, and to do individual health assessments and vaccinations. Second, we knew we also had to address the immediate medical issues among the Camp residents. For this we invited the regular participation of Street Medical Teams from the CHAS Denny-Murphy Clinic in Spokane. Medical practitioners came to the camp twice a week, tending to patients in the Resource/Access Tent, filling or replacing prescriptions, and walking through the Camp looking for anyone in need of medical attention. When Street Medical personnel weren't available, we took people needing immediate help to the Providence Community (Free) Clinic downtown. A visit by a Street Medical team, or a trip to the Providence Community Clinic was far less costly for everyone involved than an ambulance trip to a local emergency room (and, yes, we had a few of those, too).

Practical Takeaway - Work with local health officials and medical service providers to protect the health of the Camp community, and to meet the immediate medical needs of the residents.

Fencing, Counting, And Badging

On closing day at Camp Hope, a handful of dignitaries came to observe and celebrate the event. One of them, a Spokane City Council member, shared an anecdote with me that I had not heard before. It seems that, in the early stages of Camp Hope on the WSDOT property, this person had suggested to the City Administration that they take the initiative to put a fence around the Camp, badge and count the residents, and create a process for resolving the Camp by finding out what the residents needed to exit homelessness. Unfortunately, those suggestions fell on deaf ears. Not until the Camp was the size of a small town and the

Departments of Commerce and Transportation took oversight of the Camp (in September) did those earlier suggestions become a reality. Fencing, badging, and counting would become critical components of our work to resolve the Camp and move the residents forward and out of homelessness.

The first step in actively managing a homeless camp is to wrap your head around who and what you're dealing with. Fencing, counting, and badging are about securing the camp, identifying it's borders and size, along with who belongs in the Camp and who doesn't. Before WSDOT fenced the Camp and installed gates, anyone could access Camp Hope, including people with bad intentions who didn't belong there. From the armed vigilante looking for a stolen laptop (that wasn't in the Camp) to drug dealers who would drive down the center alley of the Camp and troll for customers (why else would a brand new Lexus be slowly parading through a homeless camp?), access control became increasingly important to protect the Camp residents and nearby local businesses. One business close to the Camp admitted that once the fences went up and badging was in place, suspicious activity and crime around his business noticeably fell. Once badging was completed (it took a couple of weeks), only people with valid ID badges could access the Camp. Closing the Camp to anyone not badged also stopped the uncontrolled growth of the Camp (and, yes, we had to turn people away. After all, the Camp only contained 84% of the known and counted unsheltered homeless in Spokane. The remaining 14% were still looking for a safe place to exist).

Practical Takeaway - Work with local officials to secure the Camp and to begin the process of identifying and quantifying those involved, and starting the process of assessing what they need to build an exit ramp out of homelessness.

Working Through The "Steps"

Earlier we offered 12 *steps* for moving people from the *chaos* of unsheltered homelessness to the *cosmos* and *shalom* of stability (including stable housing). You'll see those *steps* in the graphic on this page. Consider these steps as a basic outline for any model that is created to successfully resolve any encampment of people experiencing unsheltered homelessness and to move the residents forward into

CHAOS/SURVIVAL
1 - UnSheltered Homelessness
2 - A Low Barrier Shelter
3 - Assessments
4 - On-Site Services
5 - Identification Restoration
6 - Peer Support/Community Building
7 - Substance Abuse Treatment
8 - Physical & Mental Health Assistance
9 - Re-Building Life Skills
10 - Resolving Legal/Court Issues
11 - Employment
12 - Housing (appropriate & affordable)
COSMOS/STABILITY/SHALOM

something better (and, yes, these steps also tend to work for the Sheltered homeless as well). Think of them as a check-list of your essential components to work through in any plan to successfully move people forward. At the end of each check-list item we will offer a "Check-List Action Item," a recommendation intended to help you focus on what to do with what you've learned. In the spirit of *The Martian* (see our comments in the Introduction), think of these check-list items as the problems that need to be solved, one after another, in order to go home. Working with the unsheltered homeless, if you and they solve enough of these problems, achieve enough of these steps, both you and they get to go home. Think of what follows as your "How The Martian Goes Home" check-list for how to get there.

UnSheltered Homelessness - In any journey into the unknown, the first step is always the biggest challenge we face. Here, the first step of the journey is embracing and connecting with those experiencing unsheltered homelessness. They aren't Old Testament lepers, or Medieval carriers of Bubonic plague. They're people experiencing unsheltered homelessness in a homeless camp. Chances are good they don't want to be there any more than you do. A story illustrates the problem. I was standing outside the Resource/Access Tent when I was approached by two caseworkers from a local agency. "Can I help you?" I asked. "We're looking for (another case worker)," one of them replied. "Oh, they may be in the Camp," I said. "I can take you in and we can find them," I offered. Their eyes got wide and then came the moment that stuck with me, "Oh, no," one of them replied, "We aren't allowed to go into the Camp."

If you think this is an isolated case, you'd be wrong. The only actual contact most homeless service agencies have with the unsheltered homeless is when the homeless show up at the agency office looking for help. And the same problem exists among City homeless policymakers. In the 18 months of Camp Hope, no one from the City's Community Housing and Human Services (CHHS) Department ever visited the Camp or spent time getting to know the very people they are making policies about. How can you make life-altering policy for people you've never spent time getting to know and whose journey into and through homelessness you don't understand? As a Community, we will never meaningfully address homelessness until we embrace and connect with those experiencing it.

Check-List Action Item - This is perhaps the hardest action of all, embracing the reality - the true size and nature - of homelessness in your community and making the conscious choice to engage it.

A Low Barrier Shelter. In our initial assessments of 600 Camp Hope residents in the Summer of 2022, 51 of the 600 individuals assessed (or 8.5%) said they would be willing to go to a low-barrier shelter, depending on who was operating it, which translates into how well it is run and how the shelter staff treat or mistreat the guests. One of the early steps in organizing any homeless encampment should be to contact local shelters, determine which ones are truly low-barrier (accepting people in whatever condition they happen to be in, so long as they are not a threat to themselves or others), which ones have open beds, and how many beds are open and available on any given night, and their willingness to work with you as you refer people to them from the Camp. Shelter avoidance among unsheltered populations is common, and often deep-rooted due to previous negative experiences. Rebuilding trust between shelter operators and the unsheltered should be a common goal.

Check-List Action Item - Identify and contact local area shelters, discovering their actual capacity and their willingness to work with your population, including sending their staff to connect with your people.

Assessments. It's impossible to help someone build an exit ramp out of homelessness if neither you nor they know what they need. That's where assessments come in. I'm going to make a distinction between *initial* assessments and *in-depth* assessments. An initial assessment enables you to build a "big picture" road map for the general needs that exist, how wide-spread or common those needs are, and where you will need to do more in-depth assessments as you move forward (for example, a housing assessment might go into a detailed history of any prior housing in order to discover actions like evictions that could be barriers to any future housing). At the end of this Appendix you'll find "Potential Initial Assessment Questions." I've adapted the questions on this Potential Initial Assessment from an assessment we did at Camp Hope in July of 2022, plus additional questions we later wished we had asked. Hindsight is always much clearer than foresight. As I described in Chapter 13, certain assessment questions yielded answers that surprised us and guided our planning moving forward as we looked for service providers to meet the needs we discovered. And each sub-divided topic could be the subject for a later, more detailed assessment.

Check-List Action Item - Take an initial assessment of your population. Utilize the Potential Initial Assessment Questions at the end of this Chapter. Take it sooner, rather than later.

On-Site Services. Earlier, in Chapter 12, we talked about the importance of on-site services. One of our early challenges at Camp Hope was finding and partnering with organizations that could meet certain needs. We partnered with Compassion Addiction Treatment to address the issue of substance abuse. They brought their mobile outreach RV to the Camp and parked it next to the Resource/Access Tent so that they could meet, connect with, and council those who were ready to address their substance abuse without having to send them to their downtown office. Other agencies agreed to send their Peer Navigators or housing navigators to the Camp to meet with residents in the Resource/Access Tent. The bottom line is that we worked with agencies, caseworkers, and peer navigators who were willing to provide on-site assistance. It's one of the most important ways we eliminate potential barriers to needed services.

Check-List Action Item - Collaborate with homeless services agencies, caseworkers, and peer navigators who are willing to work on-site to get things done. Consider providing them with a place on-site (a tent, a mobile outreach trailer, etc) where they can meet and work with clients.

Identification Restoration. As we've previously discussed, identification restoration surfaced as a major issue for the residents of Camp Hope, as our initial assessments revealed that 98% of camp residents needed some level of ID restoration. When we speak about restoring ID, we're talking primarily about what we refer to as *core documents*: birth certificates, Social Security Cards, and Driver's Licenses (or other State issued ID). Restoring these *core documents* became the primary task of a team we established to address it. Many agencies will tell you that they have someone who is knowledgeable about ID restoration, but too often it's an *ad hoc* arrangement that sort of works. But we saw problems. *First*, existing *ad hoc* procedures were simply inadequate for the volume that we had to deal with (like 598 people needing help). *Second*, we discovered that some agencies would actually return IDs (especially SS Cards) if the incoming mail containing the ID wasn't addressed to the caseworker (rather than the client). *Third*, we needed to get the cooperation and involvement of two state agencies (the Departments of Licensing and Health) to create a one-stop shop for on-site ID restoration. *Fourth*, all of this needed to be co-ordinated by someone (preferably a caseworker) with extensive knowledge and experience in working with those agencies to help people experiencing homelessness restore lost IDs. In response, our ID Restoration lead person created a system designed to handle large volume over a relatively short period of time (once per week for 6 weeks) while arranging for both critical State Departments to participate on-site. The Department of Licensing could look to see if someone previously had an ID in the State, re-issue it, and provide a printed temporary ID on-site. The Department of Health could issue replacement birth certificates for those born in-state, or reach out to the state of their birth to request a replacement birth certificate from that state. Social Security SS-5 Forms (to request a replacement SS Card) could be filled out with an on-site caseworker and sent off. All returning mail with IDs was sent to a secure mailing address where it could be collected, photocopied, and then distributed to the client. By the time the program ended its six-week run, the Department of health had issued 106 birth certificates, and the Department of Licensing had issued 400 ID cards. Based on the total of birth certificates and ID cards issued, that's an 85% success rate with the 598 people who said they needed ID restoration from our initial assessments!

Check-List Action Item - Find an individual or agency in your homeless services community with extensive successful experience with ID restoration among the homeless. Work with them to build a system and a team of ID restoration specialists who can focus on this need and successfully process a large volume of people needing IDs.

Peer Navigator Support. As we discovered in Chapter 14 (and discussed in Chapter 22, Step 6), the Peer Navigators - people with lived experiences at overcoming many of the same issues as those experiencing homelessness - were the "secret weapons" in our work to move people forward from life in the Camp to something better. It's time now to build a team/network of available, willing, and experienced Peer Navigators. People who have successfully built their own exit ramp out of homelessness and it's related issues are the people best qualified to motivate and navigate others to do the same. These need to be stable and seasoned Peers who are not coming to their first rodeo. It is intense work, filled with potential "triggers" for those who are still in recovery themselves. We saw significant turnover among Peers due to their not being stable enough themselves to closely interact with Camp residents who were deep in their own struggles.

Check-List Action Item - Collaborate with available agencies to build a network of Peer Navigators who are specialists in their particular service field (i.e., housing, substance abuse & recovery, mental health, etc.), and are stable and mature enough to work successfully in such a challenging atmosphere without being "triggered."

Substance Abuse Treatment. There is a common mythology that substance abuse (or drug addiction) is the primary cause of homelessness. But the primary cause(s) of homelessness vary depending on whose report or study you read. Consider these three examples. *First*, according to Community Solutions (citing a HUD study), about 21% of those experiencing homelessness in 2022 reported having a severe mental illness, while 16% reported chronic substance abuse. In LA County, 26% of those experiencing

2023 Pont In Time Count Reasons Cited for Homelessness	
Reason Cited	Percent %
Lack of Affordable Housing	20%
Lack of Family or Other Support	13%
Substance Abuse	12%
Unemployment	12%
Mental Health Problems	10%

homelessness in 2018 reported a severe mental illness, and 15% reported a substance use disorder. Again, according to Community Solutions, the most reliable predictor of homelessness is a lack of affordable housing, as opposed to substance abuse or mental health issues.[149] *Second*, according to the City of Riverside (California), the top causes of homelessness are: 1) Lack of affordable housing, 2) Unemployment, 3) Poverty, 4) Low wages, 5) Mental illness and the lack of needed services (Single adult individuals), and 6) Substance abuse and the lack of needed services (Single adult individuals).[150] *Third*, according to Spokane's 2023 Point In Time Count (see the graphic on this page), the top 5 reasons cited by respondents for their homelessness were: 1) Lack of Affordable Housing, 2) Lack of Family or Other Support, 3) Substance abuse, 4) Unemployment, and 5) Mental Health Problems. A seldom acknowledged reality is that substance abuse is frequently a result of homelessness, not a cause. But either way, substance abuse remains a challenge for the unsheltered homeless community, a life-altering barrier that needs to be addressed for their success moving forward.

Meaningfully addressing substance abuse among those experiencing homelessness requires both their participation and the participation of those agencies, counselors and Peer Navigators that can provide them with the counseling, sobering help, and treatment services they need to move forward. Your initial assessments will give you an idea of who and how many might be ready to move forward toward sobriety and treatment, but you also need to know who can help. In our work at Camp Hope, the lack of adequate sobering beds in the City quickly became a recognized barrier for those seeking sobriety. For the residents of Camp Hope, the Department of Commerce provided funding to Compassionate Addiction Treatment to create a new sobering unit with 16 beds for those who were ready to start their journey toward sobriety and dealing with their substance abuse issues.

Check-List Action Item - Identify, collaborate, and build a service network with those agencies, caseworkers, and Peer Navigators that have the ability and capacity to move people in your population toward counseling, sobriety, and treatment.

Physical & Mental Health Assistance. Physical and Mental Health are related, but I'm going to divide them into two stories. Let's start with physical medical assistance. In the pre-COVID weeks leading up to March of 2020 when the pandemic changed everything, I was filming a street medical team working among the homeless in Spokane. We were in front of *The City Gate* in Spokane when I filmed an individual who came up to the lead street doctor (name withheld) complaining about his left arm. When he pulled up his sleeve to show the doc what was going on, we all caught our collective breaths. His forearm - from fingertips to elbow - had swollen up to more than twice its normal size, the result of an infected "fight bite." The street doctor managed to keep his calm composure and suggested (strongly) that his new patient go to the hospital (NOW!) and get it treated. The doc arranged for an ambulance and told the attendants that this was serious and needed to be aggressively treated. He later confided that this individual was within 24 hours of losing his arm. The good news is that two weeks later, as I was filming street medical outreach at the weekly *Blessings Under The Bridge* outreach event, the same individual showed up and announced to the street medical team that his arm had healed and that he was doing well. My point (in case you missed it) is the absolute life-saving importance of providing physical medical assistance on-site to the unsheltered homeless.

The second part of this point has to do with mental health assistance. Allow me to tell you about Robert, a resident of Camp Hope where I served as a Day Manager.[151] Robert had serious mental health issues. He would walk around the camp, interfering in other peoples business and having loud and animated conversations with no one in particular. He was also a pyro who enjoyed setting things on fire, including one of our porta potties. We finally had to remove Robert from the Camp, both for his safety and for the safety of the other residents. But we knew he had no where else to go, so we allowed him to camp alone on the property across the street from the Camp where the Resource/Access Tent was located and where we could keep in eye on him. But, the day came when Robert's mental health issues became too much for him (and us). The police were called, he reacted poorly to being confronted, and was arrested. The good news was that, as a result of that encounter and arrest, he received treatment, and was placed back on needed medications. At last report, he was in transitional housing and doing well. But what does it say about us as a Community that our jails have to be the front-line (and largest) providers of mental health services to those experiencing homelessness? What kind of expense could we as a Community avoid if we were able to offer on-site street medical assistance in the form of street psychiatry for people like Robert?

Check-List Action Item - This action step is as much a cautionary tale as it is an action step. You are going to encounter physical and mental health situations where you may have limited abilities or resources with which to respond to them. Have a plan for how you are going to respond. If there are street medical teams in your community, try to develop a working relationship with them as a first step before the ususal fall-back response of calling 911. A street medical team administering $25 worth of medications on-site on the street can prevent a $5,000 trip to the emergency room to treat a more advanced (and untreated) condition. And actual mental health workers who are willing to work on-site with your population could prevent a law enforcement confrontation that could end badly. Work to build those professional networks that can be called on when needed.

Re-Building Life Skills. Unsheltered homelessness is a thief that robs those experiencing it of many things: their health, their dignity, their relationships, and their life-skills, to name just a few. Life skills are the daily living skills you and I take for granted, things like civil communication, money management, time management, personal hygiene, respect for other people's property, and just picking up after oneself (as the former chief garbage collector for a camp of 689, I could give details that you really don't want to know, so take my word for it). Such life skills get replaced with what I call "survival skills." In survival mode, the common form of communication frequently involves yelling, aggressive posturing, lots of trauma and drama ("I'll whip you're a** if you touch my stuff"), and other behaviors best understood as forms of self-protection and survival. Such survival skills might work in a homeless camp, but they quickly become barriers that can derail their journey out of homelessness. Consider the couple who kicked in someone's apartment door at the transitional housing facility where they lived, thinking another resident had stolen their property. Unfortunately, everyone involved got removed from the facility. Those working to build an exit ramp out of unsheltered homelessness may need assistance transitioning out of "survival mode" and recovering the basic life skills they will need to maintain themselves in whatever housing they achieve.

Check-List Action Item - It's time to find, partner, and collaborate with agencies and ministries that offer classes and mentoring on such basics as cooking (check to see if a regional food bank offers classes on how to cook using products they frequently distribute), money management (how to budget for rent, utilities, food, essentials, etc.), relationship communication, job skills, responsible renters classes, etc.

Appendix: Framing A New Model Moving Forward

Resolving Legal/Court Issues. As we observed earlier in Step 10 of Chapter 21, those who have been homeless on the streets of Spokane for any length of time have probably had an encounter with local law enforcement. Such encounters frequently result in legal citations for such things as Trespassing or 3rd Degree Possession of Stolen Property (usually, a shopping cart). Some of their citations may be more serious, but you get the idea. These citations often combine with lost life-skills - such as a loss of time management skills - to produce such things as missed court appearances and bench warrants being issued for failure to appear (Did you know that an outstanding warrant prevents you from accessing any government services?). All such legal entanglements create additional barriers for those seeking to build an exit ramp out of homelessness (yes, they pop up on background checks for housing and jobs).

In working with the residents of Camp Hope, we chose to be pro-active and to help the residents address their legal issues. In addition to being one of the Day Managers at the Camp, I also served for several years on the planning committee for the annual Spokane Homeless Connect (and its sister event, the Spokane Valley Connect). At each year's event we sponsor an "All Courts Warrant Fest." For this *warrant fest*, we bring together the judges, public defenders, prosecutors, and court staff of all three Courts: Municipal, District, and Superior. Any of our homeless friends with outstanding warrants can come (without fear of being arrested, unless the warrant is for a more serious criminal charge), talk with court staff, have their warrant(s) recalled (or "quashed") and get a new court date set up. This is important because an outstanding warrant prevents the individual from accessing any government benefits. Once warrants have been recalled and court dates re-scheduled, our Peer Navigators work with the individual to make sure they get to court on time, make their appearance, and follow whatever instructions the Court declares for them (in "Therapeutic Courts" - Community Court, Drug Court, and Veterans Court - following those instructions is crucial in the eventual disposition of their cases). Participating in a warrant fest doesn't solve all of their legal problems, but being pro-active to address your legal issues demonstrates a good faith effort to obey future instructions of the Court, and judges often take that into consideration when it comes to sentencing. You can't solve all of their legal problems, but you can work with those trying to build a meaningful exit ramp out of homelessness by helping them be pro-active in addressing their legal issues.

Check-List Action Item - Find and partner with legal aid groups in your community who may be willing to help. Find out what agency or group is offering free legal clinics to help people in poverty (including the homeless) to address their legal issues. Consider organizing a warrant fest (if it isn't already an event in your community) to help those experiencing homelessness to deal with the legal problems originating from their journey through homelessness.

Employment. Yes, it's all about jobs, jobs, jobs. As we saw above in our review of the varied suggested causes of homelessness, unemployment was the second cause cited by the City of Riverside, California, and was tied with Substance Abuse for fourth-place in the 2023 Spokane Point-In-Time Count. For those able to work (without disability income or some type of housing voucher) their long-term ability to exit homelessness and maintain housing (including paying their living expenses) depends on finding meaningful employment. Many of them will need help from Peer Navigators to complete job applications. Others may need a basic job skills class (like the PEPP class we described in Chapter 11). Still others may need help with appropriate work clothes (clean clothes, work boots, etc.), or a bus pass to get to and from work.

Check-List Action Item - Find and partner with agencies offering job skill classes, and other agencies offering work clothes, transportation help, and other basic assistance for new employees.

Housing. A recent NPR story, *Why Can't We Stop Homelessness? 4 Reasons Why There's No End In Sight,* [152] highlighted four sobering realities about homelessness and housing in America.

1. More people than ever are being housed - but an even higher number are falling into homelessness
2. Rents are out of reach for many, and millions of affordable places have disappeared
3. Zoning laws and local opposition make it hard to build housing for low-income renters
4. Pandemic aid programs that helped keep many people housed are winding down

These are the "housing headwinds" faced by those looking for housing and trying to build an exit ramp out of homelessness. Finding appropriate housing (I prefer to use terms such as "appropriate" and "stable" rather than permanent) for an unsheltered population is a challenge that requires an outside-the-box approach. Let's begin with the idea of shelters. For some people, going to an appropriate shelter that offers services including laundry, showers, meals, and peer navigation help could be a good next step for them. All such shelters should function as transitional housing, designed around helping clients move on to whatever their next step will be (again, think of shelters as airport boarding areas, temporary places to wait for the plane to their destination). In resolving Camp Hope, the State Department of Commerce funded the purchase (by Catholic Charities) and remodel of a former Quality Inn to offer 80 transitional living apartments for Camp Hope residents who were ready for such a next step (we discussed this earlier in Chapter 11). We also worked with local agencies and non-profits to build a network of alternative housing options ranging from Oxford (sober) Houses, to private "Greenhouses" (managed sober houses with 4-to-6 people), to sober living houses operated by some of our agency partners. The Spokane Low Income Housing Consortium worked on compiling an inventory of local available low-income housing, including those that would accept a "Section 8" Housing Choice Voucher," [153] in order to identify additional and more traditional "stable" housing options. We could have offered additional options such as pallet houses and tiny houses if local City and County governments had been willing to lean in and partner with us to allow - and even fund - the development of such non-traditional (but effective) housing options. What was lacking was political vision and will to do things differently.

The housing idea at work here was *Housing First*, getting people into different forms of appropriate and affordable housing as a top priority. But *Housing First* simply CANNOT mean *Housing Alone*. We don't do those we serve any favor if we set them up to fail in the housing we and they have worked so hard to achieve because we failed to help them address the issues that have kept them homeless until now. We need to address such issues as mental health, substance abuse, lack of identification, lack of Peer Support, lack of meaningful employment - all of the steps we have looked at over the past two chapters. To be successful, *Housing First* has to mean *Housing And Wrap-Around Services that set people up for success*. It has to include helping them work through all of these steps we've covered, and then continuing to walk with them after they've achieved housing.

Check-List Action Item - work with governments, agencies, and service providers to identify a variety of housing options that can address a variety of housing needs. You'll need them all before you're done.

Leading By Building Shalom

A basic principle of successful leadership is that successful leaders set those they lead up for success in their absence. That includes leadership in homeless services. As we work with those we are moving out of unsheltered homelessness, we need to regularly ask ourselves, "Am I setting this person up to succeed after I'm no longer here?" Even with wrap-around services, the day will eventually come when you or I will no longer be there. Life will move on for both of us, for us and for them. None of us can predict the future, and none of us can control their outcomes. People get to make their own choices and control their own journeys. But all of us can ask ourselves if, in the time we had together, we did all we knew how to do to set those we helped on to a path that would lead to success after we're gone.

Setting people up for their future success is what leadership and building *shalom* is all about. While housing is a priority, it isn't the goal. The same is true of all the steps we've reviewed and planned for - assessing needs, providing on-site services, mental health services, restoring identification, achieving sobriety, and more. Those things aren't the goal. They are all important objectives and stepping stones toward the goal. But they aren't the goal. The goal is to empower those experiencing unsheltered homelessness (as well as those experiencing sheltered homelessness) to build their personal shalom - their personal wholeness, well-being, and peace. And by building their *shalom*, we build our *shalom*, as well as that of our community.

A Place to Exist

Check-List For A New Model Moving Forward

Securing The Basics To Survive

Food
✓ *Check-List Action Item* - Create a food plan for the camp you manage.

Water
✓ *Check-List Action Item* - Create a water plan for the camp you manage.

Garbage
✓ *Check-List Action Item* - Create a plan to regularly handle garbage in the camp you manage.

Sanitation & Porta Potties
✓ *Check-List Action Item* - Create a plan to handle sanitation in the camp you manage.

Fire Safety
✓ *Check-List Action Item* - Work with local Fire Officials to create a plan and protocols to handle fire issues and concerns.

Winter Warming/Summer Cooling Plan
✓ *Check-List Action Item* - Start early to develop your summer cooling and winter warming plans.

Health & Medical Support
✓ *Check-List Action Item* - Work with local health officials and medical service providers to protect the health of the Camp community, and to meet the immediate medical needs of the residents.

Fencing, Counting, And Badging
✓ *Check-List Action Item* - Work with local officials to secure the Camp and to begin the process of identifying and quantifying those involved, and starting the process of assessing what they need to build an exit ramp out of homelessness.

Working Through The "Steps"

UnSheltered Homelessness
✓ *Check-List Action Item* - This is perhaps the hardest action of all, embracing the reality - the true size and nature - of homelessness in your community and making the conscious choice to engage it.

A Low Barrier Shelter
✓ *Check-List Action Item* - Identify and contact local area shelters, discovering their actual capacity and their willingness to work with your population, including sending their staff to connect with your people.

Assessments
✓ *Check-List Action Item* - Take an initial assessment of your population. Utilize the Potential Initial Assessment Questions at the end of this Chapter. Take it sooner, rather than later.

On-Site Services
✓ *Check-List Action Item* - Collaborate with homeless services agencies, caseworkers, and peer navigators who are willing to work on-site to get things done. Consider providing them with a place on-site (a tent, a mobile outreach trailer, etc) where they can meet and work with clients.

Identification Restoration
✓ *Check-List Action Item* - Find an individual or agency in your homeless services community with extensive successful experience with ID restoration among the homeless. Work with them to build a system and a team of ID restoration specialists who can focus on this need and successfully process a large volume of people needing IDs.

Peer Navigator Support
✓ *Check-List Action Item* - Collaborate with available agencies to build a network of Peer Navigators who are specialists in their particular service field (i.e., housing, substance abuse & recovery, mental health, etc.), and are stable and mature enough to work successfully in such a challenging atmosphere without being "triggered."

Substance Abuse Treatment
✓ *Check-List Action Item* - Identify, collaborate, and build a service network with those agencies, caseworkers, and Peer Navigators that have the ability and capacity to move people in your population toward counseling, sobriety, and treatment.

Physical & Mental Health Assistance
✓ *Check-List Action Item* - This action step is as much a cautionary tale as it is an action step. You are going to encounter physical and mental health situations where you may have limited abilities or resources with which to respond to them. Have a plan for how you are going to respond. If there are street medical teams in your community, try to develop a working relationship with them as

a first step before the ususal fall-back response of calling 911. A street medical team administering $25 worth of medications on-site on the street can prevent a $5,000 trip to the emergency room to treat a more advanced (and untreated) condition. And actual mental health workers who are willing to work on-site with your population could prevent a law enforcement confrontation that could end badly. Work to build those professional networks that can be called on when needed.

Re-Building Life Skills.
✓ *Check-List Action Item* - It's time to find, partner, and collaborate with agencies and ministries that offer classes and mentoring on such basics as cooking (check to see if a regional food bank offers classes on how to cook using products they frequently distribute), money management (how to budget for rent, utilities, food, essentials, etc.), relationship communication, job skills, responsible renters classes, etc.

Resolving Legal/Court Issues.
✓ *Check-List Action Item* - Find and partner with legal aid groups in your community who may be willing to help. Find out what agency or group is offering free legal clinics to help people in poverty (including the homeless) to address their legal issues. Consider organizing a warrant fest (if it isn't already an event in your community) to help those experiencing homelessness to deal with the legal problems originating from their journey through homelessness.

Employment.
✓ *Check-List Action Item* - Find and partner with agencies offering job skill classes, and other agencies offering work clothes, transportation help, and other basic assistance for new employees.

Housing.
✓ *Check-List Action Item* - work with governments, agencies, and service providers to identify a variety of housing options that can address a variety of housing needs. You'll need them all before you're done.

Potential Initial Assessment Questions

Personal Background Information
What's Your Full Legal Name? (First, Middle, Last)

What was your last permanent mailing address (or the last place they received mail)?

Date of Birth _____/_____/_____ What State were you born in?_____

How long have you been homeless?

When was the last time you had housing outside of a shelter or transitional living facility?

Other than a shelter, where was the last City/Town/State where you had housing?

Restoring Identification
_____Yes _____ No - Do you have a Social Security Number?

_____Yes _____ No - Would you be willing to share it with me?

_____Yes _____ No - Do you have your Social Security Card in your possession?

_____Yes _____ No - Do you have a current State issued Driver's License or Identification Card in your possession?

What State was your last State ID card issued in? _____

_____Yes _____ No - Do you have Certified Copy of your Birth Certificate?

Why Are You Homeless?
What caused your current homeless journey/experience? (Check as many as may apply)
_____ Family Conflict
_____ Divorce/Domestic Violence
_____ Loss of Housing/Eviction
_____ Loss of Income
_____ Loss of Job
_____ Alcohol, Drugs, or Substance Abuse
_____ Criminal Justice Issues (jail, prison)
_____ Other (Describe)

Substance Abuse
_____Yes _____ No - Are you currently using? What are you currently using?

_____Yes _____ No - Have you been through sobering/recovery or medical detox/treatment before?

_____Yes _____ No - Would you accept sobering/recovery help if it was offered to you?

Current Criminal Justice Involvement

_____ Yes _____ No - Are you currently subject to any court, DOC, or legal proceeding.

_____ Yes _____ No - Do you have any outstanding warrants?

Housing Goals

_____ Yes _____ No - Are you willing to go into transitional housing?

_____ Yes _____ No - Is it your goal to get into permanent or "stable" housing of your own?

What has prevented you from getting housing?

_____ Yes _____ No - Do you have income to support yourself in housing? What's your monthly income? _____

_____ Yes _____ No - Would you accept a pallet house or tiny house in a managed village if one was offered to you?

Assessments & Caseworkers

_____ Yes _____ No - Have you done an assessment like this before? With whom?
_____

What was the result/outcome?

_____ Yes _____ No - Do you currently have a caseworker?

Their Name and Agency: _____

What are they working on for you?

When was the last time they communicated with you?

Practical & Immediate Needs

_____ Yes _____ No - Do you have a medical condition that needs attention?

_____ Yes _____ No - Do you have a working phone?

What's the number so we can reach you?
(_____) _____ - _____

_____ Yes _____ No - Do you need to replace a lost/stolen phone?

_____ Yes _____ No - Do you need help with laundry and/or personal hygiene?

What is an immediate need that we can help you with today?

Interviewer's Additional Notes

End Notes

1. The most current academic study of homeless policy in Spokane has been done by local faculty at Eastern Washington University. It compares Spokane's homeless policy with policies in other communities. See Anderson, M.B., Staal, A., Mutungi, D., Gower, K. and Agyei, C. (2023), "(Com)passionate Revanchism and the Role of Private-Sector Coalitions in the Spatial Management of Houselessness." *Antipode*. Available at https://doi.org/10.1111/anti.12966

2. Available on our Youtube Channel, *My Road Leads Home* at https://www.youtube.com/channel/UCYooVO_ZJA2e3m_kAAUUhhw

3. Segment 2 of our documentary, *The Spokane Homeless Connect*. This segment documents the annual Point In Time Count which takes place every January and works to count the number of street homeless in the City. Filmed in January 2019 at the Canon Street Warming Center in Spokane, Washington. Available for viewing @ https://youtu.be/sJAYNfAWFao

4. The phrase "the least of these" is found in the teachings of Jesus in the New Testament in Matthew 25:31-46. We treat the Hebrew word *dal* and the idea of "the insignificant poor" in detail in Segment 2, "The Insignificant Poor," in our documentary, *The Night of the Unsheltered Homeless*, available on our YouTube Channel, *My Road Leads Home*, @ https://youtu.be/_9KvXMc_MFE

5. My thinking on *shalom* has been shaped in no small part by the work of Cornelius Platinga, Jr., *Not the Way It's Supposed to Be: A Breviary of Sin* (Eerdmans: Grand Rapids, 1996).

6. The verbal form of *shalom* (*shalam*) appears 14 times in the Old Testament book of Exodus, Chapters 21 and 22, where Moses instructs the people of God about what to do in cases of material loss or theft of property. The owner who suffered the loss is regarded as incomplete and lacking wholeness. The person responsible for the loss was instructed to "make it good" or to "restore."

7. Bryant Myers, *Walking with the Poor* (Maryknoll, NY: Orbis Books, 2011), 143.

8. *The Night of the Unsheltered Homeless*, produced by Rising River Media, available on our documentary YouTube Channel, *My Road Leads Home*, at https://youtu.be/_9KvXMc_MFE

9. Marchauna Rogers, *Refocusing the Why of Evangelicalism*, (a paper submitted to Multnomah Seminary, May 1, 2021, DM832M - Framing Leadership: Communicating Vision from a Theological Foundation. Copy provided by the author), 16.

10. This was the final individual head count, conducted in late July by Jewels Helping Hands, the Camp organizer, prior to the Washington State Department of Transportation (WSDOT) becoming actively involved in the management of the Camp in September of 2022. From this peak point forward, Camp Hope began to shrink as organized efforts to move residents into housing options picked up momentum.

11. In July of 2022, at Camp Hope's peak of 689 residents, the Spokane city-wide shelter system had 711 total beds, prior to the September opening of the TRAC shelter

12. As we will explain in greater detail in Chapter 5, prior to November of 2019, when it began keeping its *Shelter Capacity Report*, the City of Spokane did not maintain or publish any official inventory of beds in the city-wide shelter system. They simply didn't know how many beds were available, or how that number might relate to the number of people experiencing homelessness.

13. Casey Decker, "Salvation Army opens large warming center in Spokane," Krem 2, January 9, 2019, accessed @ https://www.krem.com/article/news/local/salvation-army-opens-large-new-warming-center/293-9a 0a306b-8eef-4b76-bb15-91eebdc685ce. Under the Federal Case of *Martin v City of Boise* - 920 F. 3d 584 (9th Cir. 2019), temporary warming center beds cannot be counted as satisfying the requirement of having sufficient low-barrier beds to accommodate the known and counted homeless when a community seeks to enforce local "No Sit & Lie" or "No Camping" ordinances against those experiencing unsheltered homelessness.

14. Kaitlin Riordan, "Lawsuit filed over City of Spokane's response to Camp Hope," KREM2, July 19, 2019, accessed @ https://www.krem.com/article/news/local/homeless/lawsuit-filed-over-city-of-spokanes-response-to-camp-hope/293-781c454d-e8e8-48e3-b5f9-521cfe7e923e

15. *Martin v City of Boise*, 920 F. 3d 584 (9th Cir. 2019)

16. This came in the form of a City of Spokane Executive Order titled "DIRECTIVE OF THE MAYOR REGARDING ADOPTION OF AN ADMINISTRATIVE POLICY" signed and filed with the City Clerk's Office on November 13th, 2020.

17. Amanda Roley, "Spokane's sit-and-lie still in effect one year after Camp Hope," KREM2, December 6, 2019, accessed @ https://www.krem.com/article/news/local/homeless/spokanes-sit-and-lie-still-in-effect-one-year-afte r-camp-hope/293-de674a2b-2d7a-44a2-95e7-f19551ee9d4b

18. Wilson Criscione, "Despite a lack of shelter space, records show spokane police still enforce laws targeting homeless people," *The Inlander*, October 20, 2022, accessed @ https://www.inlander.com/spokane/despite-a-lack-of-shelter-space-records-show-spokane-police-sti ll-enforce-laws-targeting-homeless-people/Content?oid=20484809

19. *Our Annual Greek Homeless Tragedy*, available on our YouTube Channel, *My Road Leads Home* @ https://youtu.be/Vzaf3K53fxk

20. The event related here appears in *The Night of the Unsheltered Homeless* in a segment titled "Sweeps And Collateral Damage" starting at about the 42 minute mark. Available for viewing on our Youtube Channel, *My Road Leads Home* @ https://www.youtube.com/channel/UCYooVO_ZJA2e3m_kAAUUhhw

21. Shawn Vestal, "The City Council should use its power to force a better approach to shelter emergencies," *The Spokesman-Review*, July 9, 2021, accessed @ https://www.spokesman.com/stories/2021/jul/09/shawn-vestal-the-city-council-should-use-its-powe r/

22. These regular reports run around 19 - 8½ X 11 pages, listing camps reported to or visited by local law enforcement.

23. From audio transcript of documentary video footage, an interview I did with Julie on 6-16-2022.

24. From an audio transcript of documentary video footage captured independently by Rising River Media.

25. On more than one occasion, the City of Spokane has insisted that the issuance of a "48-Hour Notice To Remove Property" is not a law enforcement "sweep" of a homeless encampment, unless law enforcement actually physically removes the residents and their property. But, it's a technical distinction, because any sweep is a two-step process that begins with the issuance by Spokane Code Enforcement of a "48 Hour Notices To Remove Property," usually with law enforcement present. Step two of a sweep is the return of law enforcement to effect the removal of the residents (if they have not already left by this time) and the disposal of their property. I utilize the term "sweep" as I believe it is a more honest description of both the process and its intent. If you're going to vilify those experiencing homelessness as nuisances and trash to be removed, then you might as well finish the analogy by describing their removal as a "sweep" with law enforcement being the "broom." Yes, that's harsh, but unvarnished reality often is.

26. The City of Spokane cited public health and safety concerns as the justification for sweeping the Camp, but no such concerns had been raised or expressed to protest organizers prior to the "Notice to Remove Property" being issued.

27. From an audio transcript of a documentary interview with Julie Garcia captured by Rising River Media.

28. In addition to his account of the Mayor's visit, Mike Shaw, Director of the Guardians Foundation, gave this author the specific peak Convention Center shelter count number of 486, which has never appeared anywhere in print before now.

29. From the HUD Exchange: https://www.hudexchange.info/programs/hdx/pit-hic/ See also the 2022 Annual Homeless Assessment Report (AHAR) to Congress @ https://www.huduser.gov/portal/datasets/ahar/2022-ahar-part-1-pit-estimates-of-homelessness-in-t he-us.html

30. "A River of Homelessness," Segment 1 of our documentary, *The Hidden Homeless: Families Experiencing Homelessness*. Segment 1 is available on our YouTube Channel, *My Road Leads Home* at https://youtu.be/rjs3YTZU5B4

31. Shawn Vestal, "The homeless crisis is not about one camp, and it's bigger than most people realize," *The Spokesman-Review*, Wednesday, December 7, 2022, accessed at: https://www.spokesman.com/stories/2022/dec/07/shawn-vestal-the-homeless-crisis-is-not-about-on e-/

32. *The Living Wage Project* at the Massachusetts Institute of Technology: https://livingwage.mit.edu/counties/53063

33. On this topic, see also Gregg Colburn and Clayton Page Aldern, *Homelessness Is A Housing Problem* (University of California Press; First edition March 15, 2022. ISBN: 978-0520383784. Available on Amazon @ https://www.amazon.com/dp/0520383788/

34. Available on-line at https://www.theatlantic.com/magazine/archive/2023/01/homelessness-affordable-housing-crisis-de mocrats-causes/672224/

35. The author has a copy of that original spreadsheet, created by a CHHS staff person for the internal use of the CHHS department.

36. Data source: *Point In Time Count Data: PIT 2007 - 2022 by CoC*, available as a downloadable Excel spreadsheet at:
https://www.nhipdata.org/local/upload/file/2007-2022-PIT-Counts-by-CoC.xlsx.

37. Available at:
https://static.spokanecity.org/documents/ending-homelessness/everybody-counts/2019-everybody-counts-campaign-presentation.pdf

38. Historically, the *Sheltered* count divides between "Shelters" and "Transitional Housing." Based on a five year average, the "Shelters" portion of the Sheltered Count is consistently about 77% of the total, with the "Transitional Housing" portion making up the other 23%. The following numbers are the result of that historical five year average: Shelters - 780, Transitional housing - 214. Based on 780 people in shelters, and a total bed count of 722, shelters would have been operating at 108% of capacity on the night of the PIT count.

39. As of November of 2019, 10 months after the PIT Count, when the City's *Shelter Capacity Report* began tracking beds and availability).

40. Available at:
https://static.spokanecity.org/documents/chhs/hmis/reports/2020-pit-count-presentation.pdf

41. Using the historic 5-year average percentages: Shelters - 799, Transitional housing - 219. Based on 799 people in shelters, and a total bed count of 805, shelters would have been operating at 99% of capacity on the night of the PIT count.

42. A June 13, 2021 article in the Spokesman Review stated that preliminary data from the January 2021 Point In Time count showed that 992 people were counted in city shelters that month. The City of Spokane erroneously used this preliminary data to argue that the City-wide shelter capacity was 992 beds. As observed earlier, the annual Point In Time Count is always divided into two parts: "Sheltered" and "Unsheltered." Due to COVID restrictions, the 2021 Count did NOT included the "Unsheltered" part. People not staying in shelters simply weren't meaningfully counted. The remaining "Sheltered" portion of the Count is always divided between "Shelters" and "Transitional Housing." Historically, based on a five year average, the "Shelters" portion of the Sheltered Count is consistently about 77% of the total, with the "Transitional Housing" portion making up the other 23%. For 2021, this would suggest that 763 shelter beds were filled, not 992. The City's *Shelter Capacity Report* showed only 713 total shelter beds in the City-wide system at that time, which means that shelters were operating at 107% of capacity. According to the City's *Shelter Capacity Report*, that number would fall to 679 by December of 2021 at the time of the Camp Hope protest in front of City Hall.

43. Using the 77%/23% five year average discussed above we get: Shelters - 725, Transitional housing - 209. Based on 725 people in shelters, and a total bed count of 710, shelters would have been operating at 102% of capacity on the night of the PIT count.

44. Using the 77%/23% five year average discussed above we get: Shelters - 1,105, Transitional Housing - 330. Based on 1,105 people in shelters, and a total bed count of 1,095, shelters would have been operating at 101% of capacity on the night of the PIT count.

45. Ava Wainhouse, "Open drug use, naked people, stabbings: Closure of Camp Hope rocks downtown businesses," KHQ, July 11, 2023, available @
https://www.khq.com/news/open-drug-use-naked-people-stabbings-closure-of-camp-hope-rocks-downtown-businesses/article_3ca18f54-204c-11ee-a5ef-6fe8a00ebba4.html

46. At the time of the 2023 Point In Time Count (January of 2023), the city-wide shelter system had a total capacity of 1,095 beds. But 6 months later, with the closing of the Cannon Street Shelter, that number had dropped to 1,015.

47. The City of Spokane stopped publishing a *Shelter Capacity Report* in mid-2022, replacing it with an internet-based shelter dashboard accessible at https://sheltermespokane.org/ Months after its launch, the dashboard - like the Shelter Capacity Report that preceded it - remains a work in progress. The data underlying the dashboard is not available for independent inspection or correction and frequently raises more questions than it answers.

48. See *Martin v. City of Boise*, 902 F.3d 1031 (9th Cir. 2018)

49. See *Johnson v. City of Grants Pass* [D.C. No. 1:18-cv-01823-CL] September 28, 2022

50. The actual quote, "What's past is prologue" comes from Shakespeare's play *The Tempest* (Act 2, Scene 1). The quote is engraved on the National Archives Building in Washington. The "big idea" is that history sets the context for the present, an idea commonly used by military planners when discussing the similarities between war throughout history, which might explain why military planners are often accused of planning to fight yesterday's war.

51. The City of Spokane's *Shelter Capacity Report* is incomplete for the month of December, 2021, covering only the first half of the month (1st - 13th). We are reporting only low-barrier beds because this is the standard mandated by Federal Courts in *Martin v Boise* and *Johnson v City of Grants Pass*.

52. Adam Shanks, "Encampment near Interstate 90 allowed to stay put by WSDOT, for now," January 14, 2022, accessed @ https://www.spokesman.com/stories/2022/jan/14/encampment-near-interstate-90-allowed-to-stay-put-/

53. Adam Shanks, "Spokane city leaders ask: When shelter isn't an option, where do the homeless turn?" *The Spokesman-Review*, Monday, February 24, 2020, accessed @ https://www.spokesman.com/stories/2020/feb/24/spokane-city-leaders-ask-when-shelter-isnt-an-opti/

54. Adam Shanks, "Fences erected under Browne Street viaduct in effort to deter camping," *The Spokesman-Review*, February 8, 2022, accessed @ https://www.spokesman.com/stories/2022/feb/08/fences-erected-under-browne-street-viaduct-in-effo/

55. This documentary short-film (8 minutes), filmed on Saturday, March 5th, 2022, focuses on fences recently installed by the City of Spokane in the Browne Street viaduct in order to prevent the homeless from sleeping or camping there. Available on our YouTube Channel, *My Road Leads Home*, @ https://youtu.be/XoqYnFS2bE8

56. CMIS stands for "Community Management Information System," sometimes referred to as HMIS or "Homeless Management Information System." It is an database used by caseworkers and service providers to track the progress of those experiencing homelessness as they access services.

57. I created a documentary short film around a protest organized to draw public attention to the City's fence policy, *Shelters, Not Fences*, available on our YouTube Channel, *My Road Leads Home*, @ https://youtu.be/XoqYnFS2bE8

58. Robert Frost, *Mending Wall*, accessed from Poetry Foundation @ https://www.poetryfoundation.org/poems/44266/mending-wall

59. Greg Mason, "City of Spokane identifies East Trent building as spot for new homeless shelter," *The Spokesman Review*, April 12, 2022, accessed @ https://www.spokesman.com/stories/2022/apr/12/city-of-spokane-identifies-east-spokane-building-a /

60. Greg Mason, "Woodward to maintain course for proposed 250-bed homeless shelter as City Council recommends limits, alternatives," *The Spokesman-Review*, Wednesday, April 27, 2022, accessed @ https://www.spokesman.com/stories/2022/apr/27/woodward-to-maintain-course-for-proposed-250-bed-h/

61. Brianda Perez, "Jewels Helping Hands hosting 2-day service fair for people living at I-90 homeless encampment," KXLY, July 5, 2022, accessed @ https://www.krem.com/article/news/local/spokane-county/service-fair-spokane-homeless-encampm ent/293-ee845941-7055-4d9e-8b37-19eb8e3dcc0e

62. Greg Mason, 'We're doing what we can': Spokane homeless camp builds cooling tent to keep safe during expected heatwave," *The Spokesman-Review*, July 26, 2022, accessed @ https://www.spokesman.com/stories/2022/jul/26/were-doing-what-we-can-spokane-homeless-camp -build/

63. Greg Mason, "Spokane City Council approves funding to support cooling tent at Camp Hope homeless encampment," *The Spokesman-Review*, August 1, 2022, accessed @ https://www.spokesman.com/stories/2022/aug/01/spokane-city-council-approves-funding-to-suppor t-c/

64. Greg Mason, "City of Spokane puts WSDOT on notice over cooling tent at Camp Hope homeless encampment," *The Spokesman-Review*, July 28, 2022, accessed @ https://www.spokesman.com/stories/2022/jul/28/city-of-spokane-puts-wsdot-on-notice-over-coolin g-/

65. Greg Mason, "State will not take action to remove Camp Hope cooling tent despite city's notice,"
The Spokesman-Review, July 29, 2022, accessed @ https://www.spokesman.com/stories/2022/jul/29/state-will-not-take-action-to-remove-camp-hope-c oo/

66. Patrick Henkels, "Department of Commerce pays $500,000 to fund first step in moving homeless individuals living near I-90 and Freya," KREM, August 8, 2022, accessed @ https://www.krem.com/article/news/local/homeless/department-commerce-fund-first-step-homeless -i-90-freya/293-8ebb24d6-7e02-4852-9133-96b254145c9e

67. Shawn Vestal, "A quick end to Camp Hope is probably not on the horizon," *The Spokesman-Review*, Sunday, September 4, 2022, accessed @ https://www.spokesman.com/stories/2022/sep/04/shawn-vestal-a-quick-end-to-camp-hope-is-proba bly-/

68. Greg Mason, "Threatening legal action against the state, city of Spokane sets deadline for removal of Camp Hope homeless encampment," *The Spokesman-Review*, September 9, 2022, accessed @

https://www.spokesman.com/stories/2022/sep/09/threatening-legal-action-against-the-state-city-of/

69. Source: Musixmatch. Songwriters: Paul Simon. The Sound of Silence lyrics © Paul Simon Music, Sony/ATV Songs LLC

70. Nate Sanford, "State agencies push back on Spokane's order to remove Camp Hope; call deadline 'irrational'," *Inlander*, September 20, 2022, accessed at https://www.inlander.com/spokane/state-agencies-push-back-on-spokanes-order-to-remove-camp-hope-call-deadline-irrational/Content?oid=24597885

71. Colin Tiernan, "In scathing letter, state chides city of Spokane on Camp Hope response, accuses mayor of valuing 'optics' over 'action'," *The Spokesman-Review*, Wednesday, September 21, 2022, accessed @ https://www.spokesman.com/stories/2022/sep/21/in-scathing-letter-state-chides-spokane-on-camp-ho/

72. Garrett Cabeza, "Knezovich plans to 'clear' Camp Hope by mid-October," *The Spokesman-Review*, September 22, 2022, accessed @ https://www.spokesman.com/stories/2022/sep/22/knezovich-plans-to-clear-camp-hope-by-mid-october/

73. Shawn Vestal, "If dumb, angry responses to homelessness worked, we'd have solved it already," *The Spokesman-Review*, Friday, September 23, 2022, accessed @ https://www.spokesman.com/stories/2022/Sep/23/shawn-vestal-if-dumb-angry-responses-to-homelessne

74. Camp Hope Spokane Homeless Coalition Meeting, available on our YouTube Channel, *My Road Leads Home*, @ https://youtu.be/Cg0CrWEItdo

75. Daniel Walters, "Camp Hope officials say they repeatedly asked police for help removing dangerous residents — that help rarely came," *Inlander*, March 30, 2023, accessed @ https://www.inlander.com/spokane/camp-hope-officials-say-they-repeatedly-asked-police-for-help-removing-dangerous-residents-that-help-rarely-came/Content?oid=25694701

76. Celina Van Hyning, "City of Spokane responds to WSDOT deadline to clear homeless camp near I-90," KXLY, September 9, 2022, accessed @ https://www.krem.com/article/news/local/homeless/camp-hope-clear-out-deadline/293-6703fb8f-297d-4e18-a0c3-f3ec3b4a36cd

77. Garrett Cabeza, "Knezovich plans to 'clear' Camp Hope by mid-October," *The Spokesman-Review*, September 22, 2022, accessed @ https://www.spokesman.com/stories/2022/sep/22/knezovich-plans-to-clear-camp-hope-by-mid-october/

78. Celina Van Hyning, "Spokane police chief tells WSDOT he may declare I-90 homeless camp a Chronic Nuisance Property," KREM, October 7, 2022, accessed @ https://www.krem.com/article/news/local/homeless/spokane-homeless-camp-spd-letter/293-8476515a-bdce-42b0-b0a2-6805e85689a6

79. Kyle Simchuk, "Spokane police chief and county sheriff moving forward on I-90 encampment plan," KREM, October 13, 2022, accessed @ https://www.krem.com/article/news/local/homeless/spokane-police-chief-county-sheriff-moving-forward-i-90-encampment-plan/293-589aa5d8-2203-460a-87af-4ed23a7a403f

80. Kyle Simchuk, "Sheriff Ozzie Knezovich plans emergency operations center as I-90 camp clearing date approaches," KREM, October 24, 2022, accessed @ https://www.krem.com/article/news/local/homeless/spokane-county-sheriff-emergency-operations-center-i-90-camp-clearing/293-e2001bf4-524b-441d-af47-e73ea54a01e7

81. Kyle Simchuk, "Lawsuit filed in U.S. District Court looks to prevent clearing of I-90 homeless camp," KREM, October 28, 2022, accessed @ https://www.krem.com/article/news/local/homeless/lawsuit-filed-us-district-court-prevent-clearing-i-90-homeless-camp/293-69aeffe4-b531-48fc-a573-6d58ca997592

82. Emry Dinman, "Spokane County sheriff's use of helicopters, infrared imaging to survey Camp Hope at center of latest legal dispute," *The Spokesman-Review*, November 22, 2022, accessed @ https://www.spokesman.com/stories/2022/nov/22/spokane-sheriffs-use-of-helicopters-infrared-imagi/

83. Garrett Cabeza, "Constitutional rights, nuisance claims at center of complaints filed regarding Camp Hope," *The Spokesman-Review*, October 28, 2022, accessed @ https://www.spokesman.com/stories/2022/oct/28/constitutional-rights-nuisance-claims-at-center-of/

84. Andrew Biviano Interview, *The Night of the Unsheltered Homeless*, Rising River Media, October 8, 2021. Available on our YouTube Channel, *My Road Leads Home*, @ https://youtu.be/Gjh8wERRHcc

85. Colin Tiernan, "'It's like you belong again': State agencies helping Camp Hope residents get critical ID cards," *The Spokesman Review*, October 27, 2022, accessed @ https://www.spokesman.com/stories/2022/oct/27/its-like-you-belong-again-state-agencies-helping-c/

86. Two months earlier, in September of 2022, the Spokane County Sheriff had announced a plan to close the Camp by mid-October. Part of his plan was to provide bus tickets for the 600 homeless people living there so they could reunite with family. See Garrett Cabeza, "Knezovich plans to 'clear' Camp Hope by mid-October," *The Spokesman-Review*, September 22, 2022, accessed @ https://www.spokesman.com/stories/2022/sep/22/knezovich-plans-to-clear-camp-hope-by-mid-october/

87. These numbers were consistent with the 2022 Point-In-Time Count which found that 79% of those interviewed said they came from Spokane County (or "Greater Spokane"), and 74% said they came from the City of Spokane.

88. Rania Kaur, "People living at Camp Hope react to law enforcement's closure notices," KXLY, December 7, 2022, Updated Jan 13, 2023, accessed @ https://www.kxly.com/news/local-news/people-living-at-camp-hope-react-to-law-enforcement-s-closure-notices/article_af59e69c-929d-50d8-b369-7e925ae4c8c6.html

89. Patrick Henkels, Janelle Finch, "Spokane law enforcement hands out notices with intention to close I-90 homeless camp," KREM, December 6, 2022, accessed @ https://www.krem.com/article/news/local/homeless/spokane-county-sheriff-notices-close-i-90-homeless-camp/293-c248dcfd-55c7-4b32-b386-03349231ca9a

90. YouTube Link To Tuesday, December 6 Footage: https://youtu.be/m-xEc1OhQdg
YouTube Link To Wednesday, December 7 Footage: https://youtu.be/LwuevzNepKo

91. Emry Dinman, "'This camp is to be closed': Confusion, frustration after law enforcement hands out flyers at Camp Hope," *The Spokesman Review*, December 6, 2022, accessed @ https://www.spokesman.com/stories/2022/dec/06/this-camp-is-to-be-closed-confusion-frustration-af/

92. Celina Van Hyning, "Emergency restraining order sought to prevent clearing I-90 homeless camp," KREM, December 8, 2022, accessed @ https://www.krem.com/article/news/local/homeless/camp-hope-lawsuit-restraining-order/293-b6d6 bee0-3961-4ccd-b9ec-73e435e8b3d7

93. Emry Dinman, "Federal judge prevents sweep of Camp Hope through Christmas," *The Spokesman-Review*, December 12, 2022, accessed @ https://www.spokesman.com/stories/2022/dec/12/federal-judge-prevents-sweep-of-camp-hope-thro ugh-

94. The difference between the computer badged count of 377 and the physical head-count of 198 can be explained by the fact that scared residents left the Camp in the two weeks following the law enforcement visits without notifying Camp staff or surrendering their resident badges. According to the badging system, their badge was still active and they were still Camp residents. Over the next month, as it became obvious that people had left and abandoned their sites, and as their badges were slowly culled from the system, the badge count and the regular head counts slowly matched up.

95. Following the closure of the Camp in June of 2023, the Washington State Department of Commerce used Right of Way funding to enter in to a contract with Jewels Helping Hands to conduct outreach and re-connect with as many of the formerly badged Camp residents as possible and to offer them continued assistance toward housing.

96. If the concept of unintended consequences was a coin, the front of that coin would feature Robert K. Merton. The back of that coin would feature another well known person, Air Force Captain Edward A. Murphy. In 1949, Captain Murphy was an engineer on an Air Force project at Edward's Air Force Base to see how much sudden deceleration a person could withstand in a crash. One day, after discovering that a key electrical component had been wired wrong, Captain Murphy criticized the technician responsible, saying "If there is any way to do it wrong, he'll find it." The Northrop project manager, George E. Nichols, who kept a list of "laws" they were discovering, added this one, which he called Murphy's Law: "If anything can go wrong, it will" Nichols' Fourth Law says, "Avoid any action with an unacceptable outcome." Nichols would go on to work for NASA at the Jet Propulsion Lab. The doctor who rode the rocket sled in the deceleration test, Colonel John P. Stapp, formulated his own "law" after the experience: "The universal aptitude for ineptitude makes any human accomplishment an incredible miracle." (Source: USAF publication, *The Desert Wings* – March 3, 1978). Welcome to the world of "unintended consequences." Our thanks to Professor Merton and Captain Murphy. Politicians, policymakers, and people with good intentions should make a note.

97. Merton, Robert K. "The Unanticipated Consequences of Purposive Social Action." *American Sociological Review* 1, no. 6 (1936): 894–904. https://doi.org/10.2307/2084615

98. Sociologists, like philosophers, spill copious amounts of ink adding footnotes to impactful schools of thought, such as the school of thought surrounding "unanticipated consequences" formalized by Professor Merton. But his original five causes of unanticipated consequences have stood the test of time, which is why I'm using them here without alteration. Source: Wikipedia, "Unintended Consequences". Accessed at https://en.wikipedia.org/wiki/Unintended_consequences

99. Shawn Vestal, "Of the Forking Paths at Camp Hope, One Produced Results," *The Spokesman-Review*, Sunday, February 19, 2023, accessed at https://www.spokesman.com/stories/2023/feb/19/shawn-vestal-of-the-forking-paths-at-camp-hope-one/

100. Emry Dinman, "Camp Hope will close by June 30 as leaders project blame for duration of camp," *The Spokesman-Review*, May 30, 2023, accessed at https://www.spokesman.com/stories/2023/may/30/camp-hope-will-close-by-june-30-as-leaders-project/

101. Located at: https://www.commerce.wa.gov/wp-content/uploads/2022/12/Spokane-ROW-funding-allocation-summary.pdf

102. A Greek verse supposedly spoken by the 4th-century BC Egyptian King Tachos to the Spartan king Agesilaus, mocking him for his small stature. For more, see The Mountain In Labour, https://en.wikipedia.org/wiki/The_Mountain_in_Labour

103. Bradley Warren, "Governor Jay Inslee praises Jewels Helping Hands, service providers for Camp Hope closure," KHQ, June 30, 2023, acessed at https://www.khq.com/news/governor-jay-inslee-praises-jewels-helping-hands-service-providers-for-camp-hope-closure/article_2a2f6136-178a-11ee-9afd-93d33f4a5246.html

104. Ibid.

105. Following the closure of the Camp, we are working to follow up with as many former camp residents as possible and to record their on-going stories.

106. Greg Mason, "Spokane City Council approves agreement to lease East Trent Avenue warehouse for planned homeless shelter," *The Spokesman-Review*, June 27, 2022, accessed @ https://www.spokesman.com/stories/2022/jun/27/spokane-city-council-approves-agreement-to-lease-e-e/

107. Luke Baumgarten, "Spokane building official says Trent shelter is not authorized for more than 250 people," *Range Media*, December 5, 2022, accessed @ https://www.rangemedia.co/spokane-building-official-trent-shelter-occupancy/

108. Luke Baumgarten, "Trent shelter can now legally shelter 350 people," *Range Media*, December 8, 2022, accessed @ https://www.rangemedia.co/trent-shelter-capacity-spokane-building-code/. It is curious to note that the increase in occupancy at TRAC from 250 to 350 residents came at the same time as the law enforcement visit to the Camp, as if in anticipation of a large influx of new residents to the shelter . . . which never occurred.

109. "City of Spokane: 97 people at Trent Shelter, 27 from Camp Hope," KHQ News, Sep 21, 2022, accessed @ https://www.khq.com/news/homeless/city-of-spokane-97-people-at-trent-shelter-27-from-camp-hope/article_1697729c-2a57-11ed-9566-27a907ba5e4f.html

110. Carl Segerstrom, "Cut off: TRAC's remote location worsens health, contributed to amputations," *Range Media*, March 8, 2023, accessed @ https://www.rangemedia.co/tracs-trent-location-medical-care-access-spokane/?ref=range-news-newsletter

111. Amanda Roley, "Spokane neighborhood frustrated with growing calls for criminal activity near Trent Shelter," KREM, February 17, 2023, accessed @ https://www.krem.com/article/news/local/homeless/spokane-neighborhood-frustrated-criminal-activity-trent-shelter/293-c6cf54fe-4c91-49a2-b04f-9bd3d6cccb84

112. As of this writing, in mid-2023, those conditions have not changed.

113. Greg Mason, "Overview of proposed east Spokane homeless shelter leaves City Council with questions amid hopes to open this month," The Spokesman-Review, August 17, 2022, accessed @ https://www.spokesman.com/stories/2022/aug/17/overview-of-proposed-east-spokane-homeless-shelter/

114. In late July of 2023 the City of Spokane CHHS Department issued a new Request for Proposal, also known as a "Notice of Funding Availability" (or NOFA) for a new operator/service provider for the TRAC shelter with an annual budget reduced by roughly 30% from $14 million down to $9 million. As of this date, the RFP/NOFA was available on the City of Spokane's website @ https://static.spokanecity.org/documents/chhs/funding-opportunities/chhs/2023-08-01/trac-notice-of-funding-availability-v4.pdf

115. Daniel Walters, "The City of Spokane's homeless shelter system is teetering on the edge of financial collapse," Inlander, April 06, 2023, accessed @ https://www.inlander.com/news/the-city-of-spokanes-homeless-shelter-system-is-teetering-on-the-edge-of-financial-collapse-25732653

116. Carl Segerstrom, "Sexual assault, harassment reports at Trent highlight dangerous oversight gaps at Spokane shelters," Range Media, April 13, 2023, accessed @ https://www.rangemedia.co/sexual-assault-reports-trent-oversight-gaps-spokane-shelters-trac/?ref=range-news-newsletter

117. Shawn Vestal, "Trent shelter report to council charts progress, big challenges," The Spokesman- Review, December 16, 2022, accessed @ https://www.spokesman.com/stories/2022/dec/16/shawn-vestal-trent-shelter-report-to-council-chart/

118. According to Brian Coddington, Director of Communications and Marketing at City of Spokane, in a story aired on KXLY4 (ABC), some 37 TRAC guests had been placed into permanent housing. As of this writing, however, this number cannot be verified from any data released by the City or the shelter operator. See Maryssa Rillo, "TRAC operator contract set to expire: What unsheltered people say they need," KXLY, Thursday, July 27, 2023, accessed @ https://www.kxly.com/news/trac-operator-contract-set-to-expire-what-unsheltered-people-say-they-need/article_69f858c2-2ce8-11ee-9bb0-836fd47e756a.html

119. William Safire, "If You Break It...," The New York Times, October 17, 2004, accessed @ https://www.nytimes.com/2004/10/17/magazine/if-you-break-it.html

120. City of Spokane News Release, "Nadine Woodward responds to 2023 Homeless Point-In-Time Count," KHQ, April 27, 2023, accessed @ https://www.khq.com/straight_from_the_source/nadine-woodward-responds-to-2023-homeless-point-in-time-count/article_a49798f2-e572-11ed-b2d8-3f19ff582324.html

121. Source: https://www.commerce.wa.gov/uncategorized/commerce-makes-final-right-of-way-safety-initiative-funding-awards-to-city-and-nonprofit-proposals-in-latest-step-toward-closing-camp-hope/

122. The City of Spokane's 2022 PIT Count presentation is no longer posted on the City's website, and the City's 2023 PIT Count presentation does not contain this information, preventing any year-over-year comparison.

123. Emily Blume, "From Camp Hope to the classroom," KXLY, March 7, 2023, accessed @ https://www.kxly.com/news/from-camp-hope-to-the-classroom/article_e5df6600-bd59-11ed-8529-cb7f8fe888ad.html

124. Ava Wainhouse, "'I'm ready to move on': 10 homeless students graduate from Spokane pre-employment program," KHQ, March 24, 2023, accessed @ https://www.khq.com/news/im-ready-to-move-on-10-homeless-students-graduate-from-spokane-pre-employment-program/article_cb730978-caad-11ed-81d3-53759bdb7bf8.html

125. These numbers were provided by the Spokane Low Income Housing Consortium which was responsible for tracking Camp Hope housing outcomes. These numbers were current as of the end of May, 2023, just before the Camp closed.

126. Audio transcript from *The Hidden Homeless: Families Experiencing Homelessness*, Rising River Media, 2020, available on our YouTube Channel, *My Road Leads Home*, @ https://youtu.be/WnpeS2RwHLg

127. Later, in the Autumn of 2022, the City offered to grant electrical and water service to the Camp in exchange for data on Camp residents, specifically the legal names of all 467 residents gathered by WSDOT during the badging process to receive a camp badge. WSDOT declined the offer, which came with additional requirements. Nate Sanford, "City wanted list of campers' names, removal deadline in exchange for water and electricity at Camp Hope," *Inlander*, November 16, 2022, accessed @ https://www.inlander.com/spokane/city-wanted-list-of-campers-names-removal-deadline-in-exchange-for-water-and-electricity-at-camp-hope/Content?oid=24896973

128. *The Night of the Unsheltered Homeless*, available on our YouTube Channel, *My Road Leads Home*, @ https://www.youtube.com/channel/UCYooVO_ZJA2e3m_kAAUUhhw

129. Learn more about the Washington State Housing Trust Fund on the Department of Commerce website at https://www.commerce.wa.gov/building-infrastructure/housing/housing-trust-fund/

130. See *Improving Homeownership Rates for Black, Indigenous, and People of Color in Washington*, https://www.commerce.wa.gov/wp-content/uploads/2022/09/Homeownership-Disparities-Recommendations-Report-FINAL-Sep2022.pdf

131. For details on how law enforcement conducts sweeps, see Chapter 19.

132. "How can a mere 'theory' change the outcome of a case? Like this: employee shoots at their boss, misses, charged with attempted murder but found not guilty due to medication errors. Employee then sues for loss of job. A losing case: employers can fire employees who empty a revolver at their manager. Wrongful discharge is a losing theory. But when the court appoints a lawyer, the lawyer finds a federal rule that says employees with five years' service who suffer from a mental breakdown are entitled to 'mandatory mental health retirement benefits.' The employer

failed to apply for the employee's mental health retirement within the one year allowed. Employee wins that case. All that terrible evidence against the employee's wrongful discharge suit becomes great evidence for the employee's suit for the unpaid mandatory mental health retirement. That's a change in the theory, from a losing to a winning case.

133. *Martin v. Boise*, 920 F.3d 584 (9th Cir. 2019) (barring criminalization) and *Johnson v. Grants Pass*, 50 F.4th 787 (9th Cir. 2022) (rehearing denied) (applying Boise rule to civil nuisance suits). *Grants Pass* was upheld by the full 9th Circuit but there were 11 dissents and the case may be headed to the Supreme Court.

134. See Gregg Colburn and Clayton Page Aldern, *Homelessness Is A Housing Problem*, University of California Press; First edition, (March 15, 2022). Available on Amazon @ https://www.amazon.com/dp/0520383788/

135. Edward J. Watts, *The Eternal Decline and Fall of Rome: The History of a Dangerous Idea*, Oxford University Press (August 3, 2021), 6.

136. British philosopher Alfred North Whitehead once observed, "The safest general characterization of the European philosophical tradition is that it consists of a series of footnotes to Plato." Whitehead, *Process and Reality: An Essay in Cosmology* (1929), Part II, Chapter 1, Section 1. The book, originally published in 1929, is a revision of the Gifford Lectures he gave in 1927–28.

137. Madeleine L'Engle, *Walking On Water: Reflections On Faith And Art*, Convergent Books (October 11, 2016). See Chapter 1, "Cosmos From Chaos."

138. Jonathan posts his work on Twitter. His story on the Camp can be accessed @ https://twitter.com/choeshow/status/1565404824195444736?t=dTsAv1cwv6Vac5eNKMQUFQ& s=19

139. You'll find "Expect Compassionate Accountability" on page 18 of the *Mayor's Homeless Plan 2.0* at this link: https://static.spokanecity.org/documents/mayor/2022-state-of-the-city/homelessness-plan-2-2022-0 4-26.pdf

140. In the State of Washington, a 72 hour mental health hold begins with an evaluation by a county-designated mental health professional who can commit a patient to a hospital for a 72-hour evaluation if he or she is dangerous to themselves or others due to a mental disorder. The authorizing statute is Chapter 71.05 of the Revised Code of Washington. The Washington State Health Care Authority publishes a fact sheet that summarizes "The Involuntary Treatment Act (ITA)" available as a PDF @ https://www.hca.wa.gov/assets/program/fact-sheet-involuntary-treatment-act-2022.pdf

141. Sydney Brown, "County opens new 'stabilization unit' as part of jail diversion efforts," *The Spokesman-Review*, September 14, 2021, accessed @ https://www.spokesman.com/stories/2021/sep/14/county-opens-new-stabilization-unit-as-part-of-jai /

142. Treva Lind, "MultiCare targets fall to open behavioral health clinic at the Northeast Community Center," *The Spokesman-Review*, Sunday, May 28, 2023. Accessed @ https://www.spokesman.com/stories/2023/may/28/multicare-targets-fall-to-open-behavioral-health- c/

143. Lo, E., Lifland, B., Buelt, E.C. et al. "Implementing the Street Psychiatry Model in New Haven, CT: Community-Based Care for People Experiencing Unsheltered Homelessness." *Community Mental Health Journal*, 31 May 2021, 57, 1427–1434 (2021). https://doi.org/10.1007/s10597-021-00846-1

144. While writing this section I reached out to homeless service providers in the Spokane Homeless Coalition for input regarding their experience getting people into substance abuse, mental health, and medical respite beds. One licensed drug and alcohol counselor told me that even with all her professional contacts from years of working to get people into treatment, she found it "almost impossible" to get people into treatment in less than two weeks. It usually took longer.

145. You can learn more about the HOPE program, pioneered by the Mr. Diablo Unified School District, at: https://sites.google.com/mdusd.org/mdusd-school-community-service/programs/hope-homeless-out reach-program-for-education

146. Rising River Media has produced a sample training video on de-escalation in a homeless shelter taught by Marty McKinney, the director of Truth Ministries Men's Shelter. We filmed it in the shelter as Marty and his staff reviewed an incident that occurred in the shelter that required de-escalation. The video, "Module 101 - Introduction To De-Escalation In A Homeless Shelter," is available on our YouTube Channel, *My Road Leads Home*, @ https://youtu.be/SVsc52NWuLM

147. You can do your own "deep dive" into their proposal on their website @ https://spokaneunite.org/

148. In late August of 2023, the Spokane City Council, at the urging of homeless service providers and advocates, passed a resolution declaring its support for a regional homeless authority, including conditions for eventual approval and participation. Many of those conditions were framed by service providers who felt that they and those experiencing homelessness were under-represented in the leadership structure. See Shannon Moudy, "'We're still committed to the concept' | Spokane City Council pumps brakes on regional homeless authority," KREM, August 30, 2023, accessed @ https://www.krem.com/article/news/spokane-city-council-pumps-brakes-regional-homeless-authori ty/293-a35e7c42-2d3e-4677-af91-1c99ac74de48

149. See Community Solutions, *The Truth About Homelessness* @ https://community.solutions/research-posts/the-truth-about-homelessness/

150. City of Riverside, "Causes": https://www.riversideca.gov/homelesssolutions/causes

151. Earlier, at the end of Chapter 15, Julie Garcia referred to this person as Firestarter Robert. Same person, but a little different takeaway.

152. Jennifer Ludden, "Why can't we stop homelessness? 4 reasons why there's no end in sight," *National Public Radio*, July 12, 2023, accessed @ https://www.npr.org/2023/07/12/1186856463/homelessness-rent-affordable-housing-encampments

153. The "Section 8 Housing Choice Voucher" is a major program sponsored by the Federal Department of Housing and Urban Development (HUD) to "(assist) very low-income families, the elderly, and the disabled to afford decent, safe, and sanitary housing in the private market. Since housing assistance is provided on behalf of the family or individual, participants are able to find their own housing, including single-family homes, townhouses and apartments." Learn more @

https://www.hud.gov/topics/housing_choice_voucher_program_section_8